Christmas 2000

Benn, some...

we hope you

be fine

Much love

Mum

M.J.

M.J.

THE LIFE AND TIMES
OF M.J. COLDWELL

Walter Stewart

Published in 2000 by Stoddart Publishing Co. Limited
34 Lesmill Road, Toronto, Canada M3B 2T6
180 Varick Street, 9th Floor, New York, New York 10014

Distributed in Canada by:
General Distribution Services Ltd.
325 Humber College Blvd., Toronto, Ontario M9W 7C3
Tel. (416) 213-1919   Fax (416) 213-1917
Email cservice@genpub.com

04 03 02 01 00   1 2 3 4 5

Canadian Cataloguing in Publication Data

Stewart, Walter, 1931–
M.J. : the life and times of M.J. Coldwell

ISBN 0-7737-3232-2

1. Coldwell, M.J. (Major James), 1888–1974.
2. Co-operative Commonwealth Federation – Biography.
3. Politicians – Canada – Biography. I. Title.

FC581.C64S73 2000   971.063'092   C00-930027-9
F1034.3.C64S73 2000

Jacket design:
Angel Guerra
Text design and page composition:
Joseph Gisini/Andrew Smith Graphics Inc.

Printed and bound in Canada

THE CANADA COUNCIL | LE CONSEIL DES ARTS
FOR THE ARTS | DU CANADA
SINCE 1957 | DEPUIS 1957

*We acknowledge for their financial support of our publishing program the
Canada Council for the Arts, the Ontario Arts Council, and the Government of Canada
through the Book Publishing Industry Development Program (BPIDP).*

For Lorne Ingle

CONTENTS

PREFACE

This book was written with the help of the Douglas-Coldwell Foundation, which not only financed my research but also provided the preliminary work of a number of other people, including and especially Anne Scotton of Ottawa and David Heaps of Princeton, New Jersey. These two assembled a good deal of the original material, such as two sets of *Memoirs*. The first of these was a series of tape recordings collected in 1963 by A.M. (Sandy) Nicholson, for years a friend and CCF colleague of M.J.'s; the second a number of chapters Coldwell wrote as a scholar at Carleton University in 1971. Neither of these *Memoirs*, referred to in this book's Notes as *Memoirs 1*, covering the Nicholson tapes, and *Memoirs 2*, M.J.'s own writing, was ever finished. With some occasional forays into later years, they mostly covered the period of the 1930s, especially the early years of the decade (although, unaccountably, not the Regina Convention and the launching of the CCF). Then, there was a collection of tape recordings done in the early 1970s, called *Reminiscences*. These came about through tape recordings done by Clifford Scotton, Anne's father and National Secretary of the New Democratic Party from 1966 to 1976, and by Carl Wenaas, who had been M.J.'s secretary for a time. Again, they were never completed, and the book to which they were to lead was never written.

Other work was done by Walter Young, who was M.J.'s chosen biographer, until his sudden illness and death foreclosed the possibility of a biography. His papers contained a number of interviews and other original material, as did M.J.'s own papers, now housed in the National Archives of Canada, in Ottawa, with other collections in Regina and at the University of British Columbia (where they form a part of the Walter Young Collection). The National Archives also produced a great number of radio scripts, articles written by M.J., letters, newspaper and magazine clippings, and an extensive, and very personal, talk he gave to the Public Archives History Club in 1966.

Because this process produced so much material in M.J.'s own words, I had hoped to write what would amount to a ghosted autobiography with notes, but there were too many gaps in the story to permit this. Still, it seemed to me that the best witness to the events described was the man himself, so I have used extensive quotations from these various sources.

I am grateful to all those who did the spade work to begin this process and to the many others who helped with interviews, notes, suggestions and clippings. Responsibility for the contents of this book remains with me.

Finally, Mrs. Margaret Carman of Ottawa, M.J.'s daughter, was an invaluable source of information and insights, as well as of photographs that cover the entire span of her father's life. The remarkable daughter of a remarkable man.

WALTER STEWART
STURGEON POINT, ONTARIO

INTRODUCTION

He was a man in whom decency flowed as naturally as blood.
— DAVID LEWIS, *THE GOOD FIGHT*, 1981

THE LIBRARY AND THE ARCHIVES IN ROSETOWN, SASKATCHEWAN, ARE BOTH housed in the same nondescript little building just off the main street and down the way from the three grain elevators. Rosetown, in turn, is a pleasant little town (Pop. 2,571, the signs tell us) in west-central Saskatchewan, about an hour's drive southwest of Saskatoon, at the junction of highways 4 and 7. It is not particularly known for its roses — the town name comes courtesy of James Rose, the earliest settler in the area, just after the turn of the century[1] — but takes a good deal of pride in its nine-hole golf course, tennis courts, swimming pool, curling arena, ball diamonds and "soon to open driving range."[2] I had thought that it might take at least equal pride in its place as the geographic centre of Rosetown-Biggar, the federal electoral riding that gave Canada M.J. Coldwell, but no.

"Who?" said the fortyish lady in charge of the desk at the archives.

"Major James Coldwell," I said, adding quickly, "He wasn't a major; that was his first name."

"Never heard of him," said the lady.

"He represented this riding in Parliament for twenty-three years," I said, "from 1935 to 1958," and she said, Oh.

"He was the leader of the Co-operative Commonwealth Federation for eighteen years," I said, and she said, The which?

"You have 569 files of local history in your archives," I said — I had been reading the town brochure. "There is bound to be something on him there."

1

"Take a look," she said, waving an arm towards the shelves. "The archivist is away."

I took a look and came up with a clipping from the Rosetown *Eagle*, which still flourishes as the district newspaper. It informed me that a man named "M.J. Colwell" had managed to win a victory in the 1935 federal election as the CCF candidate for Rosetown-Biggar. In fact, he had a substantial plurality of 2,500 votes over the Liberal candidate. "Libs Win in Ottawa," the paper added, to get the important point across.[3] That was it.

I went back to the car, cursing, and my wife wanted to know why. "They've never heard of M.J. Coldwell," I grumbled. "Just like Biggar." Biggar is the other metropolis of the riding, straight north of Rosetown, straight west of Saskatoon. When we asked the two high school girls manning the information booth there about M.J. Coldwell, we drew the same blank response.

"M.J. Coldwell," I repeated.

I could see in the eyes of one bright young thing that she was considering asking me what team he played for, but refrained.

"Do you know who Jean Chrétien is?" I asked.

"Sure," said one. "He's the prime minister."

"He's the Liberal," added the other.

"Conservative."

"Liberal."

I rolled my eyes, they giggled, and I left. They were high schoolers, expected to be ignorant.

"M.J. is disappearing from history," I complained. "Here is a man who has made an incalculable contribution to Canadian public life, and the people in the middle of his own riding have forgotten all about him already."

"Then tell them," said my wife.

Major James William Coldwell was born in Seaton, Devon, England, in 1888, came to Canada in 1910, became a schoolteacher, school principal, education activist, alderman, member of Parliament and leader of the Co-operative Commonwealth Federation, the CCF, predecessor of the New Democratic Party. He led that party from 1940 until after his defeat in 1958 and, in the words of *Colombo's Canadian References*, "He presided over the party's great wartime gains, and the subsequent postwar disillusionment, with force and dignity."[4] I like that "force and dignity"; they were his hallmarks. But they are not the reason I stake his claim to a place in Canadian history. His importance was threefold. In the first place, he led a party that had been dismissed as a collection of cranks, oddballs and collectivists by most of the populace into a secure place on the left wing of Canadian politics. J.S. Woodsworth, the first leader of the CCF, was venerated as a man who stuck to his principles, but they were not principles that most of the nation wanted to share with him. He was, as Frank Scott, one of the great figures of the party, once said, "a crusader, not a Parliamentarian."[5] He was not interested in the party as an organization, and opposed the appointment of David Lewis as a salaried national secretary, because he thought the CCF should remain an entirely voluntary movement, whose self-evident goodness would persuade the people to follow, without all the bother of poll captains, fund-raisers and professional organizers. There was a strong whiff of the sanctimonious about him, which was all very well, but uncomfortable; moreover, he was surrounded by a ragtag and bobtail of a party whose vociferous adherents ranged from disciples of Social Credit economics, like William Irvine, on the right, to a gaggle of uncritical admirers of the Soviet Union, on the left. Woodsworth was more venerated than followed, at least outside his own riding. And, with him at the helm, it was not hard to dismiss the party he led as, at best, a swarm of impractical idealists, or, at worst, collectivists, crypto-Communists, Trokskyites — take your pick.

The *Regina Manifesto,* the banner under which the CCF began its life, was full of passionate rhetoric, including this magnificent peroration:

> No CCF government will rest content until it has eradicated capitalism and put into operation the full program of socialized planning which will lead in Canada to the establishment of the Co-operative Commonwealth.[6]

Which was all very well, no doubt, but a hard sell in a nation that had done very well, in its own view, under capitalism, with all its faults, and wasn't immediately anxious to trade it in for socialized planning. David Lewis, in his autobiography, called this sentence "an indefensively extravagant assertion that was used by opponents in a devastating way."[7] Coldwell, typically, never directly attacked this strident call to arms, but spent a good deal of time and effort in an attempt, which finally proved successful, to replace the *Regina Manifesto* with a statement of principles that sounded less scary around the grain elevator — for he knew, instinctively and by experience, that the farmers on whom so much depended for his party were, at base, active and enthusiastic capitalists, in practice, if not always in theory. He was a firm believer in socialism, but he knew they had to be persuaded, not shouted, into agreement.

Don't mistake me. M.J. revered Woodsworth, followed him willingly, replaced him, when the time came, with great reluctance; but replace him he did when common sense dictated that as the only possible course. Common sense was M.J.'s great contribution to his party, and, as Charles Lynch — an admirer, but no ally — was to put it:

> M.J. Coldwell's greatest contribution to Canadian politics was that he made socialism respectable. A measure of his achievement is that, when he died at age 85, Canada had become the most highly socialized country in the western world, without anybody really noticing.
>
> He coloured us unobtrusive pink.[8]

Well, M.J. was dead when Lynch wrote those words, and there is nothing like passing on to improve a politician's reputation. Some may doubt, as well, that Canada in 1974, when M.J. died, was more highly socialized than, say, Sweden; but the fact remains that, because of his parliamentary skills, leadership ability and open, ordinary decency, Coldwell was able, after a long struggle, to overcome the image of Canadian socialism as something connected to the gulags, something as oppressive, intolerant and ideologically driven as the Soviet Union, and to replace that view with one of democratic socialism as one way to ameliorate the obvious inequities of unbridled capitalism. Listening to his rich, calm voice explaining the virtues, as he saw them, of a strong central government driven by a program designed to meet the needs of all its people, and not just its elites, it was impossible to dismiss him as a crank, or a zealot, or a danger to the public weal.

Coldwell's second achievement was to make a Movement (he and most other CCFers customarily spelled it with a capital M) into a party, and again, this was in contrast to his predecessor's approach. It made him not merely a standard-bearer but an effective working politician. Woodsworth always saw his role as a missionary one, and said as much to M.J.; he was the visionary, pointing the path to a new Jerusalem, lighting the way, but he never expected to sit in the councils of power. He spent most of his life planting powder kegs under the seats of power, and very effectively, too.

Coldwell didn't expect to be prime minister, either, but he did expect to influence public policy frequently and persistently in his time — and he did — and he did present his party as a serious alternative, rather than just a national nag. It was this capacity to appeal to a much broader band of the electorate that made the Liberal governments who dominated all his political life grudgingly give way, and steal from the CCF some of its most popular ideas. It was the fate of this party to be plagiarized.

In this accord, we are all in M.J.'s debt, whether we know it or not. It goes too far to say that, without him, we would never have had the social safety net that we now seem so intent on shredding; but without his leadership, his constant pressure for reform and the fact that he had to be taken seriously we would never have had these measures as soon, or as fully, as we did. As democratic socialism became harder to demonize with Coldwell as its ardent advocate, the social policies proposed by the CCF were subsumed, swiped, adopted and adapted by successive Liberal governments, who then spent decades boasting about having invented policies that were, in most cases, force-fed to them by Coldwell and his colleagues.

Finally, the third major contribution I claim for Coldwell has nothing to do with his specific politics, and everything to do with his personal qualities. Politics and politicians have a low name in Canada — as they do in most of the nations where they represent the only real alternative to tyranny. We don't like them much and we don't trust them much; we see them as self-serving, hypocritical, unprincipled. But it isn't true: as a group, politicians are at least as worthy as, say, the journalists who spend most of their time smearing them; it's just that the low opinion in which they are held is part of our national life.

Then there are those individuals, in every party, who restore our faith in the process. People like Howard Green and Robert Stanfield in the Conservative party; Guy Favreau and Walter Gordon among the Liberals; Stanley Knowles and M.J. in the CCF; Allen Blakeney in the NDP — people whose transparent honesty, decency and humanity convince us that it is worthwhile going on with a process that sometimes, frankly, makes us despair.

M.J. was not a man of overwhelming charisma; he never became prime minister; his private life — which remained intensely private — was marked by one great love, for his wife, Norah; he does not earn his place in history by towering oratory, low skulduggery or sexual escapades. But he was a great parliamentarian, an effective reformer, and he wielded an influence that went far beyond the councils of his own province and party.

Time to meet him, then, on the one public occasion when he uncharacteristically lost his temper and acted in a manner most unparliamentary — and with good reason.

PART I

A
GENTLEMAN
RADICAL

CHAPTER ONE

THE MAN IN THE AISLE

If I had to name the best twelve parliamentarians in Canada
during the last 50 years, I would place the name of M.J. Coldwell
on that list and not too low on it. He brought a civilized mind
to politics. — GRATTAN O'LEARY, LIFELONG TORY, 1974

M.J. WAS BOILING MAD. HE CAME ROLLING UP THE CENTRE AISLE OF THE House of Commons, waving a clenched fist, in a red-faced rage that was almost as astonishing to onlookers as the bizarre performance of the Speaker that had set it off. M.J. did not get mad, everyone knew that; not like this, anyway, not arm-waving, shouting, stomping angry. This white-haired, somewhat chunky, raging figure was quite unlike the calm, judicious, humorous and even-tempered man who had earned the collective esteem of almost everyone in the House. He was a gentleman; always had been, always would be; an English gentleman, at that, reared and burnished in County Devon, on the south coast of England, of sturdy conservative stock and tradition-polished beliefs. He had been transformed by experience and conviction into a Prairie radical. But a gentleman Prairie radical, a chap who said "My dear fellow," when what he meant was "You idiot!" and "I beg to differ" when he meant "Shut up and listen!" He was neither a saint-in-training, like J.S. Woodsworth, nor a rough diamond, like Clarie Gillis, the Glace Bay coal-miner who represented Cape Breton South in Parliament. (Gillis had gone into the mines when he was fourteen and risen to become a self-educated union leader.) M.J. was a gentleman. And here he was, thundering imprecations at the Speaker, René Beaudouin, in a most ungentlemanly fashion. George Drew, the Progressive Conservative party chieftain and leader of Her Majesty's Loyal Opposition, was bowling up the centre aisle of the green chamber right beside him, it is true, but that was quite a different matter. Drew was a bellower by nature; he was given to theatrics; this was just another performance for him. For M.J., it was no performance; his rage was wrenched out of him; he was defending something almost as precious to him as his beloved Norah — Parliament itself.

It began when the Liberal government of the day, an odd collection of talent and turmoil, ability and arrogance, was trying to push the Pipeline Bill through Parliament to meet an arbitrary deadline. The deadline had been set by Clarence Decatur Howe, Prime Minister Louis St. Laurent's "general manager of the economy"[1] and Minister of Trade and Commerce. He had given a charter to construct a pipeline to take surplus natural gas from Alberta to Montreal, via an all-Canadian route north of the Great Lakes, to an American-controlled company, Trans-Canada Pipelines Limited. The preliminary work to facilitate construction had begun, surrounded by the usual controversy and conflicts of interest that always seem to accompany such projects, but it was progressing nicely despite the entrenched opposition of some Conservatives, led by Howard Green of Vancouver, who suspected that the whole project was a boondoggle aimed at moving the gas to American markets, not Canadian ones,[2] and most of the small but resolute band of CCFers (twenty-three in a House of 265 seats), led by M.J.

He had two objections to the project. The first was to the way the line was being built. He and his party thought it ought to have been constructed and owned by the Canadian government, not private American interests, and he had been pressing that point of view since the subject first came up in Parliament, in 1952.[3] Canadian taxpayers would be taking most of the risks, Coldwell complained, because the government would be intimately involved in the financing; but the profits would all flow to the shareholders of the five huge American firms that had organized Trans-Canada. To M.J., it was a "sell-out" that would bring "enormous profits for private United States economic buccaneers."[4] His second objection was to the way in which the legislation was being rammed through Parliament. That was because the Liberals wanted construction to be completed before the next election, which had seemed entirely possible, until a snag developed.

In April 1956, only a few weeks prior, the company had announced that it was going to be unable to raise the financing necessary to build the part of the line that was to run between Alberta and Winnipeg. Money was available

for the Ontario and Quebec sections of the line, available in God's own
plenty, and already rising were the noxious fumes of special deals struck in
that part of the land, involving the sale of rights that seemed to produce great
profits for a few lucky speculators before the first shovel had been stuck in
the ground. But the section across the Prairies was something else again. The
New York bankers, upon whose financing the whole measure depended, if
you left out the government end of things, felt that the pipeline was not a certain money-maker unless the gas was going, as Howard Green had suspected,
to American markets, and they wouldn't put up the $80 million necessary
without an assurance that this would be the case.

On April 17, several members of the executive committee of Trans-
Canada went to Ottawa to tell Howe that Trans-Canada needed $80 million
for the Alberta-Winnipeg leg, and it needed the money by June 7 if construction was to begin that year. If it didn't begin that year, the line would not
be in place to form the centrepiece of the government's boasts of economic
progress when the voters next went to the polls. We couldn't have that.

C.D. Howe, never one to linger over fine points, said, in effect, never mind,
boys, leave everything to me. If those bankers won't put up the money, I will.
We'll lend you the $80 million out of government petty cash, and you can
repay us later. The main thing is to get those pipes a-rolling. He gave the company a guarantee that Parliament would do his bidding, and told them to get
on with the building.[5] To make this proposal work, the necessary legislation
had to clear the House of Commons by June 1 at the absolute latest, so it could
be rushed through the Senate and receive royal assent on June 7. Accordingly,
when Howe introduced the Pipeline Bill on May 13, 1956, he attached to it a
motion to impose closure at each stage of debate. Closure was rarely used in
Canadian parliamentary procedure then, although it is more common now;
it had been applied for the first time in Canada to ensure speedy passage of
the Naval Aid Bill in 1913, but that was on the threshold of a world war. (It
was the Conservatives who imposed closure on that occasion, which Liberals
had used ever since as an example of the way Tories abused power.)[6] This was
not a world war; it was just Clarence Decatur insisting on having his own way
and in his own time, as usual. Closure meant that debate was to be limited,
not because parliamentarians were faced with a filibuster after all arguments
had been exhausted but before debate had even begun. Blair Fraser, *Maclean's*
magazine's parliamentary correspondent, a long-time and sturdy supporter

of the Liberals on most occasions, called this tactic "truly outrageous."[7]

When Howe introduced his measure, Stanley Knowles, the CCF member for Winnipeg North Centre and the party's expert on House rules, shouted, "The guillotine!" while other members bellowed, "Dictatorship!" and there began the noisiest, rudest, roughest debate that has ever rocked the Canadian House. William Kilbourn, the historian, described an atmosphere of "cackling, whistling and catcalls, jabbering interruptions, strained laughter edging on hysteria."[8] MPs banged their desk lids, sang, shouted, hurled bits of paper about and behaved like a school of seals on speed.

Most of the uproar came from the Conservatives, and some of it was more low comedy than high melodrama, as when Donald Fleming refused to obey the Speaker's call to order and remained standing until there was nothing for it but to expel him from the House, whereupon Ellen Fairclough, who had obviously come prepared, whipped out a Red Ensign (then Canada's official flag) and draped it over Fleming's empty desk. John Diefenbaker, then a backbench MP, intoned solemnly, "Farewell, John Hampden." (Hampden was imprisoned for refusing to pay a forced loan to Charles I. Fleming's eventual fate was even worse; he became Diefenbaker's finance minister.) In reply, the Liberals got up a chorus to sing "There'll Always Be a Pipeline" to the tune of "There'll Always Be an England." They sang it loudly, but badly, and it went into Hansard, along with an equally off-key version of "I've Been Working on the Pipeline."

Howe, who had never had much regard for the clumsy mechanics of Parliament anyway, introduced each clause of the bill by reading only the marginal notes of explanation, rather than the clause itself, and then imposing closure. Parliament was effectively gagged — at least on the substance of the bill, though not, it seemed, on the methods used to push it through.

At the end of fifteen days of uproar, during which Coldwell, Knowles and other CCF MPs kept up a steady but decorous — at least in comparison with the other parties — drumroll of motions, points of order and questions of privilege, the debate came to its climax in the late afternoon of Thursday, May 31. Prime Minister Louis St. Laurent had moved the closure motion for the seven clauses of the bill, and all Speaker René Beaudoin had to do was shepherd this through, backed by the Liberal majority and by the Social Credit Party, whose members favoured the pipeline and claimed that its opponents were "following the Communist line."[9] Instead, when Colin

Cameron, the CCF MP for Nanaimo, got up to raise a question of privilege, expecting it to be rejected, as had been every other point that seemed likely to frustrate or delay the government timetable, Beaudoin was receptive. Cameron read from two letters to the editor that had appeared in the *Ottawa Journal* criticizing Beaudoin for his handling of the debate. The Nanaimo MP pretended to be shocked by the letters, which were an insult, he said, to the Speaker; he wanted to advance a motion to bring the writers before the House to explain themselves.

Beaudoin was intrigued. A vain man, he was flattered that one of the impudent opposition was leaping to his defence. He thought Cameron was working along the right lines, although, of course, his motion was in the wrong form — and the Speaker proceeded to reword Cameron's proposal, in amendments that the astonished MP instantly accepted. The motion was put, seconded, and debate began.

Conservative Leader George Drew then rose and launched into a long speech on the rights and duties of the Speaker — a speech that could not be curtailed, because it was outside the closure motion. Drew spoke until closing time, 10 p.m., and gave notice that he intended to continue to speak all the next day. If he did so, there went Howe's June 1 deadline. That night, a number of impressive limousines were seen outside Beaudoin's Ottawa house, prompting a suspicion that he had been called on by Howe and/or other members of the cabinet. He also consulted Walter Harris, the Liberal House leader; and, early the next morning, J.W. Pickersgill, the party's parliamentary strategist, appeared at Beaudoin's place to discuss the problem with him.[10] When the House met on June 1, the Speaker announced that he had made a mistake in accepting Cameron's motion the day before. Even though he himself had drafted it, the measure was not in order. But he had already accepted it, and debate had already commenced, so he was going to ask the House, "which is master of its own proceedings," to vote that it "should be placed in exactly the same position as it was when I resumed the chair yesterday." In short, he would turn back the clock to May 31 at 5:15 p.m., and rule against Cameron after all.[11] Then he would impose closure and force the vote on the government's entire bill.

It was when he put this course of action to the House that M.J. came rushing out of his seat down the centre aisle and waved his fist under the Speaker's nose. What he said was unclear on the official House of Commons Debates records; the Hansard reporters, overwhelmed by all the shouting, got down a few "Some hon. Members, 'Oh, oh.'" and this enlightening passage:

> **Mr. Drew:** Mr. Speaker —
> **Mr. Fleming:** Mr. Speaker —
> **Mr. Fulton:** Mr. Speaker —
> **Mr. Knowles:** Mr. Speaker —
> **Some hon. members:** Hail, hail, the gang's all here.
> **Mr. Drew:** Mr. Speaker, do I understand that you will do nothing…
> **Mr. Coldwell:** Mr. Speaker —
> **Some hon. Members:** Oh, oh.[12]

And so on. All good, clean fun, but the problem was that it left the reporting of what was actually said to the journalists in the Press Gallery above, and one of them recorded Coldwell as having called Beaudoin "a bloody fool."

It is worthwhile, I think, to record what M.J. rose to say the very next time the House sat:

> **Mr. M.J. Coldwell (Rosetown-Biggar):** Mr. Speaker, I rise on a question of privilege. On page 1 of the *Ottawa Citizen* of Saturday, June 2, the following sentences appear:
>
> Then, white-faced, but determined, the Speaker moved the next vote. The Opposition could restrain itself no longer. Coldwell, shaking his fist, advanced on the Speaker. "You bloody fool," he shouted over the bedlam.
>
> Mr. Speaker, I wish to say that never in my life anywhere, at any time, in any place have I used those words to anyone. Earlier above the din I had sought to be heard on privilege. I advanced toward the table and I said: "You are a dictator, Mr. Speaker," and I repeated "dictator" several times. Again, let me say that I have never in my life used the foul language attributed to me.[13]

And he meant it. Parliament might be under attack, the rules of the House might be bent into pretzels, Chaos and One Night might be overtaking the nation, but M.J. did not want the world to think that these matters had caused him so to lose control of himself that he would use the word "bloody" to describe a fellow human being, even if he happened to be a self-important, fat-headed and easily twisted human being, like René Beaudoin.

The Pipeline Bill went through, but the image of the Liberals using their majority to trample the rights and customs of the House of Commons remained with many voters and became the centrepiece of the next election. In that election, held in June 1957, the Conservatives, under John Diefenbaker, who vaulted into the leadership after Drew's resignation in the autumn of 1956, managed to eke out a narrow minority government. The CCF came back with twenty-five seats, although they dropped marginally in their percentage of the popular vote, and the Tories went on to win in a landslide when Diefenbaker cashed in his minority seven months later, in March 1958. The CCF was reduced to a rump of eight members, and M.J. Coldwell was one of the casualties; it was the end of his parliamentary career.

The voters had chosen to reward Diefenbaker, because he was seen as the man most likely to unseat the arrogant Liberals. Coldwell was a decent enough fellow, no doubt, but he was a socialist, after all, and he lacked that instinct for the jugular, that sense of the dramatic, the wild language and savage rhetoric that made Diefenbaker so effective on the stump. The kind of man who worries about whether people think he said "bloody" does not have the edge, many voters felt, that it takes to run a nation like Canada.

Possibly the voters were right. Coldwell did not have the killer instinct; he was an effective debater, but a fair one; he kept to the rules, never mistook an insult for an argument, never fudged his figures (and if a mistake did get on the record, he set it straight at once), never indulged in those soaring flights of oratorical splendour that sounded so impressive on the stump but, read in the cold light of day, were seen to be full of sound and fury, signifying very little. This was the only time he ever lost his cool in Parliament, and he was a little ashamed, although there was certainly no need to be. A rougher debater — Tommy Douglas, say, or David Lewis, two of those who were later to lead the New Democratic Party — might have made more of this. Each of them had a whiplash wit, whereas M.J.'s humour was gentle, and never personal. M.J.'s concern was for Parliament, not points, and he was genuinely upset that the record might show that he used such blunt language, even under duress.

It is hard not to contrast this scene with that of Prime Minister Pierre

Elliott Trudeau, a far more potent politician in terms of collecting votes, when he told opponents in the House to "fuck off," and then denied that he had ever used the phrase.[14] Trudeau had greater electoral appeal than Coldwell; it does not follow that he was a worthier man.

M.J.'s strengths, and weaknesses, were the product of his upbringing, as they are for most of us, so if we want to understand what made him tick, it is necessary to go back to where he came from — Seaton, County Devon, England.

PART II

THE LAD FROM DEVON

Seaton is a parish, village or station on the S.W. Railway, 10 miles from Honiton in the eastern division of the county of Devon. The living is a vicarage, annual value £260 15s, with residency of 1½ acres of glebeland, in the gift of the Hon. Mark Roule. There are schools for boys and girls, built by Sir W.C. Trevelyan, Bart. The acreage is 2,712, the populace about 2,155. Seaton is a pleasant village and watering place, on the English Channel, and of late years has become a resort of invalids seeking to obtain relief by sea-bathing. The neighbourhood abounds with a durable free-stone, called Beer-Stone.

Risdon says the Danes landed here in 937, and we have it on the authority of Leland that there had been "a notable haven here, but now a rigge or barre of stones at the mouth."

— J.G. HARROD & COMPANY'S *ROYAL DIRECTORY OF DEVONSHIRE AND CORNWALL,* 1818

CHAPTER TWO

SEATON DAYS

The Bath House provided residents and visitors with cold sea-water
baths. It was run by a Mrs. Woodgate, who charged 2s 6p for a
hot bath, 2s for a tepid bath and 1s for a cold one. If you ordered
a bath, but did not take it, she charged you half price.
— TED GOSLING, *COLYTON AND SEATON IN OLD PHOTOGRAPHS*, 1994

THE YEAR WAS 1888, AND IT WAS DRAWING TO A CLOSE. QUEEN VICTORIA WAS
on the throne, had been there since 1837, and the celebration of her Golden
Jubilee a year ago had given the nation great joy (it would be eclipsed by her
Diamond Jubilee a decade hence). The Empire, propelled by the extrava-
gances of Sir Charles Dilke, who spoke of a "world that was growing more
English every day," and Rudyard Kipling, who proclaimed the "white man's
burden," and Britain's mission to bear the brunt of it, was swelling day by day.
British shipping made up almost half of the globe's tonnage,[1] which made
the nation an enthusiastic proponent of free trade, and British banks and
investment companies bestrode the financial world. At home, the Second and
Third Reform Bills were transforming politics, enfranchising skilled artisans
and even "agricultural workers with fixed abodes" — not women, of course,
nor the lower classes — and the members who represented the new voters
were still of solid old gentry stock. Home Rule for Ireland, the issue that
dumped William Ewart Gladstone from office in 1886, was still the thorni-
est question in domestic politics, along with Free Trade, which the Gladstone
Liberals favoured and the Disraeli Conservatives opposed.

Abroad, it had been necessary to place Egypt under protection; it had
been a pleasure to make Her Majesty Empress of India, and, in Africa, Soma-
liland, Uganda, Kenya and the Sudan had all recently been swept into England's

protective embrace — for their own good, you understand, as well as for the imperial interest. It was a pretty good time to be born a Briton. There were problems, of course; the rise of the factories had de-populated much of the countryside and created, instead of the promised prosperity, urban decay, child labour, choking pollution and vast poverty beside vast wealth.

Grumbling had been heard in some quarters over the continuing wide gap that existed between rich and poor, and this grumbling was beginning to find political expression, to varying degrees and in various places. A long depression in agriculture and a steady decline in some industries (caused mainly by competition from such protectionist countries as the United States, Germany, France and Japan) was causing even more than the usual hardships among the working classes, and unions, even industry-wide unions, were beginning to be established, to the consternation of the Better Classes. The misguided ravings of that German, Karl Marx, who had done much of his research in the Reading Room of the British Museum, thank you very much, were percolating through the underclasses of Europe, and even found an echo in England, now and then. *Das Kapital* was translated into English in 1886 and was much discussed at meetings of the Fabian Society, formed in 1883, which hoped to solve the economic conundrum through a rather weird combination of democratic socialism and eugenics.[2] Edward Bellamy, the American journalist and lawyer, first published *Looking Backward* in 1887, and it was raising eyebrows in Britain a year later. This utopian romance pictured an ideal world of state socialism in the year 2000, and propounded a paradox at the heart of capitalism that is no closer to a solution today than it was then:

> Your system was liable to periodical convulsions, overwhelming alike the wise and unwise, the successful cutthroat as well as his victim. I refer to the business crises at intervals of five to ten years, which wrecked the industries of the nation.[3]

However, these were sideline carpings in the main; the vast majority of sturdy Britons marched mentally with Benjamin Disraeli, the Conservative prime minister, who believed — or, at least, who constantly persuaded the Queen that he believed — that the inequities of society, while regrettable, were unavoidable. In the unending search to improve the Empire and the

Race, some were bound to suffer, because, as sociologist Herbert Spencer had pointed out, adapting the biological theories of Charles Darwin to sociology, Nature worked her wonders to provide for "the survival of the fittest"[4] and the consequent removal of the rest. Just as Nature improved the various species by automatically selecting their highest forms, so society would approach perfection only by giving its elites free rein to express themselves. And, mind you, without state interference:

> There cannot be more good done than that of letting social progress go unhindered; an immensity of mischief may be done in the artificial preservation of those least able to care for themselves.[5]

This philosophy went well in Seaton, where a comfortable — well, for some — complacency had settled on the land. Here, in a pretty little village near the mouth of the Axe River, William Major James Coldwell was born, on December 2, 1888.

Although it is somewhat larger — a population of about 6,000, three times that of a century ago, has pushed suburbs out in three directions from the sea — Seaton today is clearly recognizable as the place M.J. remembered as a child. There is the beach, the Esplanade behind the beach, a road running behind the Esplanade and a series of streets fanning out, with no particular logic or direction, over the hills behind. The surrounding countryside is still a place of hills and dales, sun-dappled meadows and shady nooks, or, to put it in the purple prose of the time:

> Seaton, with its trim little sister, Axmouth, stands at the mouth of that beautiful and interesting Devonshire trout stream, the River Axe, whose sparkling waters, after leaping merrily through a most picturesque and fertile valley, rush with a song of gladness over the shingle into the sea, as if eager for the embrace of Mother Ocean.[6]

When this was written, shortly after M.J.'s birth, Seaton was struggling back to prosperity after a long spell of slack activity. The place had once been the site of a Roman encampment, and the Romans worked — or, more probably, put the locals to working — salt pans along the foreshore in the first century of the Christian era.[7] Even before that, Seaton had been visited by the Phoenicians and, after that, by the raiding Danes. When William the Conqueror came calling, his bureaucrats put Seaton into the Domesday Book, with a value of sixty shillings.[8]

Throughout the late Middle Ages, it was a bustling port, indeed the only port of consequence between Exeter and Portsmouth along the Channel coast, but the harbour was gradually blocked by the rocks, sand and pebbles brought in by the sea as the centuries rolled by, until Leland, the historian, reported during the reign of Henry VIII that "Seaton is now but a mene thing, inhabited by fisscharmen. It hath been far larger when the haven was good."[9]

All right for the fisscharmen, who took mackerel, pollock, bass and whiting, and for the huntin' and shootin' gentry, who hounded foxes in the winter and took duck, geese, widgeon, snipe and moorhens in the nearby marshland; not so good for local merchants and would-be manufacturers. There was also, as a secondary industry, the business of smuggling, which particularly flourished in Beer, a two-mile hike over the hills from Seaton, and less than thirty miles from the coast of France. Beer was the birthplace of Jack Rattenbury, known as "the Rob Roy of the West,"[10] and like that Scots rebel was famous for helping others, after he had helped himself. Tennis, cricket and hunting were the sports of the nobs; dodging the "gaayers" to bring in brandy kegs was one of the chief recreations of the rest.

The ruin of her harbour saved Seaton from the factory onslaught, but left her a scant, if snug, place, which derived as much of its wealth from nearby farms as from the sea. Then came the Napoleonic Wars, which cut the British traveller off from continental watering holes (although it didn't impact quite so heavily on the smugglers, many of whom kept on with their business throughout the war); and then came the railways, which vastly increased the number of travellers and turned them to the seaside resorts along the Channel, where, the locals assured them, the sea water would cure all their ills, possibly because it was so damn cold. Lyme Regis, about seven miles east of Seaton, flourished, and became a setting for scenes in Jane Austen's novels.

Seaton flourished, too, by being greatly daring. In the mid-1800s, nude bathing was common along these shores, but by the 1880s, the forces of Victorian propriety had entirely triumphed, and not only was there no nude bathing but mixed bathing was also banned, and, indeed, men and women used entirely separate beaches. At most resorts, the yards and yards of black cloth that made up a swimsuit were donned in changing houses that were separated by sexes as well, with the men's at least a hundred yards from the women's. At Seaton, however, Mrs. Woodgate ran a single Bath House, where you could squat and get squirted with hot or cold water, or make a dash for the beach, within a few dozen yards of heavily wrapped persons of the other sex. Shocking, but true.

Still, proper order was maintained, because the resorts attracted "those who were seeking havens of social decorum, where they could avoid the close presence of the lower ranks of society."[11] There were, for example, no "nigger minstrels" allowed, and the noisy, flashy amusements that were popular at places like Blackpool were entirely eschewed.

There were no pleasure piers at Seaton; rather, the visitors — most of whom came by train, some of whom came in tourist steamers that anchored offshore and ferried their charges to land — took rooms in the single hotel, or in the boarding houses that dotted the village. They would arrive, complete with a huge canvas bath, which was installed and filled by bucket from the sea, unless they chose to patronize Mrs. Woodgate's, and they would stay for most of the summer.

Under this prodding, Seaton's population doubled between 1881 and 1893. One of the new arrivals was M.J. Presumably — we do not know, but it was the custom — he was born at home, Number Five, Major Terrace, just off what was then Sidmouth Street — now Queen Street — perhaps two hundred yards above the Esplanade. His father, James Henry Coldwell, was born in Wales (it says something of this shadowy figure that M.J. thought he was born in Hereford, but James Henry gave his birthplace as Wales in the 1881 census), apparently of Huguenot parents. Here is M.J.'s vague explanation:

My father was a hop-grower in Herefordshire, and I don't know the whole story behind the family difficulties but one brother went to the United States, my father went down into Devonshire and he engaged in buying and selling cattle, and sending some of the meat away to London. He opened a small shop in the town and failed. He lost some little money he had himself and most of my mother's.[12]

Mother was Elizabeth Farrant, a far clearer, stronger personality than James, though no more beloved; James Henry seems to have been a man of great charm. She was the daughter of Anne Farrant, wife of Walter Farrant and daughter of James Major the Elder, M.J.'s maternal great-grandfather. They married late; Elizabeth Farrant was born in 1850, and was in her late thirties when M.J. came into the world at Major Terrace.

James Major, a successful builder in Seaton and nearby Beer, had purchased a large plot of land from Sir Walter Trevelyan, part of an orchard owned by the baronet, in 1838. The price was £80, a considerable sum in those days. Here, he built two houses, one for himself and one for his first-born, James Major the Younger. Then, in April 1869, when the elder Major was ailing and wanted to provide for all six of his grown children (he died the next year), he deeded this land to them, collectively, under a clever but complicated indenture.[13] At that time, he could not leave property to his four daughters — it would pass instantly into the control of their husbands — so he left the land to the husbands with an understanding that it belonged to the women. When the Married Women's Property Act was passed in 1882, the husbands dutifully turned the parcels over to their wives. Under the indenture, six houses were to be built, side by side, along one part of the property, with a garden at the other side and a carriage drive between. (The garden went where the two original houses had been.) The houses were to be built by agreement — that is, each owner had to approve of the plans for the others — and every two houses were to share a well. The simple solution was to build the lot of them together to the same design, and since Walter Farrant, Elizabeth's father, was a builder he got the contract. He did a fine job of it, and the row of houses, behind a sturdy wall, march off along the terrace today much as they did when M.J. was born. His grandmother, Anne Farrant, was given Number Five Major Terrace because she was the fifth of the six children, and she passed it in turn to her daughter Elizabeth, M.J.'s mother, a rather stern-looking woman who probably had much to be stern about. It is not surprising that his mother named M.J. for her grandfather, the land-giver, although "Major" was an awkward tag to bear. (It came from an old German word, "Malger," which meant "council-spear" and signified someone in authority; it thus became a military rank, as well as a family name, and M.J. was stuck with it. He used it in England, but became M.J. soon after coming to Canada.)

In short, M.J. and his sister, Winnifred, were born in comparative affluence, which vanished when their father, who suffered from some undiagnosed illness, lost his money and Elizabeth's, trying to be a butcher. Elizabeth then took out a mortgage to provide funds, which she used to refashion

Number Five as a boarding house, and took in boarders from the sea-seeking hordes that rode the trains from London. Later, in 1899, she sold the house, again to provide funds, and set up another boarding house (they were called "first class apartments," not rooms) around the corner on what became Queen Street. Finally, in 1902, she moved to 9 Seafield Road, where *Kelly's Directory* shows her still renting rooms in 1923, when she was seventy-three. She supported the family and educated her two children by renting out rooms, and there was never any money to spare.

Still, M.J. was brought up amid a cloud of relatives, in a sort of family compound, until he was old enough to be sent out of town to school. One of his great-uncles, John Needs, was a customs officer, not a bad thing to be in those days, and it was he who provided the £400 it cost to build Number Five. (He held a mortgage that paid 5 per cent interest, but only the interest was paid annually by Anne Farrant; the principal continued.) Another great-uncle, William, was an innkeeper, and ran The George, which still stands about a tankard's throw from Major Terrace.

M.J.'s early memories of Seaton were entirely happy ones, reflecting a comfort, security and sense of order that seemed to continue even when money became scarce. The portrait he paints of his days there reflects this:

It was into an old world environment that I was born. My mother's family had lived in the Devonshire village for many generations. Their tombstones dot the grassy churchyard where the shadows of the tall elms and the cawing of the rooks lend an eerie air to the place where the rude forefathers of the village slept. In the little ancient parish Church where Norman, Gothic and perpendicular architecture tell a story that is the history of medieval England, my parents were married and I was baptized.[14] *I do not remember this, of course, although I have heard of it, both from the coachmen who drove my parents to the Church and from the aunts who were present at my Christening.*

…The house I was born in was one of six rather nice and roomy houses in a row in front of which was a delightful lawn where daisies grew in abundance and where we children made daisy chains. Lawn and houses were surrounded by a massive wall and the entrance from the street was guarded by an iron gate of substantial dimensions…

I well remember the arrival of my baby sister when I had reached the somewhat mature age of two years and four months. Then "Rowley," as I called her, (i.e., the maid) dressed me in a new sailor suit[15] *so that I might greet my sister properly. She stood me on the kitchen table to adjust my sailor hat. It had an elastic under the chin which she let slip from her fingers so that it hurt me and I remember crying long and loud…*

…My first few years are filled with memories of that lawn with the swings under the tall willow tree, with the kindly figure of an old great-uncle who sat nearby on a rustic seat when the weather was fine and read the daily paper. But there was another kindly figure who stopped at the gate every day and sometimes gave us one of his peppermints after he had poked us with his walking stick. With him is associated my first recollection of death, for, sometime afterwards, I saw a group of people pass very quietly and very slowly, and four men carried something on a shutter from a shop. Captain Purchase had dropped dead. A few days later, as I was playing on the lawn, I saw a long procession filing down the street, and on the shoulders of six top-hatted men was borne a polished wooden box. My old friend was being carried to his resting place…

We seemed to have many visits from aunts and grown-up cousins who were very proper and very precise, and before whom I was always told to behave. They made a deep impression upon me in my little world surrounded by the high stone wall.

Then come memories of the great world outside — the tall white cliffs to the west, the equally tall or taller red ones to the east, beyond which lay the little Dorset port of Lyme Regis, where, years afterwards, I learnt that the ill-fated Duke of Monmouth landed in his disastrous attempt to wrest the throne from King James the Second; an attempt which cost him his head and sent many in that countryside to the gallows and to slavery across the seas.[16]

When the weather was fine I drove with my father to see flocks of sheep and herds of red cattle and spent many a happy hour riding through those lovely lanes, fragrant with honeysuckle and new-mown hay.[17]

M.J. went to school first at the Infants' School, now a community centre, about 100 yards up Sidmouth Street from his front door, where he was taught by Miss Gush, a friend of his mother's — "a lady with curls hanging down her back"[18] — who taught M.J. his letters and how to sing "All Things Bright and Beautiful," as well as Bible stories.

I welcomed the shorter ones so that I could learn to recite them quickly before my father took me to the parish Church on Sunday mornings.[19]

To get a fuller portrait of M.J.'s childhood, as he remembered it, I cannot do better than give it to you in his own words — not least because he has a clear, direct style:

Looking back, there seems to have been so much to do. As we grew older, we wandered through the lanes hunting birds' nests in the spring and catching the brightly-coloured butterflies as summer wore along. There were primroses, violets, daffodils in the spring, blackberries and nuts to gather in abundance in the fall before school began, and then Christmas. Those Christmases with stockings, chimes and waifs who sang the carols. I well remember the village painter who played a big bass viol, the fiddlers and the cornet player, who, as the night wore on and frequent offers of refreshment from hospitable villagers were accepted, seemed to find their instruments strangely out of tune!

There were Christmas parties, too. One I remember well, for staying with us at the time was an orphan cousin whom my mother had brought up, twenty years older than I, who I learnt in later years was something of a practical joker. He suspected that I might be asked to say Grace, so he took me aside and taught me one to say. Lo and behold, I was asked to say Grace and solemnly I repeated what he had just taught me, which was — "For what we are about to receive, may Mr. and Mrs. G pay. Amen."

I learnt to swim. When, I do not remember, but I was very young. Then I was allowed to go out in the boats with the fishermen, from whom I learnt to bait the hooks and draw the crab and lobster pots from the bottom of the sea. They told me stories; stories of my great-grandfather, whom some of the older men had known; stories of an uncle and of cousins who had been drowned at sea. Sometimes the gales blew and the great Atlantic rollers broke over the pebble ridges, so that the boats were piled high up the village streets. There were shipwrecks, too. One stormy November night, when I was six, my father came in just as I was going to bed and said that Jim Newton and Ernest Watts, two fishermen, had just rescued a dozen men whose whale-boat from the sunken Norwegian schooner Ran *had attempted to land at the height of the storm and in the darkness of the night. Years afterwards, old "Jeem," as we called him, and his son-in-law "Watts" wore their Royal Humane Society medals proudly on gala occasions.*

…About this time, too, someone presented me with a billy-goat, a set of harness and a two-wheeled goat cart. We did not keep it long, but long enough for me to participate in the annual Guy Fawkes parade on the Fifth of November.

That was a great night, with a huge bonfire on the shore when Guy Fawkes was burnt each year in effigy. All this was preceded by a parade in aid of the Devon and Exeter Hospital and Eye Infirmary. People at the crowded windows dropped coins into tin boxes on long poles as the torchlight procession passed by. On this occasion I was dressed as "Little Lord Fauntleroy," with pale blue knee breeches, laced cuffs and a big blue hat with the huge white ostrich feather from my mother's wedding outfit. But how it rained! I remember I was drenched, the ostrich feather lost its curl and folded up into a sort of woebegone skewer. I got second prize in the costume contest, in spite of the stubbornness of the billy-goat, who had to be lifted along from time to time.

There were no picture shows. Sometimes there were lantern lectures at the Assembly Hall,[20] and, once or twice a year, a circus or menagerie, with clowns, acrobats and lion tamers, who placed their necks in the lion's jaws. These were great occasions, and school closed for the afternoon.

I well remember my father taking me to hear a wonderful machine that had been brought to town. We placed something resembling a doctor's stethoscope in our ears, paid a penny, and listened to the first gramophone, and a nasal voice telling us that we were hearing an Edison-Bell record.

In 1898 or 1899, I am not sure which,[21] the Bath and West of England Agricultural Society held its annual show in Exeter, and I went with my father. As we approached the show field, we stopped to watch a weird thing pushing slowly up the hill. The thing was preceded by a man carrying a red flag as a sign of danger. How it shook and sputtered and stank! My father laughed and said there were some people fool enough to think that these things would take the place of horses! That was the first automobile I ever saw.

…Another clear memory is of the visits to our village of an old dentist named Stringfellow, who was treated with kindly tolerance, for everyone thought the old gentleman was crazy. You see, he spent many years and much money trying to perfect a flying machine. It turned out that he had discovered the right wing-principle, but the internal combustion engine which made so many things possible was only in its infancy.[22]

In 1901 — the year Queen Victoria died, to be succeeded by the rascally Edward VII — M.J.'s parents decided that, despite the financial burden involved, he would have to go to school in Exeter. Winnifred, by this time, was in an excellent school for girls in Seaton, and M.J. had graduated to a

school established by Sir Walter Trevelyan, but it was not of a calibre to prepare him for college or university, which is where his mother was determined
he should go.

*At last it was decided that I must go away to school. After much discussion about
expense and all the rest of it, for my father was not well and had not prospered
in these years, it was decided that I should go to Hele's School in Exeter, some
thirty-five miles away.[23] Season tickets on the railway were reasonable in price,
and so I journeyed to that city every day, catching the seven o'clock train each
morning and returning home at half-past six at night. Now a new life opened.
There was football and field hockey in the winter and cricket and aquatic sports
in the summer. Those train trips were very interesting, though much of my very
heavy homework was done in travelling to and from school.*

*On Fridays, market days, the trains were always crowded and, although we
had Second-Class season tickets, we sometimes found it difficult to find seats if
we happened to be detained at school. I shall never forget one of these Friday
trips. The four-forty was just at the point of departure. I rushed to the first
second-class compartment I could see. I opened the door, and a hand grabbed
me and I sat down hard in the only vacant spot. I felt something give under me,
and guessed what had happened. The compartment was well-filled with gentlemen who had been attending some meeting in Exeter. Quite evidently, they had
been imbibing freely, and the gentleman next to whom I was seated was a prominent county squire. Just outside the city there was a short tunnel, and the train
was not lighted. When we reached this, I grabbed something from under me, and
quickly threw it on the rack above and behind me, and at the next station, I
transferred myself to another compartment. A few stations further on, I watched
the passengers leave the train and saw what I had suspected — the prominent
country gentleman got out wearing a very dilapidated top hat!*

*School days were happy. I often think of the boys with whom I worked and
played. Alas, many of them found resting places in Flanders Fields and in far-
off Mesopotamia, to which the Wessex Brigade was dispatched early in the war,
for I belong to the generation which was largely lost in the Great War. No doubt
partly because of this, I hate war and have hoped that collective security might
protect another generation from being lost.[24]*

*Boys at school were, I think, more mischievous than now. Discipline was
harder, punishment more severe, and a relaxation of such discipline resulted in*

more daring breaches of school law. We had one elderly master who, in a certain form, gave us one hour of Latin exercises every afternoon. Just after noon, he'd come in, assign the exercise, and promptly take a nap. At the back of the room was the boarded-in, ancient fireplace. In this alcove stood a huge wicker basket, where we deposited waste paper. One afternoon, another boy and I were seated in the back row of desks, with a rather fat boy between us. I do not know what bewitched us, but we tried to put our fat friend in the basket. The boys tittered, and we struggled. Suddenly, we became aware of an ominous silence in the room. We looked around and, behold, the master was awake and striding towards us with the cane. I can still feel the sting of that cane, but, worse than that, we were assigned the task of writing the chief parts of a thousand Latin verbs.

Still, it was an excellent school, presided over by a splendid headmaster, Edward H. Shorto, who was associated with it for over fifty years. He exercised a remarkable influence for good over the boys, because he himself trusted us, and we tried not to let him down. He was greatly mourned when he died a year or two after I left the school. I attended his funeral, a boy among many men of all ages whom he had taught.[25]

Hele's School, where M.J. was taught, and occasionally caned, from the age of thirteen to sixteen, does not appear to modern eyes the mini-paradise that M.J. remembered. The building still stands,[26] on the New North Road in central Exeter, just across from the railway station where M.J. debarked and embarked every day. It was named for Elize Hele, who died in 1636, leaving behind a comfortable fortune for "charitable works." However, nothing was done. Two centuries later, the trustees, greatly daring, elected to devote £500 to building a school in Exeter, with another £300 annually for maintenance.[27] Exhausted by this activity, the trustees did nothing more until the passage of the Education Act of 1870 provided some public funds to support schools. A mere fifteen years later, Hele's was opened, with 86 pupils, all boys, of course, between the ages of thirteen and sixteen. The stone-block building was heated, if at all, by coal-burning stoves, and there was no artificial light provided — which had the advantage that, in mid-winter, boys could not be detained much past four o'clock, because the building was pitch-black.

Three of the six classrooms occupied a single large chamber, and were separated only by curtains. This meant that each of the teachers might start with good intentions and a quiet tone, but would gradually become louder and louder to overcome the competition from behind the curtains, until all were bellowing. One teacher, a retired ex-sergeant major with brass lungs, was considered to have an unfair advantage.[28]

When M.J. attended, from 1901 to 1905, the school was under the firm direction of Edward Shorto, an austere gent who always wore formal clothes, with a tail-coat, high collar and "a vast, red silk handkerchief."[29]

There was no assembly hall, no gym and no science equipment or laboratories. The boys were taught reading, writing, arithmetic, English grammar, Latin and history, with a strong emphasis on England's role as the centre of the universe. Many of the boys did not make it all the way through, and the "Remarks" column of the school register contains some terse notes on these leavers, such as:

"Drowned while bathing,"
"Burnt in the theatre fire,"
"Advantageous removal to another school,"
"Gone, and never paid any fees," and
"No reason, bad boy."[30]

We can see that M.J. loved Hele's, even if it is a little hard to work out why. In the winter, he would rise about six a.m., walk about a mile to the Seaton station, where he would catch a branch-line train to Colyford, stand on the windswept platform for about twenty minutes, and then catch the through train from London to Exeter. The trip was repeated in return each night, five days a week, often in the miserable conditions Coldwell described more than half a century later.

I'll never forget those mornings of getting up in the dark, perhaps with howling gales of wind and heavy rain. The station was right beside the river, between the river and the town proper;[31] on the one side you had the sea, and on the other side, the marshes — open land, nothing to break the wind on either side, and I remember how wet I used to get, although I was well dressed; they always saw I was well dressed. I used to wear a sou'wester hat, a tarred coat, and heavy boots, leggings and knee-britches. I left an overcoat at the station, to wear in town, and before I left, I would drop the slicker and sou'wester, and put on my coat and hat. Many a morning I went into that train very, very cold and wet.[32]

Hele's school building is now used as a student centre for the University of Exeter, and has been completely rebuilt inside. But the values it deposited in M.J.'s young mind were never really rebuilt, and they were not such bad values at that. He learned a lot about such abstractions as "fair play" and "honour" and "tradition," along with his Latin declensions; corny civilities that were to govern his conduct for the next seven decades.

More of the same awaited him away from school, and, again, the best possible source for this is his own writing:

Interest in politics began early. I must have been very small when I was taken to the Assembly Hall to hear the Member for the division upon one of his infrequent visits to the district. You see, elections came once in seven years, and the West Country rural divisions were, in many instances, merely pocket constituencies for the Conservative Party. I can see the fine, bearded figure of Sir John Kennaway, M.P., who was a typical nineteenth century Tory squire of the anti-Home Rule evangelical variety. He was a fine type of English gentleman who devoted forty years of his life to the House of Commons and was seldom, if ever, known to speak. I don't remember much about the meeting except that I fell asleep!

That old Assembly Hall had many interesting associations for me. Old-fashioned "Penny Readings" still lingered in the English villages. There were still many people who could read only imperfectly, and so they, with others, assembled once a week during the winter to hear someone read. There, I learned to love Dickens. I have a vivid recollection of my introduction to the humour of The Pickwick Papers, *illustrated by lantern slides — the glorious first of September, the shooting party, and Mr. Pickwick in the wheelbarrow trundled along by the inimitable Samuel Welles.*

I grew up in this old world, rich in stories of Raleigh, whose boyhood days were spent in the nearby seaside village of Budleigh Salterton, while within easy walking distance were Ashe Houses, where John Churchill, first Duke of Marlborough, was born at Bevey Manor. The home of the Courtenays, barons of medieval times, lay in ruins within three miles and, on the hills beyond the River Axe, were the barrows dug to defend the countryside from Danish invaders after the Romans left the shores of Albion.

Under the cliffs were smugglers' caves and, looking out to sea, the flashing lights on Portland Bill and Shark Point marked the eastern and western limits of Torbay. Ships plied to and fro and the iron-clad vessels of the Channel Fleet anchored now and then within easy reach of the shore. Lying in the grass on the cliffs, I read the sea stories by Kingston, Henty, Kingsley and others, who laid the scenes of some of their stories along those very shores. Thus the love of literature, of history, and of the English countryside became almost the marrow of one's bones. This was the England of the English people — peaceful, simple and kindly — an England that one would like to see again; different to the congested slumdom I saw in London and other cities afterwards.[33]

CHAPTER THREE

AN EDWARDIAN IN EXETER

*Male students lived in licensed lodgings. Landladies were required
to keep a record of our incomings at night. Except for Saturdays
and Sundays, the rules were 9:00 o'clock, but infrequent permission
to attend the theatre, concert or public functions was not too
difficult to obtain.*

*Men and women students were not supposed to associate
except at lectures, and loitering to chat in the corridors was strictly
forbidden.*   — M.J. COLDWELL, "I REMEMBER," 1963

THE ROYAL ALBERT MEMORIAL MUSEUM STRETCHES ALONG QUEEN STREET
in downtown Exeter, County Devon, between Musgrave and Gandy Streets,
and looks very much as it did when M.J. Coldwell first walked up the stairs
and through its central arch in 1905 after graduation, with high marks, from
Hele's preparatory school, half a mile away. However, when you enter through
the front door today, there is nothing to suggest that, when M.J. came here,
the place was a combined art college, technical school, museum, library,
domestic science institute — with "instruction in such womanly subjects as
cooking, dress-making, and domestic economy" — as well as a place to provide "courses of instruction for assistant and pupil teachers."[1]

It had been opened as the School of Art, with premises over the Lower
Market on Milk Street, in 1855, and was transformed by two events. The first
was the death of Prince Albert, in December 1861, of typhoid, at the early age
of forty-two. This led to a mania for naming things after the prince, and in
due course, a vast Victorian edifice arose on Queen Street as the Prince Albert
Memorial Museum. It opened in 1865, and soon functioned as both a
museum and "free library." The second event was the establishment of

34

a special duty on beer and spirits in 1890, with the proceeds allotted to local authorities to spend on technical instruction.

They were going to brew brains out of beer. Exeter collected £900 in 1890 alone and, under the prodding of a local education enthusiast, one Miss Jessie Montgomery, decided to move the School of Art into the museum and expand it to cover other subjects, including manual training (later dropped). In 1893, it became a university extension college, connected with the University of London and, in 1899, changed its name to the Royal Albert Memorial College,[2] with the museum, art school, library and college sharing the same premises. The teaching end gradually became known as "University College, Exeter," which is how M.J. referred to it. The museum was entirely separated from the college in 1909, and the college moved to grander grounds a couple of miles away. It is now the University of Exeter.

Despite what was inevitably called "the whisky money," funds were short, so, when the board of education offered training schools grants of £20 for every certified teacher, the Royal Albert went into that line, in 1901, with twenty-five women students. Greatly daring, the authorities expanded the program to include men in 1903, although they were, of course, strictly segregated to prevent who knows what-all happening at the back of the class.

The great advantage of this program was that the students could learn and teach — for a pittance, but enough to cover school and travel costs — at the same time, and could then decide whether to go on to higher education. M.J. spent another two years riding the train from Seaton, learning for two or three days a week, including most Saturday mornings, and acting as an assistant and fill-in teacher for the other days, depending on when he was needed. Most of this teaching was in Beer Church School, in the village of Beer, two miles along the coast from Seaton.[3] He was attached to the Teachers' Training Centre, rather than the more formal, full-time teaching program at the college, although both were operated out of the same premises. During these years, 1905–1906, he joined the school's rugby team, although he was still only a part-time scholar.[4]

In 1907, when he was closing in on his eighteenth birthday, he and his parents had to make a crucial decision. That summer, M.J. sat for, and won, a King's Scholarship, which would pay tuition at the college, but nothing for living costs. He could enter either a three-year course, leading to a bachelor of arts or science from the extension program, or a two-year course leading to a teacher's certificate. "I decided on the two-year course, which was less expensive, because they had to keep me in Exeter."[5]

It was a decision that would change his life — and Canadian history.

M.J. shared rooms in a house around the corner from the college with Vernon Boyle, of Bideford, near Seaton; he was the nephew of family friends, and although he and M.J. had never met before they wound up in the same rooming house. Boyle was in the three-year program, on his way to a bachelor of science degree. He was also a gifted artist, and later gave M.J. a number of watercolours he'd painted in their rambles around the countryside together. The two men remained firm friends and frequent correspondents until Boyle's death in 1956.

M.J. wrote a number of times about his happy days at Exeter, including this bit about costs:

Our "digs" were comfortable. Accommodation and board were ridiculously low in price by modern standards. For the use of a sitting room on the bedroom floor, a bedroom each and the use of the bathroom, we paid 15 shillings a week each. Pocket money, half a crown a week, supplemented by an extra shilling or two very occasionally, sufficed. Those of us who smoked could buy a tin of cigarettes, Players, Gold Flake or Capstan, for one shilling. Woodbines were five a penny. And for those who liked a glass of beer, it could be obtained for three half-pence. After an evening lecture, we would sometimes treat ourselves to fish and chips, which cost us tuppence or tuppence half-penny.[6]

Included in the price were three meals a day, "really excellent food," M.J. recalled, and the duties of making sure the students, maddened by Woodbines or glasses of beer, did not misbehave themselves.

To qualify for the placement of students, a landlord (or, more usually, landlady) had to be licensed by the college, which required the provision of "a warm, well-lit room for evening study."[7] But that wasn't all, not by a long shot.

"The rules...also required landladies to record in a diary the time at which students returned to their lodgings if they came in after 9 p.m.; if a student came in after 11 p.m.,"[8] the landlady had to report the fact to the college the next day. Occasionally, permission would be given for one of the nineteen- or twenty-year-old students to stay out past 10 p.m., to attend a play or concert.

M.J. never objected to the strict rules that bound his daily activities, and which included three daily prayer sessions — Anglican, of course. Discipline, order and tradition had always been the hallmarks of his life, and the notion that he would object, at the age of nineteen or twenty, to being told when to go to bed, even when to pray, never entered his head. Not only he, but his entire family, were, in the words of a family friend, "blue to the core."[9]

Classes were held in a couple of lecture halls in the museum, but more often in makeshift rooms "badly lighted, worse heated and barely habitable,"[10] in two old houses on Bradninch Place, behind the college, the same street where M.J. and Vernon lived. Because the museum didn't open until 10 a.m., if there was a morning lecture before that time, the students had to go through "the Stokehole," a battered door off Queen Street that led through the furnace room — the college possessed one of the first coal-fired central heating plants in the area, which was a scientific marvel, but provided very little heat. Today, museum employees still enter before hours and leave after hours by the Stokehole.

Despite the drawbacks, M.J. loved the college and remained fiercely loyal to it, as I learned in a roundabout way. One morning in the spring of 1998, while I was cross-questioning the inquiry desk inside the museum entrance about M.J. — "Who?" — a young man passing by said, "Did you say Coldwell? Wasn't he a mayor or something over in Canada?"

"He was a member of Parliament."

"Then we have his buffalo," said the man, who turned out to be Fred Ferguson, the museum's collections manager. And so they do. In the middle of the display area in the museum's main room there stands a veritable buffalo of giant dimensions and shaggy mane, looking faintly reproachful from his post on a bit of shaggy green rug, representing the Canadian Prairies, against a painted Prairie background. A small plaque in one corner announces that it was donated through the good offices of M.J. Coldwell, a student on these premises in 1955.

The way of it was this. In 1954, M.J., then an MP, ran into a Miss Brigden, of Winnipeg, another Devon exile, who reported that she had visited the Royal Albert the year before, and it didn't seem to have many wildlife exhibits. Could he help? M.J. contacted Jean Lesage, then federal minister of northern affairs and a friend of M.J.'s, who promptly offered a list of possibilities, beginning with skunks, gophers and muskrats, and working up through bears, timber wolves and beavers to "the head, hide and feet of a Canadian buffalo."[11] This led to a flurry of letters and wires, back and forth, in which the museum curator pressed for a whole series of animals — "Porcupine, Woodchuck, Fisher, Kit Fox…a Jumping Mouse and, if possible, a Mink."[12] But especially a buffalo. What he got was buffalo bits and a bill for $84.10 for "Labour, Crating and Shipping" via the Canadian Pacific Steamer *Maple Dell* on January 23, 1955. Governments did not throw money around in those days. The buffalo is still there, looking fit and fine, if a little morose.

M.J. was an excellent all-around student, who did well at academic work, played on the rugby team, edited the school magazine *RAM* (for Royal Albert Museum) in his second year, and took part in increasingly disturbing, if always proper, debates. In his first debate, M.J. defended, successfully, the proposition that "Charles Dickens's novels are true to life." When he rose to speak that day, M.J. was clearly in pain, from an injury he had received in the afternoon during a rugby-football match. (In his final year, he hurt his knee so badly that he had to give up rugby.) Nearly sixty years later, he remembered the applause, which was as much for pluck as speaking skill.[13] The *RAM* reported the debate this way:

> Mr. Coldwell, in the debate on Dickens, by his references to the great novelist's early struggles, caused the tears to flow unchecked down many a manly cheek and the sympathetic sigh to flutter from the depths of many a womanly heart.[14]

He did not fare quite so well in the political tussles.

We had some professors who were quite obviously radicals, and we had a contingent of young people from Wales, who were also either very left Liberals or Socialists, and, of course, I came from a very Conservative home. My entry into debates was to try to put these people right, and therefore I tried to defend the Conservative cause as it was understood at that time, particularly Chamberlain's Tariff Reform,[15] Imperialism, and all the things that went with it. Well, it wasn't very long before I was reading everything that these radicals quoted and over a couple of years I was to all intents and purposes a supporter of the newly-formed Labour Party.[16]

The Labour Party emerged in 1900 out of the Labour Representation Committee, an amalgamation of the Independent Labour Party, founded in 1893 by Keir Hardie, the Fabian Society and the Social Democratic Federation, a Marxist group founded by Marx's English translator, Henry Mayers Hyndman (who later took his group out to form the British Socialist Party). The founding meeting defeated two motions, one for a party based upon "recognition of class war," another that only "members of the working class" would be accepted as parliamentary candidates. Instead, the 129 delegates agreed with Hardie's argument that the party must have "flexibility for development." The former Scots coal-miner trilled, "It has come. Poor little child of danger, nursling of the storm. May it be blessed."[17]

At first, the Labour Party supported the Liberals, who were advocating what was, for the time, a distinctly radical approach, embodied in the famous "Budget of 1909" introduced by the Chancellor of the Exchequer, David Lloyd George. To understand the turmoil in which M.J. found himself, it is helpful to look at the background.

In 1905, a royal commission was established to examine the New Poor Law — essentially, an early-nineteenth-century updating of the Elizabethan Poor Law of 1601, which retained that legislation's underlying principle that poverty was, at bottom, the fault of the poor. The commission found that the law was not working very well. There were more poor than ever, and despite the constant assurances that jobs were to be found, if only the slackers would look hard enough, they remained elusive. Even the best endeavours of the workhouses to drive what we would now call social welfare bums out to shift for themselves, by making life so miserable within the institutions (a variation of the same basic approach of many modern governments), did not seem to produce employment. Moreover, the private charities on whom most of the burden for caring for the underprivileged fell were, at best, indiscriminate, and at worst bereft of reason. The commissioners described a woman who was so moved by a Sunday sermon on the perils of the poor that she took to the streets to distribute champagne and grapes to London's helpless hordes.[18]

The *Majority Report of the Commissioners* abandoned the cosy notion that most of society's ills were caused by sinful sloth, and suggested that instead of deterring the poor from applying for assistance by making its availability as harsh and spare as possible, the government should recognize that at least some poverty was a direct result of the way the industrial system operated — the argument we appear to be revisiting today. There ought to be an old age pension, the commissioners concluded, free hospital treatment for those in need and more residential homes for orphans and foundlings. These would be provided in the main by the existing charities on a voluntary basis, but, where it was required — and especially in the matter of old age pensions — the necessary funding would come from government.[19]

All of this was directly contrary to the doctrines on which M.J. had been raised, which left the poor pretty much to the care of Lady Bountiful, church charity and the workhouses. But worse was to come. A *Minority Report* of two commissioners took the debate to another stage. This report was written by Beatrice and Sidney Webb, early members of the Fabian Society and supporters of the Labour Party (Beatrice Potter, daughter of a wealthy industrialist, had married Sidney James Webb, a senior civil servant and economist; together they helped to launch the London School of Economics in 1895 and the *New Statesman* in 1913). They proposed scrapping the Poor Law entirely and bolstering private charity with state social services to protect everyone, not merely the poor, against illness and misfortune. It should be the task of government to provide a framework of prevention, in place of the vicar's daughter, and a state-supported pension to support not only the poor, but the general populace, in old age.

Indeed, the Webbs argued, in a series of books and tracts, that private charity was doing more harm than good, since it relieved some of the symptoms of poverty without attacking the base cause, which was an industrial system founded on the exploitation of one class by another. Voluntary agencies would always be needed to supplement the state, but the main burden ought to be borne by government. The Webbs, reflecting European experiments, foreshadowed the welfare state, with its underlying principles of universality and government funding of the major elements of social care. Their *Minority Report* was a direct attack on the private charity system then in place and was swiftly relegated to a footnote of history, although its arguments continued to percolate through debating societies such as the one at Exeter College.

The *Majority Report* fared rather better, and the budget of 1909, drawn up by Lloyd George and adopted by Herbert Asquith's Liberal government, embodied an entirely new approach to social problems.

"Four spectres haunt the poor," Lloyd George told Parliament. "Old age, accident, sickness and unemployment. We are going to exorcise them."[20]

His budget proposed just that, not by having the state take over the work of private charities, but by having it supplement them to a degree unheard of in England, though well known in continental Europe. It provided for a system of social insurance, including non-contributory old age pensions, labour exchanges and a fledgling program to provide at least some unemployment and sickness insurance. This would be financed in part by contributions from earnings, but also from land and income taxes; the general purse would be called on to take at least part of the place of Lady Bountiful; the dreadful deed would be accomplished by a tax of nine pence on the pound up to an income of £2,000 and a shilling in the pound above that level.

The House of Lords rose as one man to veto the budget, and Asquith asked King Edward VII to create enough new Liberal peers to overwhelm the old Tories and get the budget through. Edward hated this idea, so he dithered and did nothing. (In the end, just as M.J. was preparing to leave England, the Liberals fought and won a new election on the basis of the budget of 1909, which became the budget of 1910, with the support of Labour members.)

This was the debate that was going on all across the nation when M.J. was attending Exeter, and that city was itself in the middle of a period of transition. On the one hand, "the path to local advancement and social status continued to lead through Conservatism and the Church of England;"[21] on the other, change was in the air everywhere.

The economy was still based on the horse, and, on Fridays the "principal inns of the city rang with the clangour of wheels and horse-hoofs on the cobbles, and the farmers came in by gig and trap for the most important market of the week."[22] The large fortunes in this city of 48,000 came from banking, brewing, coach-building, hat-making and church furnishings. The locals took pride in their community, and the city books showed the largest contingent of "foreigners" to settle there in 1901 — 610 males and 809 females — came from London.[23]

If the church provided guidance, the army provided heroes; there was — and remains — a terrific statue erected to General Sir R. Buller, who led Devon troops in the Boer War, just down the street from where M.J. was training as a teacher. Families, even if only of modest wealth, had maids, cleaners and yard boys — almost one-quarter of the city's population at this time consisted of domestic servants, who knew their place and kept it. A run-of-the-mill house cost about £375, a handsome, detached house with a large garden, about £1,650. Eggs sold for eight pence a dozen, butter for ten pence, and you could buy a hogshead of strong cider for less than ten shillings.[24] A hogshead held sixty-three gallons.

However, traditional political patterns were crumbling, and while Exeter had gratefully returned Conservative members since 1865 — in the 1901 general election, Sir Edgar Vincent defeated the Liberal candidate, Allan Bright, by a margin of more than ten to one — the times they were a-changin'; by 1906, Sir George Kekewich, a radical educator, had won a narrow victory for the Liberals. His campaign was based on a direct attack on the clergy and the "licensed trade" — that is, pub owners and brewers — who were engaged in a joint campaign to keep down the rising middle class. Kekewich wanted the schools to be run by the state, not the church, and he was a strong supporter of the Lloyd George budget. (When the House of Lords defeated the budget, temporarily, as it turned out, a local lord gave £300 pounds to provide a dinner for the city poor, in celebration.)[25] Kekewich was considered a traitor to his class, and his own family voted noisily against him, but he won by 88 votes, mostly cast by men who had never voted before in their lives.

Extending the franchise had led, just as its opponents feared it would, to the lower orders wanting to muscle in on power, and the local councils were being taken over by "men of the new class" who insisted on holding meetings in the evening because they could not afford to give up a day's work to attend.

Even the outhouse was under attack. The Exeter Chamber of Commerce called a meeting to hear a paper describing the city's successful adoption of the septic tank system.[26] In 1907, the New London Inn turned its back on coaches, and opened a garage for fifty of the new horseless carriages. Where would it all end?

There was an increasing impatience with the continuing poverty that was beginning to threaten property values, if not the social order. The medical officer of health reported to Exeter Council:

> Many of the houses are occupied by people of the very lowest class; the mode of living of this class of people is so well known that I need not describe them; they are a terror to landlords and a continual source of trouble to the sanitarian authorities.[27]

Workhouses were still about the only answer the Conservatives, M.J.'s party, could advance to meet the crisis. If a family fell destitute, it was shifted into one of these dim, dark, dirty, dank hovels, run by the local Corporation of the Poor, or else put on Outdoor Relief — which usually meant the meanest tasks of road repair, weed clearing and manure hauling. In 1906, after having rejected the proposal for several years running, the Exeter Corporation of the Poor voted to give an extra shilling to the inmates for Christmas.

It was not easy to keep defending these remedies, which, along with prayer and obedience to the established order, were supposed to bring prosperity, and M.J. found himself in trouble in the debates, particularly against a young radical, Reginald Northam, whose father was an engine driver on the London and South Western Railway — the one M.J. rode from Seaton. Northam went far beyond the Lloyd George position, to support the Labour Party and the welfare state proposals of the Webbs. Although a skilful enough debater, M.J. found himself more in sympathy with Northam's arguments than his own.[28]

The radicals and socialists quoted from Fabian pamphlets, from Bernard Shaw and other socialist authorities which I made it my business to read whenever I could. The result was, of course, that I not only became interested in radical and socialist ideas, but gradually acquired some of them.[29]

Needless to say, there were no politics in the *RAM*; M.J.'s writings there reflected pretty faithfully the ideals of a young Edwardian male, full of chivalry and applesauce, such as this Soliloquy to My Pipe:

Talking about matches, do you remember how she would laugh when I allowed you to go out, and how she would burn her fingers when lighting you again? In confidence, old friend — she told me in a letter this morning that she was longing to see you — and me — again. Let's hope it will be soon! Twelve o'clock! Good night, old chap! Thanks ever so much for your company, and the visions of her that you have conjured up.[30]

She was Norah Gertrude Dunsford, who had given M.J. the pipe. A bright, vivacious, comely young woman with a magnificent mop of auburn hair, she was the daughter of the well-to-do J.T. Dunsford, publisher of the *Bridgwater*

Mercury in Bridgwater, Somerset, and part owner of a chain of West Country newspapers. M.J.'s daughter, Margaret Carman, remembers:

> My mother was definitely an "English lady," in the old sense of the word. She was of straight Anglo-Saxon ancestry, and a very friendly and gentle woman, who loved children. She came from a fairly well-to-do family, and was one of four children from a second marriage (the first family died in a tragic fire). Her father, John Thomas Dunsford, was a journalist and had some newspapers in the west of England. It was told by the family that he didn't even tie his own shoelaces! He was a staunch Conservative and, after his second wife died, used to discuss the morning news over the breakfast table with his female housekeeper.[31]

Bridgwater is about thirty miles from Exeter, and it was natural for Norah to go there to train for teaching — one of the acceptable trades for intelligent young women like her. She lived in the College Hostel on Castle Street, where most of the female teachers-in-training boarded. The hostel was converted from a fine old Georgian house overlooking the ruins of Rougemont Castle; it had been bought for the college by a syndicate formed by Jessie Montgomery, the same woman who had been behind the move and expansion of the institution in the first place. The rules for female students were the same as those for men — Lord knows they were strict enough for anyone — and began with an injunction not to waste valuable time chatting with each other in the corridors between sex-segregated classes. This received all the attention it deserved — even a number of the professors saw no harm in the inevitable flirtations that sprang up — and M.J. and Norah were soon fast friends. M.J. never said how they first met, but apparently they flirted in church, risking thunderbolts, and met at college functions such as the debates, athletic contests and even sing-songs.

They were jolly affairs usually held in one of the restaurants where we would sometimes have a meal together, then adjourn to a room where we sang[32] and smoked and those who wished could get half a pint of beer or cider. Looking back, I realize that these privileges were not abused. Sometimes we were joined by one of the members of the staff, but they had no effect upon our conduct. We welcomed and enjoyed their company. We had a few students from Germany who joined us on these occasions. We got on well with them in spite of the fact that the clouds of war were visible in the distance.[33]

As young people will, Norah and Major — the name she knew him by — managed to get together quite often, despite the rules. The best thing was to get away from the college in a hired carriage, which M.J. drove.

I could go out in the country with Norah and there was an inn to which we went, about five miles away, and they'd put on a fire in one of the rooms, and we'd get a very nice tea for a shilling. There would be bread and butter and perhaps a cake and some jam and a pot of tea. If we wanted eggs and perhaps some Devonshire cream for a special treat if one of us had a birthday or something, well, then we paid an extra sixpence each.[34]

They were bound to get caught, and they did, but not until close to the end of their second and final year of teacher training, when a professor spotted them having tea together, not five safe miles away, but at Deller's Cafe downtown, and they were carpeted. Thus, at the age of twenty, Norah had to write to her father, and M.J. to his mother, for permission for them to talk to each other. J.T. Dunsford came down to the college to check out young Major before he gave his permission; Elizabeth Coldwell was content to write.

So for the last couple of months we were not breaking rules at all; we met and went for our walks together and the occasional afternoon tea and so on.[35]

The couple became engaged in December 1909, the year of their joint graduation as certified teachers. Margaret Carman, their daughter, has a portrait of them together, taken as an engagement portrait, early in 1910. M.J. is wearing a formal suit, with vest, stiff collar and tie, Norah a high-collared white blouse and dark skirt. Her hands are clasped properly in her lap. They are an extremely handsome couple, who look as if they are doing their damnedest not to smile and spoil the solemnity of the occasion. M.J. is a clear-eyed, square-jawed youngster, with a high forehead and carefully slicked-back hair. Norah's hair is parted in the middle, lush and full. They are abrim with vigour and confidence, on the brink of a lifetime of faithful love — and adventure.

By this time, M.J. had come detached from his traditional Tory roots, but he remained the man he was, highly intelligent, somewhat naive, politically aware, historically informed and steeped in the British virtues — steadfastness, decency, loyalty and a sense of honour. He retained, all his life, an attractive innocence based on the notion he had grown up with, that most people were well motivated and that traditions were not to be lightly discarded. His brain and his experiences made him a democratic socialist, but he was psychologically an Edwardian Tory all his life. He was, and remained, an unashamed monarchist:

I remember the visit of Prince Alexander of Teck and the Princess Alice to the College in 1908. The Princess was of course a sister of Mary, Princess of Wales, afterwards Queen Mary and the grandmother of our present Queen. Almost forgotten now is the fact that Royalty was none too popular at the time, but they were a charming couple and they were well-received when they passed through the lines of the assembled students.

The Princess was a very charming and beautiful woman in youth and age and the Prince was a tall, handsome figure of a man.[36]

It was a time of curtsies and deference, as well as social and political debate, and it is hardly surprising that M.J. reflected this dichotomy.

After graduation, M.J. intended to leave England, with all its turmoil, and seek a job in Australia as a teacher, but his father-in-law-to-be persuaded him otherwise. J.T. Dunsford had twice visited Canada on business trips and came back convinced that this was the real land of opportunity. M.J. listened and then fired off a letter to the deputy minister of education in Alberta, D.S. McKenzie; he had seen an advertisement that Alberta required teachers. He got back a reply saying that if he turned up in the spring of 1910, there would be a teaching position available.

To M.J. spring meant "when the snowdrops came through the ground in January, and the crocus bloomed and the daffodils bloomed in February,"[37] so he booked passage on the steamer *Grampian* on February 9, 1910, and wound up in Canada in mid-winter.

CHAPTER FOUR

PRAIRIE PROSPECTS

Good-bye God, I'm going to Canada.
— A YOUNG GIRL, ON CROSSING THE CANADIAN BORDER IN THE 1930s[1]

M.J. LANDED IN HALIFAX ON FEBRUARY 19, 1910, AFTER A "PRETTY rough" sea voyage, accompanied by a friend, one Jack Newbury, who was also headed west, looking for a teaching job — and who turned around before long and went right back to England.[2] The next day, a Sunday, they took a train up to Saint John, New Brunswick, where they completed immigration formalities and then embarked by rail for Edmonton, where the department of education was located, via Calgary, stopping only briefly in Montreal on the way through. They liked Montreal.

The sun was shining brightly, there had been lots of snow, and the streets were piled high with it, because in those days, there was no snow removal. I remember the wonderful sight along the streets of sleighs with horses, and their tinkling bells, coachmen sitting up front with their rugs around them, and the people behind all wrapped in furs. We climbed Mount Royal, and looked across Montreal under the snow — a beautiful view. That night, we took the train west.[3]

M.J. had no job as yet, only the hope of one; he had a little, but not much, money, and he had left behind not only Norah, but almost everything and everyone familiar for this leap into the wilderness. He knew that it would take some time — probably at least five years, he and Norah calculated[4] — before he would have enough money to bring her out to join him; it was going to be a lonely life. Canada at this time had a population of just over seven million, of whom 394,000[5] lived in Alberta, the new province created, along with

Saskatchewan, five years earlier. It was a nation of young people — fewer than 15 per cent were over the age of forty-five, and most of the population, especially on the Prairies, lived on farms.[6] While the cities had such amenities as street lighting and even, to M.J.'s amazement, as we shall see, dial telephones, much of the nation was backwards, undeveloped and politically crude.

These early days are the ones that seem to have been etched most clearly in M.J.'s mind, and he described them in some detail, in various sections of his two sets of *Memoirs,* both the taped interviews conducted by Sandy Nicholson and the written version he began to prepare, but never finished, at Carleton University, and in the *Reminiscences* taped later. What follows in this chapter and the next is drawn from these three sources, straightened out in time (for some reason, he dealt with his life in Saskatchewan in and around his earlier experiences in Alberta, and never got around to transferring references that clearly belonged in one chapter to another), and with some additions from later writings:

Before I left England, I went up to say goodbye to some of the College professors, and one, Professor Hart, our history professor, for whom I had great regard, took a rather dim view when he learned I was going to Canada, and north-western Canada, at that.

"Now," he said, "have you a revolver?"

"No," I said, "I haven't a revolver."

"I think you should get one," he said. "People need revolvers there, everybody carries them."

The other question was if I could chop wood. He was quite sure I'd have to chop wood, and I said I'd never done it. He obviously thought I was headed for trouble. For all I knew, he was right.

When we left Saint John for the west, we weren't travelling colonist on the train, we were travelling tourist, so we were quite comfortable. We had been advised before we left England that if we wanted to save money, we could take a little kettle and frying-pan with us, and we'd be able to buy bacon and eggs and bread and so on, and do our own cooking in the tourist car. In those days, there was a stove at the end of the car, and we cooked on this as we went along, buying things at the occasional divisional points along the way.

What I remember most of all as we travelled through eastern Canada was miles and miles of snow and forest, and not much else. We pulled into Winnipeg at night, and went out to get a cup of coffee, dressed in our English clothes, and sporting bowler hats. I wore what was known as a "Christie stiff." We walked down Main Street until we came to a cafe that was open, and went in to have a cup of coffee. The fellow who served us said, "Are you cold?"

"No, not particularly."

"Well, can't freeze you fellows," he said. It was, in fact, about 40 below, if I recall correctly. We went back to the train and the next thing I remember was being awakened at Qu'Appelle, Saskatchewan, to say goodbye to a young fellow who had been on the ship with us, and was getting off there. Then we went on to Regina, which I don't remember at all, and then Moose Jaw.

Oh, it was a bitter day, snowing and blowing, when we went for a short walk in Moose Jaw, about nine or ten o'clock in the morning. All that day we travelled through what is now south-western Saskatchewan and southern Alberta on the way to Calgary, through a land of blowing snow and rolling hills, with only the occasional little wayside station along the way, and I remember thinking, "Well, if this is the kind of country I've got to live in, I'm going to save my money and get back to Britain as fast as I can."

When we got to Calgary, to change trains for Edmonton, we walked across the street from the station and had a very good breakfast in a Chinese restaurant — bacon and eggs and toast and tea — for twenty-five cents.

When we were approaching Edmonton, I got a bit of a shock. There was no railway bridge across the river to carry the C.P.R. line into town; at Strathcona, we had to pile out and change to a bus. I got talking to the gentleman beside me on the bus, as we were crossing the low-level bridge. There were some little trees visible from the bus window, and I said, "I suppose those are peach trees?"

He laughed and said, "Whatever gave you that idea?"

I explained that, before leaving the old country, I had been to a meeting called by a Canadian immigration agent, who had shown pictures of Edmonton, featuring girls picking peaches in an orchard.

My seat-mate laughed again. "Oh, those immigration agents, they play all kinds of tricks," he said. "Those are poplars. If you want to see peaches growing, you'd better go five or six hundred miles over the mountains to British Columbia."

In Edmonton, the only address I had was on a letter of introduction to Archdeacon Gray of the All Saints Anglican Church, so we got the bus to drop Jack and myself there. We simply knocked on the door, and, when he asked us in, told him we were newly-arrived from England, and needed a place to stay, at reasonable rates.

"Oh yes," he said, "I think I can do that for you." And he walked across the room and picked up the telephone and dialled the Castle Hotel. I was astounded. This was the wild and woolly west, and they had dial phones, which we were not to get in Britain for another thirty years! I was quite impressed.

The Archdeacon was also good enough to call the Deputy Minister of Education for us, and Mr. McKenzie said to send these young men along to him on Monday morning. So, on Monday morning, February 28, 1910, we went along to the Board of Education offices, where Mr. McKenzie said, "Well, we've got over 350 schools in Alberta; it's a bit early to send you out into the country, but there are one or two schools that would be happy to have you at any time."

One of these that he particularly recommended was in the middle of a ranching area — "The railway is going through, there will be a village there before very long; it's called New Norway.[7] I'll telephone down."

So, he telephoned the secretary of the school board at New Norway, a fellow called Jack Hodges, who invited me down the next morning. Well, I couldn't get there the next morning, as it turned out. I took the train to Wetaskiwin, which is about thirty miles south of Edmonton, where I had to switch to the Camrose branch line. At Wetaskawin, I went around to look at the local school, while I was waiting, which looked fine to me, and then I took the branch line as far as a village called Rosenroll, about sixteen miles from New Norway, where I would rent a buggy to drive the rest of the way. I had to stay in the one hotel at Rosenroll, which turned out to be difficult, because they were in the process of moving it. The railway had gone through about two miles west, you see, so they were moving the entire town over to the railway, and renaming it Bittern Lake. The hotel was jacked up on blocks, ready to move, and the moving crew were my fellow guests. I had a very good supper of pork chops, and then went into the lobby, a sort of rotunda, but very small, and the work crew were all gathered there around a big, red-hot stove, spitting tobacco all over the place. I'd never seen this before, and it turned my stomach; I went out into the cold and was relieved of my dinner.

When I went to bed, it was bitterly cold, and I got every stitch of clothing out of my suitcase, and put it all on, and managed to get to sleep at long last. The next day, I drove to the Dowling School District, the district around New Norway, where I was hired on the spot, to begin teaching at the Dowling School for *an annual salary of $660 a year. I was to board with a local rancher, Frank Flint, and his wife, and pay them $15 a month. Mr. Flint was the chairman of the school district, and this was a standard arrangement. It was quite a long walk from the Flint home to school — very much longer on cold winter mornings — but I was young and hardy, and it didn't bother me.*

The school I taught, Dowling School, No. 511, was new, a frame building, which had been taught the previous year by C.O. Hicks, later, like me, President of the Canadian Teachers' Federation. I had no pupils beyond Grade Seven, although I tried to prepare one young lady for Grade Eight. She failed English — she was of Norwegian descent, so perhaps that was not so surprising.

I got on well with my pupils, none of whom was more than fourteen years of age, and became quite friendly with their parents, and other families in the district, especially Mr. and Mrs. Butler, who had three children in the school, and also came from England. As a newly-arrived Englishman, I had some difficulties in the first few days. I was giving a lesson in arithmetic, involving weights, and one of the brighter boys said the answer I gave was wrong. I was a bit puzzled when the answer at the back of the book proved him correct, until he asked me why I had used 112 pounds as the value of a hundredweight, rather than 100. In Britain, of course, it was 112. Another time, I put a list of words on the board for a spelling lesson, and another student disputed my pronunciation of "tomato" — which I called, in the British fashion, "tomahto" — and was smart enough to ask me how I pronounced "potato." When I told him, he asked me "Why not pronounce tomato like potato?" A very good question, indeed.

The Flints' home was really rather primitive, and consisted of two homesteader's log shacks drawn together. The area had just emerged from the homesteading stage, although there were people who were still proving up their land before obtaining title. The homesteader received 160 acres of land, which he chose himself, in return for an agreement to spend at least six months in each of the next three years on the land, build a place to live in valued at $150.00 or more, and break fifteen acres within the three-year period. He usually managed to acquire a team of oxen, which would cost in the neighbourhood of $150, a wagon, plough, and a set of harrows and a seeder. He would either buy a reaper, or make arrangements with a neighbour who had one. And he would either buy or borrow a mowing machine to cut hay for his oxen, and his cow, if he had one. Many of the homesteaders were bachelors, who did without milk and bought butter or, if they could not afford that, lard, which was the basis of their *flapjacks, and could be used for frying. Prairie chickens were plentiful, as were ducks; there was no closed season, so that, in the summer months, they provided the homesteaders and small ranchers with plenty of fresh meat. For most of the rest of the year, the diet would be salt pork, or, when they became better fixed, salt beef from a steer butchered the previous fall.*

In some districts, where the homesteaders and farmers were better settled, they organized "beef rings" to supply themselves with fresh beef during the summer months. Usually, the arrangement was that sixteen families would each agree to slaughter a good steer during the sixteen weeks beginning about the middle of May and ending about mid-September. From this, each family received a roast, a boiling piece, and some steaks.

At the Flints, who were relatively well-to-do, the food was plentiful and good. It was common to use hot cakes or flapjacks instead of bread for breakfast, with a goodly amount of butter and syrup, accompanied by eggs and salt bacon. I took my lunch to school, and quite often, it consisted of bread and butter, the fried breasts and legs of a prairie chicken or wild duck, or, in the winter, a domestic chicken.

This was the diet of the well-to-do Alberta country home at this time. Struggling homesteaders, however, lived on flapjacks, lard, syrup and coffee or tea.

As soon as the homesteaders could obtain money or credit, they would build frame barns or homes, and one of my pleasant memories is of the bees connected with the building of a barn. As soon as the roof was on, there would be a dance, to the accompaniment of an old-time fiddler. Always, there was plenty of food and, for those who indulged in hard liquor, there would be a jug or two of rye whisky, which could be bought for about $5.00 a gallon. I can remember few who drank to excess. Tobacco was cheap. Those who could afford it bought little sacks of Old Chum, which cost twenty-five cents for a quarter of a pound. A few people smoked cigarettes, and those who rolled their own used Bull Durham, the favourite smoke of the cowboys. Older men chewed tobacco. Mr. Flint urged me, when I had a bad toothache, to try a chew off his plug, and I was violently sick, so that I never attempted to chew tobacco again. I was content with my pipe.

The countryside was a prairie-park land, with bluffs of poplar and willow interspersed with small ponds, called "sloughs," a name that was new to me. Two railways were being built — the Canadian Northern from the south up to Edmonton, and the Grand Trunk Pacific from the east. New villages were being established along the right of way, and New Norway was one of these.

Frank Flint was a small rancher, and from time to time his cattle were rounded up and driven from the open range, where they spent most of their time, to his homestead. I enjoyed riding with Frank, looking for stray animals, and I found the branding of calves in the spring, interesting, but cruel. They were not only branded, but de-horned, vaccinated and sterilized, that is, castrated, all at once. To my surprise, none of them died. At this time, the range where we went riding consisted mostly of lands set aside to be sold to improve educational facilities in the province. There were also some lands owned by the Hudson Bay Company and the Canadian Pacific Railway. The price of land in 1910 was about $7.00 to $10.00 an acre.

There were no Sunday church services in the neighbourhood, although there was a small building opposite the Flint home, owned by the Methodist church. I took a service there, on one occasion,[8] but so few came, I did not repeat the experiment.

From the outset, I liked the park lands of this prairie region. When the snow went in the spring and the willows began to show their yellow tinge, to be followed by the soft green of the poplars, the country was indeed beautiful. The sunsets were a source of never-ending wonder to me, and, during the winter, the magnificent displays of northern lights, sometimes in colour, were breathtaking.

One morning in April, two months after my arrival, a young man walked into the school and sat down in my class. The children were in an even happier mood than usual, because they had succeeded in making me an "April Fool" — I cannot remember how, and they were laughing and talking together. When I enquired of the visitor what his business was, he told me he was G. Fred McNally, the District School Inspector. He stayed at the school most of the day, and I carried on in my usual way. I had an excellent report, in which he noted that he was particularly struck by the short periods of physical instruction I had given, morning and afternoon. Later on, he asked me to address the district teachers' convention at Wetaskiwin, on the Swedish course on which my exercises were based.[9]

As the school year drew to a close, Mr. Flint asked me what I intended to do for the fall school year, which would begin at the end of August. When I told him I intended to keep teaching, he asked me if I would stay at No. 511, but I said they weren't paying me enough. He replied that they had never paid any teacher as much as I seemed to want, but a few evenings later he presented me with a contract that was much improved, and I signed. He then told me that, had they known I was an Englishman before I came down to New Norway, they would have told me not to bother to come. Later, I realized that some newcomers from the United Kingdom, mainly young men from wealthy families, were not popular in Alberta. Many of the settlers were of Norwegian or Scandinavian descent, and did not appreciate the airs and graces of the young lords.

At the end of June, 1910, I saw my first hail storm. First, there were the murky clouds gathering over the hills to the southwest, followed by the rumble of thunder, and then the rain, then high wind and hailstones as big as pigeon eggs. The children were terrified as the hail smashed through the windows and piled up on the floor. The storm did not last long, but, when I went outside, there were several inches of ice on the ground. I had certainly never seen anything like this in Devon. I dismissed the school and sent the children home. When I went home, Mr. Flint told me that, with all the ice around, we would have ice cream for supper. This was made in a small freezer, turned by hand. Cream was always plentiful at the Flints!

Most of the crops were smashed down in the hail storm, and Mr. Flint, who carried insurance, received compensation for an 80 per cent loss on his oats. The year before, he had reaped sixty bushels to the acre, less than the average in a new land where it was not unusual for oats to yield eighty or ninety or even one hundred bushels per acre. However, the crop recovered as the summer wore on, and he ended up with both a crop and the insurance, so that he did quite well out of that harvest.

Frank Flint had come from California, before he homesteaded in Alberta, and, based on information he picked up somewhere along the way, he frequently predicted that oil would be found in Alberta, because there were showings of a greasy film on one or two of the sloughs in the neighbourhood. Forty years later, of course, oil was found on the land which his son Chauncey had inherited, and Chauncey became one of the oil-rich men of the province.

During my sixteen months in Alberta, I learned to appreciate the friendliness and kindness of the settlers. If someone were riding through the country and happened to call at the house around six o'clock, there was always an invitation to join us at the table, to put the horse in the stable, and to stay overnight.

Mr. Flint was quite a horse trader and I remember, early in my first spring, a young man riding a very fine-looking saddle horse rode into the yard. It was about six o'clock, and the usual invitation was extended and accepted. Next morning, we went out to take another look at the horse. Mr. Flint asked the boy where he was going, and he replied that he was going up to the Peace River country to take up a homestead. Mr. Flint suggested that pulling up stumps was not the kind of work for this kind of horse, and proposed to trade him instead, for a nice little mare that would raise him some colts. The lad asked how the little mare was on the haul, and I expected Frank to be swallowed up by the opening earth after the description he gave that young fellow of the mare's ability to haul. However, the lad was not tempted, and went on his way. On another occasion, Frank fared better.

We had gone up to Wetaskawin, where Frank wanted to buy a small engine to pump water for the cattle, because it was awful tiring to do it by hand. I spent the day wandering around the little town while he bargained for an engine. In the barn at the ranch, he had a very fine-looking black horse, which he had been carefully curry-combing each evening. On the way back, he told me that he had made a trade with a Mr. Bearisto, the local implement agent, to take the horse for an engine, with the exact terms to be settled once the engine was delivered, and the horse inspected.

The following Tuesday, when I arrived home from school, I heard a gasoline engine chugging merrily away, pumping water for the cattle. We had supper and then Mr. Bearisto started back for home, with the new horse hitched to the back of the Democrat wagon he was driving. Frank watched him go up the road for a bit, and then remarked, "Well, I wonder how far they will get tonight?"

I said, "Oh, Wetaskawin is not very far by road. They will surely get home this evening."

Frank said, "Well, they may, but I never owned a creature like that before. She looks wonderful but, after she has gone eight or ten miles, she just collapses, and will go no further."

I was shocked. "Surely you didn't make a trade for the engine with a horse like that."

"You bet I did, and I got ten dollars, to boot."

Nothing more was said on the subject for a couple of weeks, and then Frank asked me to drive to Wetaskawin on a Sunday. I accepted. It was a beautiful May morning and we set off early, not long after daylight. When we got to Wetaskawin, we drove immediately to the implement dealer's and found him sunning himself in front of his office. As soon as he saw Flint, he rose and I never heard more foul language than he delivered at Frank. I stood by and listened to the row. I thought they would come to blows but, after a bit, Frank said, "Well, you remember when I came to this country four or five years ago, you soaked me on a cattle deal, and I have just been laying for you ever since; now I figure we are even."

Flint put the horses in the livery barn, and he and the implement dealer went off together, in the general direction of the local saloon. I didn't see them until late that afternoon, and they were both in a merry mood. Driving home, Frank burst into what I suppose he thought was melodious song from time to time; he was thoroughly satisfied both with his trade and his visit to Wetaskawin.

Well, there were few amusements, I guess. I taught Frank and some of his hands, as well as some of the neighbours, the new game of bridge, as well as bezique, a game for two players that helped to while away many a long winter evening.

I brought a number of my college books with me from England, and I began to set aside, on Friday afternoon, time for the reading of some interesting — and suitable — book. I introduced my students to Sir Walter Scott's Ivanhoe and Kenilworth. In later years, when I met some of my former pupils, some of them remarked that I had given them an introduction both to good English literature and to history. I regard this half hour or hour of Friday afternoon reading and discussion of good books as probably one of the most lasting influences I exerted during my years of teaching.

Before I began to teach in the fall of 1911, Mr. Flint suggested that I should buy a horse to get me to school. I asked him to buy me one, since I knew nothing about prairie horses. He remained silent for a minute or so and then said, "No, I won't do it. You are so green, I would skin you alive on any horse deal." Probably true. However, when school opened again, he loaned me a very fine saddle horse, which I rode for the entire year. When I offered to pay him for it, he would take nothing. He said that I had ridden with him and the boys, looking for stray animals, and had often rounded up a couple of wandering milk cows on my return from school in the afternoon. When I left, I made him a present of a couple of good English pipes.

Weather was of key importance to us, even more so than it had been along the sea in Devon. In the winter, the brutal cold would be interrupted by periods of deceptively mild days, although we were not in the Chinook region of Alberta, and then the cold would settle in again. One bitter cold day in January, 1911, the temperature went to sixty-three degrees below zero. I rode to school as usual, but only two children who lived nearby turned up, so I dismissed them. When I got back to the house, Frank asked me if I was cold, and when I said no, he asked *me if I would ride up the road, about two and a half miles, to see if a neighbour could let them have two or three pounds of butter, as they had run out. I was well-wrapped, wearing a heavy cloth coat with a fur collar, chaps on my legs, and heavy woollen mitts. There was a curious belief that new immigrants from Europe could withstand the intense cold during their first winter on the prairies. I have no idea where it came from, but I do not, in fact, remember suffering unduly, although I often awoke to find everything frozen in my room, and a rim of frost on the edge of the blanket from my breath.*

I spent New Year's Eve, 1911, with a young man named Gould who had recently arrived from Dorset, and was working in the newly-erected store in New Norway. Chauncey Flint, Frank's son, and I drove the team and cutter over to the hamlet for the celebrations, during which a high wind and blizzard arose. When we started for home in the morning, the trail had disappeared, and we could see nothing but a wall of white. I was somewhat dismayed, but Chauncey was quite undisturbed, and just let the team work the thing out by themselves, while we snuggled down into the horse blankets, and covered up. The team trotted along for quite a while, and then suddenly stopped. Chauncey got out and found that they had brought us to the corner of a fence, about half a mile from home. We were soon back at the ranch house, around a red-hot stove, enjoying hot coffee and toast. This was my only experience of driving blind in a prairie blizzard, and it was quite enough. It was not unusual for people to get lost in these winter storms, sometimes with fatal results.

While I was teaching on the prairies, I was also learning. I began to be aware of the low prices the ranchers received for their cattle, sometimes as low as two and a half cents a pound on the hoof, while, at the same time, they paid top dollar for supplies — particularly farm implements. Most of the ranchers and homesteaders were forced to buy on credit, and the interest rates were exceedingly high — usually not less than 12 per cent. Then again, when the homesteaders had proved up, they usually mortgaged their new property to pay the debts they had incurred, and often this resulted in the loss of their hard-won farms. It was then that I began to relate the conditions here to those I had been familiar with in the industrial areas of the United Kingdom. This strengthened my growing belief that government activities along socialistic lines offered the ultimate solution to both urban and rural problems.

In the spring of 1911, my second spring on the prairies, we experienced a very bad bush fire. I had opened school in the morning, but soon after a neighbour rode up to warn us that there was an out-of-control fire being driven our way from the south, by a high wind. Soon after, the smoke became quite thick, so I dismissed the school, rode back to Frank Flint's, and spent the rest of the day riding here and there to keep the fire from jumping the road allowances. Much of the poplar and willow bush around us went up in flames, but the ploughed land around the homestead made a good fire break, and we escaped any serious damage. The animals fled before the fire, down into the valley of the Battle River, and we spent quite a few days rounding them up again.

About this time, I took a gamble that was to have great, and happy, consequences for me. The West was exploding with growth throughout this decade, when the drive to bring immigrants in to settle the prairies was at its height, and real estate speculation was perhaps the most popular sport available — dangerous for some, profitable for others. During my first Easter break, in 1910, I had gone to Edmonton, where this fever was at its height, and bought a lot in a sub-division that had yet to be developed, for $100, paying $10 down, and agreeing to pay the balance in instalments. The assistant city engineer was boarding at the Castle Hotel, where I was staying, and when I told him what I had done, he remarked that newcomers were usually persuaded to buy worthless property. He advised me to forget it. I made no subsequent payments, and the deal was cancelled. Now, a year later, I accepted an invitation to visit Archdeacon Boyd at the Railway Mission in Edmonton, again over Easter, and while I was there, I enquired about the value of the lot I had purchased, and forsaken, twelve months earlier; it had increased substantially. Thereupon, I bought two lots, for $550 each, with $50 down and payments of $25 a month. That December, I had a telegram from the real estate firm offering me double the amount I had paid, and I accepted at once. This meant that, instead of having to wait five years to go back to England to be married, I had the money to do this now. Norah and I could settle down; I wrote her at once.

But we would not be living in New Norway. In the spring of 1911, my first full year at the Dowling school, I had gone up to Saskatoon to visit Norah's brother, Jack, who had a job as clerk in the Canadian Northern Railways office. While there, I heard that there was a new, two-room, school opening at Sedley, about thirty-five miles southeast of Regina, on the open plain. I applied for the job of principal of this school in writing, and got back a letter of acceptance almost by return mail.

So, I left Alberta and went east to Sedley to open the school on August 15, 1911.

When I presented myself to the school board, they were obviously startled to find that they had engaged such a young-looking man as principal — at the magnificent salary of $900 per annum. I was then twenty-two. It turned out that about the only thing they read on my application was my first name, "Major." They thought it meant that I had served in the army, and could therefore discipline the boys who were, in their opinion, rather wild. In fact, the first clash I had was with the board itself. The building allotted for the new school was in dreadful shape, and I told them the doors would not open until the place had been cleaned up and painted. School started one week late.

It took me about a month to get the pupils disciplined, and thereafter, I had no difficulties.

Sedley was a pleasant and prosperous trading centre in a wheat-growing area. The business people were all Anglo-Saxons or Scottish. The only French Canadian families were those of the station agent and the doctor. The school board chairman was a Scotsman, John Auchmuty, the Massey Harris agent, who had recently returned with his bride from Scotland, and was living in a very fine, modern house. The district round about was typical bald, prairie country. When I arrived in August, 1911, much of the land was newly broken, or had not yet been ploughed. There were hundreds of acres of wheat, however, and some flax. The summer had been favoured with plenty of rain, and the crops were heavy — I have never seen finer wheat than I saw on that first week-end, when Mr. Ferguson, a member of the school board, who had a McLaughlin Buick, invited me to drive out with him. The wheat stood shoulder high, with fine green heads, but, unfortunately, that Sunday evening it turned cold, and a heavy frost followed. The crops were badly damaged. This was the original Red Fife wheat, slow to mature, and subject to frost damage. The crop was mown, gathered in heaps, and burnt. The following spring, a few bushels of a new variety of wheat were distributed. This was Marquis wheat, developed at the Ottawa Experimental Farm by Charles Saunders, in 1907. It was a quick-maturing variety which was usually ripe early enough to avoid frost damage. It became the foundation of the wheat economy of the prairies; by 1920, more than 15 million acres were planted with Marquis.

Not long after I arrived in Sedley, quite a large group of German-speaking Russians came in from the Volga area of Russia. They were a hard-working, thrifty people who were determined to develop their land and give their children better opportunities than they had had. Like other curious townsfolk, I went *down to the station to see them detrain from their Colonist car. Men left the train first, and were greeted by friends who had settled in the district earlier. Then the womenfolk emerged, with the children, and, while the men exchanged greetings and stood around, the women unloaded all the bundles and baskets of belongings for the onward trip to out-lying farms. These new settlers, along with an increasing contingent of newcomers from Quebec, were to change the complexion of the town very much before long.*

During the year before I was married, I lived with three other lads in a small, rented shack just large enough to take our beds, a table, four chairs, a stove and some book shelves in its single room. We took our meals at the local hotel, until one of us discovered a cockroach in a piece of apple pie, after which, we went to the local restaurant, kept by a very fine Chinese gentleman, Charlie Wah, who looked after us as if we were his own sons. If one of us were confined to the shack with a severe cold, Charlie would drop around to see us, and would send over hot soup and meals to the stricken man.

My shack-mates were a student minister in the Presbyterian church — which I attended, since there was no Anglican church anywhere near — two clerks from nearby business establishments, and a teller from the Northern Crown Bank, Sandy Leslie, who became a lifelong friend. The four of us had a very happy time together. We were frequently invited out for meals and for evenings of bridge, or the discussion of magazines and books, which we read and exchanged.

I was taking an increasing interest in politics, by this time. Before I left Alberta, I had heard a good deal of criticism of the Laurier government for its failure to designate Frederick Haultain, who had been the prime mover in obtaining provincial status for Alberta and Saskatchewan, as premier of one of the two provinces. Little did I realize what his name would come to mean to me. I was also very interested in, and in favour of, Sir Wilfrid Laurier's proposal of a reciprocal free-trade agreement with the United States. This became the centrepiece of the federal general election held in September, 1911, and I would certainly have voted Liberal in that election, except that, having arrived in Sedley in August, I did not have the vote. Sir Wilfrid was defeated and replaced by Robert, later Sir Robert, Borden.

Provincially, I became concerned with the problem of education, increasingly so over the next little while. I had misgivings concerning both the Separate School question[10] *then agitating much of western Canada, and the manner in which many of the local public schools, including Sedley, were becoming, in effect, part of the Roman Catholic School system. Had I been able to vote in the 1912 provincial election, there is no doubt that I would have cast my ballot for the Conservative candidate, because of my dislike of the manner in which, under a Liberal provincial administration, the schools were developing along increasingly sharply-drawn religious lines.*

Also during this first year, I made some very good friends, who, I knew, would help to make Norah very welcome. One or two British ladies in the area found the countryside, well, uninviting, and looked back with longing to the lush green countryside from which they had come, as did some of the women from the eastern provinces, and the United States. In December, when I knew that I would be able to return to England the next summer, and bring Norah back, I told the Board that my intended wife was a trained teacher, and they immediately offered her a post at Sedley school. I was very careful to give Norah, in my letters, as accurate a picture as I could of the bald prairie and the kind of life lived there, so there would be no unpleasant surprises awaiting her.

Finally, that first year of teaching at Sedley drew to a close, and I was on my way back to England, after a rousing sendoff from Sedley by my friends. I left by train on Monday, July 1, 1912. The day before, a violent tornado struck Regina, destroying much of the centre of the city, including the handsome new Metropolitan Church, the Telephone Exchange and the Y.M.C.A. News of this disaster was carried in the British papers, where my father-in-law saw it, and he was very concerned, because he assumed that I was in Regina for the week-end, to await the train east. He didn't say anything to Norah, but he did worry, and set out to track me down and make sure I was all right. This turned out to be complicated. I was to have taken the Allan Liner, Virginian, from Montreal on July 5, together with a Scottish friend, my roommate, the student Presbyterian minister, who had gone on to Montreal ahead of me. I had sent him the money for my fare — we were to share a second-class cabin. For whatever reason, he did nothing about it until it was too late, and the only accommodation we could get was in third class. When Mr. Dunsford telegraphed, twice, to ask about the presence of a Major Coldwell in second class, he was told that there was no such person. And when he inquired after me by telegraph in Sedley, Regina and Winnipeg, I was nowhere to be found. When we were three days out of Montreal, the Captain sent a steward around to enquire if, by any chance, I was Major Coldwell. I said I was, and he rushed away to the Captain, leaving me

61

none the wiser as to why he was asking until after I arrived in Bridgwater, and Mr. Dunsford told me what he had done.

On my arrival in Britain, I went to my old home in Devon and, after spending a week there, I went to Bridgwater for the wedding. My best man was my college chum, Vernon Boyle, of Bideford. We decided to have a quiet wedding and I wore a business suit rather than tails. We were married on July 22, 1912. The church was crowded. The surplice choir attended and the bells pealed from the tower. When we left the church, some girls had baskets of roses and spread them along the short path to the waiting carriage. We spent our honeymoon at Babbacombe, Torquay, and then paid a brief visit to my mother and father, and to Norah's family at Bridgwater.

Next morning, quite a crowd of people were at the railway station to see us off on our way to Canada. I had intended to take with us a small suitcase, but Norah's brother, Fred, who had undertaken to look after all our baggage, had given this to the porter, who put it in the luggage compartment of the train. We had to change trains at Crewe, to catch the one that would take us to Liverpool for our ship, and our luggage never made it — instead, it went on with the train up to Carlisle, near the Scottish border. As a result, we boarded the liner Victorian with nothing but the clothes we stood in, and ten shillings I had in my pocket. Our travelling funds, about $300.00 in Canadian funds, had gone to Carlisle in my small suitcase.

Aboard ship, I went to see the purser, and explained our predicament. He asked me if I had railway transportation, which I did, and he then lent me $40.00, approximately eight English pounds at the then-applicable exchange rate, holding our railway tickets as security. I then dispatched a telegraph message back home, asking that one hundred pounds be sent on by wire to Montreal, where I would pick it up. We bought toothbrushes, combs, shaving gear and other necessities aboard ship, and fellow passengers were good enough to lend us enough bits and pieces of clothing to see us across the ocean.

At Quebec, where the Victorian docked, we decided to take a look at the city, and climbed the hill above the river to the Plains of Abraham. It then began to rain heavily, and we hurried back to the ship, soaked to the skin. We had no change of clothes, so there was nothing we could do but huddle in our berths while the steward and stewardess took our clothes away to dry.

At Montreal, a fellow Englishman on board who knew of our predicament offered to lend me ten pounds. Of course, I refused, until he pointed out that we were arriving on a Sunday, and we would not find any banks open to cash whatever money had been telegraphed there. In the end, we stayed overnight in Montreal, and then I was able to cash the Western Union draft, and retrieve our pawned railway tickets from the purser. We travelled west without further disasters.

Before I left England, I had had a letter from Sandy Leslie, my bank-clerk friend in Sedley, asking me to telegraph the time of our scheduled arrival at Francis, the station immediately preceding Sedley. He would borrow one of the two cars in town and meet us at Francis, so we could reach Sedley without having to undergo the boisterous and embarrassing welcome which would be, otherwise, quite certain to occur. This was successfully accomplished.

At Sedley, we had been invited to stay for a few days with Mr. and Mrs. George Carson, until our furniture arrived from overseas, via Regina. All went well with this, and we were able to move into our newly-rented home just before school opened.

The ladies of the village called as soon as we were settled, and Norah began to form friendships that lasted over the years. Among these was a friendship with Thérèse Grondines, elder daughter of the station agent. Norah introduced Thérèse to Sandy Leslie, and they soon became engaged. Sandy was a Presbyterian, and sang in the choir of the Presbyterian Church, while Thérèse came from a devout Roman Catholic family. Sandy approached me to ask my opinion as to whether he should take instruction to join the Roman Catholic church, and I replied that this was a matter he would have to decide for himself. He decided in favour, ironically enough, not long after he and I had been admitted as members of the Masonic Order, in the local lodge, Bruce No. 36, at Francis. The antipathy between the order and the Roman Catholic church was well known, and Sandy resigned.

My wife enjoyed both settling into our new home and the delightful autumn weather, which is usual in Saskatchewan. The crisp, cool air and bright sunshine were in contrast to what we had experienced during English autumns. We prepared for the winter season, and Norah was soon busy canning peaches, plums and other fruits in the homes which she visited. This was a new experience for her, but, after observing how it was done, she put up a plentiful supply, and continued to do so until she became an invalid, twenty years later. I had put in a good garden in the spring, and my bachelor friends looked after it while I was absent, so we had vegetables to store in the cellar of the comfortable little bungalow we occupied at this time, and which was heated by a large, nickel-covered stove in the living room, and a Quebec heater. Our cooking was done on a Detroit Gasoline Range, which increased my insurance on the contents of the house, but which was quite satisfactory.

Earning a joint salary of $1,600 a year, we were among the better-off residents of the village. On several nice Saturday afternoons, I hired a horse and buggy from the local livery stable, and we drove out into the country. The golden fields of grain, the harvest operations and, early in the fall, the wealth of yellow daisies, gave an attractive appearance to the bald prairie. Snow and cold came in November, and the winter was a stormy one. We were invited to spend Christmas Day with some friends, the Stewarts, who lived some nine miles southwest of Sedley. I hired a horse, and, since it was mid-winter, a cutter, and we set off from the village. The road was narrow and slippery, and we had not gone far when a dog suddenly ran out in front of us. The horse shied, and the cutter immediately tipped on its side, dumping us unceremoniously in the deep snow of the roadside ditch. Neither of us was hurt, but the cutter was a wreck. Fortunately, other friends were coming along to join us at the Stewarts, and they dragged the remains of our bedraggled vehicle back to town, before we all went out to the Stewarts for a happy visit. Norah appeared to enjoy the whole experience, but indicated that she was not anxious to take any more rides along the icy roads with me as the driver.

We attended several country dances that winter. Well-wrapped young people, perched on straw on the bottom of a wagon-box mounted on bobsleds, would race away to an enjoyable outing at some nearby house or hall. Visits to friends and exchanges of books also made this winter and the next enjoyable for us.

The second winter we spent in John Auchmuty's splendid home. The Massey-Harris agent's new Scottish wife had gone back to the home country for a long winter visit, and we rented the home, and then took John in as our guest — both landlord and tenant at the same time.

Norah never complained about the cold — or anything else, for that matter — but she must have felt it, as I did, on those frigid mornings when we would go to the school to find everything frozen solid, even the ink in the inkwells, until the stoves could do their work and bring the temperature up to at least a bearable level.

Norah was a splendid teacher, popular with her young charges — she taught the lower grades and I the upper — as well as with parents, and, indeed, everyone. The next spring, she was awarded the highest marks of any primary room in the district by the school inspector, James Duff, a fact that made us both very proud.

One of the many friends I made in Sedley was Simon Israel, a very fine and intelligent Jewish storekeeper who, with his little family, had rather cramped accommodations behind his small general store. He was a Socialist from Eastern Europe, a constant reader, and a very well-informed man who kept up my interest in the new political changes that were coming over Europe.

During the three years I spent at Sedley — from mid-1911 to mid-1914 — the English-speaking element, who began to move out as more and more eastern Europeans immigrated into the district, used to wonder what the country would be like with the influx of poor peasantry who were settling in large areas of Saskatchewan.[11] *From the vantage point of today, what one can say about the fears of many Anglo-Saxons is that they were entirely groundless. The children and grandchildren of these people who looked so depressed have secured an education — many of them are graduates of our colleges and universities, and are occupying respected and influential places in the fields of education, the professions and business, not only in the western provinces, but all across Canada. To these settlers, Saskatchewan and Canada owe a huge debt for the great contribution they made to the development of the prairies and the welfare of the West. Any fears my compatriots had in the early part of this century have proved to be entirely groundless. Because my wife and I taught many of the children of these immigrants, we conceived a deep liking for them, and formed a deep respect for the parents whom we got to know.*

At the same time, changes were coming to Sedley that would soon turn my eyes elsewhere. As the proportion of Roman Catholics, particularly of French Canadian background, increased, there was a stronger and stronger feeling that the Sedley School should be run on more religious lines, and, in particular, Roman Catholic lines. I had no dislike of Roman Catholicism, having been raised in a very High Anglican way, but I did have concerns about the increasing intrusion of religion into the school system. In 1914, a new school board was elected, with a Roman Catholic priest as chairman, and, not altogether surprisingly, they wanted to see a Roman Catholic in my position.

By a happy coincidence, James Duff, the school inspector who had given Norah such an outstanding review, knew of a new school about to be opened in the village of North Regina, a separate community adjacent to the Saskatchewan capital. He was happy to recommend me for the principalship of this new school, so I applied for the job, and was accepted. So it came about that, in July, 1914, we said farewell to our many friends in Sedley — of course, we would often come back on visits over the later years — and packed to move to Regina.

We arrived there on August 4, the day war broke out.

PART III

THE MAN FROM REGINA

Saskatchewan, Saskatchewan,
There's no place like Saskatchewan.
We sit and gaze across the plain,
And wonder why it never rains,
And Gabriel blows his trumpet sound:
He says: "The rain, she's gone around."

— FOLK SONG

CHAPTER FIVE

THE RELUCTANT POLITICIAN

If you had a lit-tle more wood, and a lit-tle more water, and here and there a hill, I think the prospect would be improved.
— SIR JOHN A. MACDONALD, DESCRIBING REGINA, 1886

THE NORTH REGINA SCHOOL WHERE M.J. WAS APPOINTED HAD NOT BEEN completed when Norah and M.J. moved on August 4, 1914. Instead, the school ran for its first months in four rooms above Marshall's store, on what is now Coldwell Avenue. There were four teachers, but Norah was not one of them; she was carrying Jack, the boy who would be born in April 1915. M.J.'s starting salary was $1,400 a year, almost as much as both had earned at Sedley, with a promise of a $100 raise every year.

Schools at this time were very much under the control of the local school board, which was often more concerned about the possibility that a teacher might lead the children to perdition by keeping company with men, or going to the awful extreme of sucking up sundaes in a downtown shop, than with what went into the little heads scholastically. Here are the rules laid down in a contract for a female teacher in Ontario in 1915:[1]

1. You will not marry during the term of the contract.
2. You are not to keep company with men.
3. You must be home between the hours of 8 p.m. and 7 a.m. unless attending a school function.
4. You may not loiter downtown in ice cream stores.
5. You may not travel beyond the city limits, unless you have the permission of the chairman of the board.

6. You may not ride in a carriage or automobile with any man, unless he is your father or brother.
7. You may not smoke cigarettes.
8. You may not dress in bright colours.
9. You may under no circumstances dye your hair.
10. You must wear at least two petticoats.
11. Your dresses must not be any shorter than two inches above the ankle.
12. To keep the schoolroom neat and clean, you must: sweep the floor at least once daily; scrub the floor at least once a week with hot, soapy water; clean the blackboards at least once a day; and start the fire at 7 a.m., so the room will be warm by 8 a.m.

M.J., being male and strong-minded, was never subjected to rules quite this bizarre, but many of his fellow teachers were, and it is not surprising that he became determined to do all he could to improve conditions and obtain some sort of uniformity and job security — which meant going directly against the whole school board system.

His new school was located in a working-class area, with very few amenities, no sidewalks and no adequate services, such as snow removal. The outbreak of war led to a much improved employment picture, but it was still an area of low wages, long hours and no backchat to the employer. Still, the Coldwells were self-sufficient, friendly and adaptable. They rented a house near the school (M.J. described it briefly as "small; the bedrooms had sloping ceilings"[2]) and settled down to what they confidently expected to be a happy normal life of teaching and raising a family.

However, within weeks of their arrival, M.J. was drawn into local politics, much against his will.

We had no post office in North Regina, and a meeting was called, downstairs from the school, in Marshall's store, to do something about this. Because I was a school principal, it was automatically assumed that I would take the chair at this meeting, and I did. Among the honoured guests attending was the former Conservative candidate for the riding, and the Conservative organizer. The federal government was that of Robert Borden, a Conservative, and it was suggested at this meeting that the way to get a post office was to form a local Conservative association. I would have nothing to do with this, of course, but a motion to form a Conservative association was duly passed, and the post office was duly awarded. A Conservative was appointed postmaster. It was my first taste of patronage politics in Saskatchewan.[3]

Federally, the Conservatives ran the patronage, but they held only one of the eleven federal Saskatchewan seats; from 1906 onwards, the province was in the unrelenting grip of the Liberal party, and machine politics, backed by patronage and, where necessary, bribery, ruled.[4] Doubtful voters were subjected to the pressure of friends or the persuasion of promises — usually to build a road to help get the crop to the railway. Party supporters were taken for granted between elections, unless they began to grumble, at which point they were brought around by the same methods as doubtful voters. Conservatives were ignored: "It was no use arguing with them, or bribing them; they might change their politics, but that would only be by their suddenly seeing the light."[5] However, a good deal of effort went into keeping Conservatives out of positions of influence in the constituency. If a strong Conservative cleric was under consideration in a riding, for example (it was a time when the political views of clerics were influential, and they showed no hesitation in advising their flocks as to how they should cast their ballots), the Liberal organizer would contact party workers on the church appointment committee to block the nomination. If possible, where well-known Conservatives intruded, in spite of the precautions taken, they were neutralized to keep the poison from spreading. "A small furniture dealer in town might, for instance, be told that if he and his family did not transfer their allegiance from the Conservatives to the Liberals, they would get no government business."[6]

Like many others, Coldwell was repelled by this crude approach to party politics and resolved to have nothing more to do with it. However, he was soon drawn into educational politics. The process began when Walter Scott, the minister of education, as well as Liberal premier, invited the teachers who were involved in marking the province-wide grade eight examination papers, which included M.J. — it was a nice way to earn a little extra money — to "consider ways and means of improving education in the Province."[7]

This they did, in ways that were both unexpected and unwelcome to those in authority. Some of the sub-examiners with whom M.J. met were familiar with the newly formed National Union of Teachers in the United Kingdom, and M.J. was soon involved in drawing up a series of proposals that included job security: firm contracts, "instead of being appointed and dismissed at the whim of members of the School Boards, who, in many instances, were uneducated;"[8] a system to negotiate salaries; a pension plan, which would be financed by contributions from the teachers; and a provision to establish larger units of administration to replace the local school districts — and thus, again, provide some job security. These recommendations were instantly rejected on the grounds that they "were not the kinds of suggestions which Premier Scott sought."[9]

The sub-examiners, feeling ill-used, promptly called a meeting of teachers to form an organization, which, avoiding the pejorative "union" label, became the Saskatchewan Teachers' Alliance. The first secretary of the new organization, William Howard, who actually ran the new group on a day-to-day basis, was very soon appointed to a job in the Department of Education. He was replaced by Alex MacLeod, principal of Victoria School in Regina, who, in turn, was swiftly wafted to a new post — Inspector of Schools. M.J. took over the secretary's position, which he had to abandon in July 1915, when his son became seriously ill.

M.J. wrote about this traumatic episode:

Our first child (John Major) was born on April 17, 1915. Norah had been very busy during the winter preparing for his arrival. She had a hand-operated sewing machine which she had brought from England, and, besides keeping up with the Red Cross work for the soldiers overseas, she had prepared a layette and other things necessary for a baby. A friend who was also a carpenter made an oak crib. Our doctor, R.R. Rodger, was a kindly, middle-aged practitioner, who recommended a midwife, who would come before the baby was born, and the baby would be delivered in the house. When the midwife told me that I should phone for the doctor, he came along late at night, but Jack was not born until the next afternoon, April 17. I am afraid Norah had a rather painful experience, but the baby was a fine healthy boy, weighing seven and a half pounds.

Norah discovered, however, to her disappointment, that she was unable to feed him. Those were the days before formulas were understood. We were not able to find anything that agreed with Jack, and for six months we struggled along with a child who grew weaker and lighter — indeed, he went down to below four pounds, and all our friends thought that we were not going to be able to save him. During that hot summer, Jack seemed to be almost lifeless, and, at one point, I telephoned the Reverend Frederick Stanford, Rector of St. Peter's Church, to baptize our baby privately.

One Saturday afternoon in October, we took him to see Dr. Coles, a child specialist who had been recommended by our own doctor, and who had placed Jack on a diet of a few drops of cream, with warm water, several times a day. It was a lovely afternoon, and Norah placed the baby in the perambulator, well wrapped, and I wheeled him along the sidewalk.

The wife of a railway worker, whose name I have forgotten, stopped me to enquire after the baby. I said he was very weak, and very sick. She looked at him and then remarked, "My mother told me that I was like that, when I was a baby. She saved me by feeding me Benger's Food." I knew of Benger's as an English invalid preparation, and we were willing to try anything, since Dr. Coles had nothing more to suggest. I telephoned the Regina Trading Company, and they sent out a tin that same evening. Next morning, we read the instructions very carefully, and made the food in a mixture of hot water, as prescribed for an infant under six months, but it looked lumpy and horrid; obviously, something was wrong. I suspected that North Regina's notoriously hard water was the problem, so I went over to the new school, where there was a cistern system to gather soft water from the roof. I fetched a pitcher of this home, we mixed it up, and the resulting concoction was smooth. We let it cool down to the proper temperature, and Norah proceeded to feed the baby a few drops. He took it, and kept it. That night, for the first time, Jack slept without crying from hunger pangs. To make a long story short, he began to gain steadily on Benger's Food. We increased the strength. We saw, at first, a gain of a quarter of a pound, then as much as half a pound a week, until, by Christmas time, we had a contented and thriving baby.[10]

Clearly, when you are hovering over the crib of a baby near death, other matters assume a lesser importance, and it is not surprising that M.J. gave up the secretaryship of the newly formed teachers' alliance during this period. With Jack's return to health, M.J. became involved again and was very much part of the growing movement to unionize teachers, which gradually spread right across the country. The Alberta Teachers' Alliance was founded in 1915, followed soon after by a similar group in British Columbia. By 1919, there were organizations in the three Prairie provinces, as well as in Ontario, and they met in Vancouver that year to form the Canadian Teachers' Federation, which remains the national umbrella group for what are, in fact, trade unions.

By this time, to his own amused bewilderment, M.J. was running for office, for the Regina city council, after dabbling again briefly, first in provincial, then federal, politics. The provincial election of 1917 was won handily, again by the Liberal machine, but during the campaign, there was a Liberal meeting at the North Regina village hall, to be addressed by J.A. Calder, who had replaced Scott as the provincial minister of education. Coldwell was nominated from the floor to chair the meeting, but he refused, because, he said, he wanted to ask the minister some questions about provincial education policies, and as chairman, he would not be able to do so. Calder agreed to submit to M.J.'s questioning at the end of his speech and found himself subjected to a grilling that the audience enjoyed hugely, but he did not. Years later in Ottawa, M.J. noted, when he was an MP and Calder, very nearly blind, was a Liberal senator, "he'd hear my voice in the hallway along the way to the Senate chamber and he'd say, 'Ah, there's Coldwell, there's Coldwell. I know Coldwell; he took the chair from me many years ago in Regina, you know.'"[11] In the 1917 election, Calder won, and the Conservative nominee in Lumsden, the riding that then included North Regina, and for whom M.J. voted, lost.

The federal vote was the "conscription election" of 1917, and the first trip to the national polls since 1911. Sir Robert Borden had held off calling an election, despite the vigorous objections of Sir Wifrid Laurier, the Liberal Opposition leader, that it was his constitutional duty to do so. Borden argued that it would distract from the national war effort, which he hoped to invigorate by establishing conscription. On July 6, 1917, the Military Service bill became law, allowing the forced enlistment of Canadians "for the defence of the nation"; this was the first time in our history. This legislation created a vast gulf between Canada's two founding peoples, because while almost every Anglo-Saxon citizen favoured conscription, most French Canadians shared the view of D.A. Lafortune, the MP for Jacques Cartier, who declared, "Do not tell me this is Canada's war. Canada did not make war on anybody... The statement that this is Canada's war is just mere imagination."[12]

Then Borden announced the formation of a Union government, including both Liberals and Conservatives, to bring the nation together to fight the war. Laurier refused any kind of co-operation, and denounced this attempt to make him responsible for a conscription policy that was bound to be unpopular with his French Canadian followers and that he had no hand in drafting. "As in the play of children," he said, "they asked me: close your eyes and open your mouth and swallow."[13] Mackenzie King, his up-and-coming lieutenant, was so dismayed at Laurier's decision, which was bound to deliver an election victory to Borden that might have been shared by both parties, that he went into a sulk and withdrew until after the election.[14]

M.J., the lad from Devon, was very much in favour of conscription. He had not been able to join up, with his young family and his necessary work, but he wanted to do so, and he thought conscription would give him a way out, by taking the responsibility for the decision out of his hands.[15] When he was asked to help in the election that came on December 17, 1917, he was more than willing. Then he discovered that the fix was in. This is his own description of what happened.

When I received the letter describing my duties at the polling station, I discovered that voting was on an expanded voters' list which included women, for the first time. However, only women who had a husband or next of kin serving overseas could vote. Norah's brother was in the Canadian army and she was, therefore, eligible. The letter that came to me also informed me that any naturalized citizen claiming the ballot should be asked for his naturalization papers. The letter stated that it was quite likely that some of these naturalized citizens, the majority of whom were opposed to conscription, would not have their certificates with them, and so, we were reminded that a voter, once having entered the polling place, if he left it to go home and get his papers, could not return. Obviously, since this was not made clear to the general public before the election, this was designed to deny such persons a vote.[16]

If there was neither logic nor fairness in allowing women the vote only if they were closely related to soldiers already posted overseas and thus almost certain to vote for the Union government, it was even worse to deny the vote to naturalized citizens, most of whom had no interest in pursuing a conflict that, as most of them saw it, was an imperial quarrel between British and German interests, rather than "the war to end all wars." The War-Time Elections Act was described by historians as everything from "a colossal gerrymander"[17] to "an attempt without parallel except in the tactics of Lenin and Trotsky to ensure the dominance of one party in the state."[18]

To Coldwell and many like him, it was simply another proof that party politics in Canada were no place for an honest man. He considered himself too busy for such matters, in any event, with his school work and increasing role in the church — he became a lay reader in the Anglican Church and spent one summer as a replacement minister at a small church in the Cypress Hills, in southwestern Saskatchewan. He received no pay, but was grateful to work for free housing. He was never drafted.

Towards the end of the war, he and Norah were both active in helping to succour victims of the deadly epidemic of influenza that struck Regina and, in fact, all of Canada. Norah was one of the early sufferers, but quickly recovered and spent many long hours helping others.

By this time, the Coldwells were solidly established as good neighbours, helpful people who could be counted on in a crisis, and it was not surprising to anyone but M.J. that he would be drawn into politics, this time at the municipal level. In 1919 he received a telephone call from the secretary of the Regina School Board, asking if he would care to submit an application for appointment to the city school staff. Although he was now making $2,100 a year and the Regina minimum for a principal was only $1,900, he decided to make the move from North Regina to the city, where opportunities were likely to be greater.

He was appointed to Dominion-Park School and then, within the year, appointed as the founding principal of Frederick Haultain School, named for the man who had helped to create the province back in 1905. He took over the new school in September 1920. If you call at the Haultain School today, and ask the principal about M.J. Coldwell, he has no idea whom you are talking about, although there is a plaque saluting M.J. just outside his office door.

M.J. moved his little family into a rented house near the east-end school and found that conditions in the neighbourhood were even worse than they had been in the north end. There were no sewers, no sidewalks, no snow removal, not even gutters to channel the flow of heavy rains or melted snow off the streets, so that his young charges were arriving at school with wet feet, shivering and miserable. He began to speak out about this and other municipal problems, and was soon butting up against the real estate developers who controlled city council and did not want any money spent on sewers and sidewalks in this poor section of the city. M.J. began holding night classes in Haultain School for the benefit of returning veterans, and a group of them approached him to run for office in 1920. He declined. For one thing, he was too busy; for another, it was not considered proper for a schoolteacher, particularly the principal of a public school, to be involved in politics.

However, conditions continued to deteriorate, and within a year he became convinced that nothing would change unless he took action himself. Accordingly, when Mrs. Austen Bothwell, one of the most prominent members of the local Council of Women, nominated him to run for city council, he accepted cheerfully. This body was elected at large — that is, there were no ward systems, and the candidates collected votes all across the city. Most candidates were clearly connected with one of the two old parties, but M.J. ran as an Independent, on a program of improving conditions in the parts of the city where people had been neglected, and holding down electricity rates, which were then very much under city control.[19]

Another of the candidates was a man named Charlie Gardiner, a postal worker who represented the Workers' Party, which turned out to be a Communist front. Gardiner approached M.J. with a proposal that they join forces, because the city then had a single transferable voting system. You would indicate your first, second and third choices on the ballot, and if your first choice was dropped off when the votes were tallied your second vote counted among those left. Gardiner was offering to try to swing his second votes to M.J. if he would do the same for him. He could also, he said, offer the support of the Regina Trades and Labour Council. M.J. refused. He said, "Well, Mr. Gardiner, I am not comprising with anyone. I am going to run as an Independent, and I am going to run alone."[20]

If he changed his mind, Gardiner said, he was to get in touch with his campaign manager, Jack Esselwein, a painter and active unionist. M.J. had no way of knowing it, but Esselwein, whom we will meet again, was an RCMP officer, and a plant.

M.J. was elected second on the city-wide ballot, while Gardiner was defeated. Almost at once, the issue was raised that it was not proper for a school principal to be on council, and a constitutional lawyer was called in. He told the school board that the way to get Coldwell off the city government, if that was what they wanted, was to defeat him at the polls.[21] Legally, there was no possible objection. M.J. was re-elected four times to two-year terms — three of these times, he got more votes than any other alderman in the city[22] — because he was seen as an indefatigable worker for all his constituents, but especially those who were less well off. He became a member of the city Relief Committee, which was responsible for the care of these men, and his first spectacular political affray came out of this situation. This is the way M.J. remembered it:

It was brought to my attention that the unemployed men in the city, particularly the younger men who had no homes, were in very bad circumstances indeed. Many of them — and there were quite a few returned veterans among them — were living in flop-houses and getting by on two meals a day allotted by the city. I went to see the Relief Officer, as he was then called, to ask that something more be done for them, but he told me that I had been listening to a lot of twaddle, and these fellows were simply agitators. I decided to find out for myself.

One of the restaurants where the men could use their meal vouchers was in the east end of the city, not far from Haultain School. The complaint was that the food here was particularly bad. Over the Christmas holidays, I let my beard grow, and got out an old suit of clothes that I used around the basement, and rubbed some soot on my face and then wiped it off, so that I would look like someone who had just come in on a freight train.

Just as I was leaving the house, on my way to City Hall to collect a meal ticket, there was a phone call from John Brownlee, the secretary of the Teachers' Alliance, and he asked me to meet him down at the Alexander Hotel, where he was staying.

I said, "Well, it's a bit awkward; I've got something I want to do."

He said, "I'm right near the station, where are you going?"

"City Hall."

"That's very close. Couldn't you drop in?"

I could see no alternative, so I went down to the Alexander and found John sitting in the lobby. When I went up to him, he looked right past this seedy bum, and kept his eye on the door, so I said, "Well, John, how are you?" He was taken considerably aback, but at least I knew my disguise was a success.

I went from there next door to City Hall, where they issued the meal tickets in the basement. I waited until I knew the principal official, who might well know me, was out to lunch, and then got in line. I was asked a great many questions, such as where I came from — Saskatoon, I said — my name — I cannot remember what name I gave — and my circumstances. Finally, and grudgingly, I was given a fifteen-cent meal ticket, which I took over to the Blue Moon. I was directed to a seat in the corner where people like me were served and presented my ticket for the fifteen-cent meal. What I got was some potato, some turnip, and a piece of meat that would have fitted neatly into the bowl of a tablespoon. I have no idea what it was. I called the waiter over and complained that I had had no soup, and no dessert, which were supposed to be provided, and he told me, "Well, the city won't pay more than fifteen cents, so what you got is all it's worth."

I went home, shaved, and went back downtown to a meeting of the Relief Committee, where I again laid a complaint against the Blue Moon. Again, I was told by the Relief Officer, a chap named Mr. Bertwhistle, that I had been listening to agitators.

"No, I have not," I told him. "I went there and had a meal."

Well, there was a great fuss over that. How had I gotten a ticket, and who had given it to me? When I answered these questions truthfully, I was accused of obtaining a meal under false pretences — perfectly true, of course — and I probably would have been charged, except that no one was anxious to have this come out. It did come out, though; somebody told a reporter from the newspaper, and there was a story which caused J.K. McInnis, one of the city's richest men, to claim, "This man Coldwell wants to hoist the Red Flag on the City Hall."[23]

One of the other fiery politicians on the council with M.J. was a Boer War veteran.

He had fought on the Boer side, and then came to Canada, settled in Regina and got into the real estate business. He was a fellow who often expressed himself very strongly, and one day he said to me, "Now, Alderman Coldwell, if I'm going too far in attacking people, I wish you'd try to stop me. Just give me a tug on the sleeve," he said. "I'll understand, and I'll stop." Well, he was a man who liked to take a long drink on a hot day, and at one council meeting, after taking on quite a little of John Barley's own product, he began to attack the Exhibition Board in a very personal way. After a certain amount of this, I got hold of his sleeve and gave it a tug. He paid no attention. After some more of his attacks on the Board I got hold of his coat and gave it a tug. He kept right on. Finally, I grabbed the leg of his pants and gave an almighty tug, and he looked at the Mayor, and he said, "Mr. Mayor, when Alderman Coldwell stops pulling my pants, I'll proceed."[24]

Coldwell became a kind of people's tribune, battling not only to improve conditions in his area, but to keep electricity rates down and to improve the water supply, which was notorious for its hard quality and evil odour. M.J. later claimed that he ran into a man who told him that, after moving to the city, "he could now credit the Biblical account of Christ walking on water. He had never believed it until he bathed in Regina water."[25]

Despite these pleasures on the municipal level, M.J. was becoming more enmeshed in the wider world of politics, as he saw increasingly that the old parties had little or no interest in doing anything substantive on behalf of either the workers or the farmers of the province. The Winnipeg General Strike, brought to a brutal end in May 1919, witnessed the suppression of civil liberties Canadians had taken for granted for decades, including the right to free assembly, and also witnessed the rise of a new figure in politics, James Shaver Woodsworth, the Methodist minister from the north end of Winnipeg who was one of eight agitators arrested for "Conspiring to bring into hatred and contempt the governments of Canada and the Province of Manitoba and to introduce a Soviet system of government."[26]

Resisting a cut in wages, which is what set the strike off, was seen by many Canadians as the road to Bolshevism. But not by Coldwell. What he saw was that the rules were changing, and that if anything was to be done for the good of the people he represented it would not come through the old parties. He was interested and sympathetic when the Progressive Party was formed by T.A. Crerar, a Manitoba farmer and president of the Grain Growers' Grain Company, a new co-operative designed to help the farmers in their perpetual battles with the banks and commercial grain companies. Crerar was brought into the Union government of Manitoba in 1917, but quit in disgust at the party politics that drove policy and, not coincidentally, kept farm prices low and farm costs high, by applying high tariffs to farm implements and removing them from crops.

One problem with the Progressives was that they did not regard themselves as a real party, any more than did most of the farm-based parties that sprang up across the country. They were so convinced that party politics were bound to lead to compromise, if not outright corruption, that they would not aim for government, only for positions in opposition where they could vote, pure of heart and full of feeling, for those measures they approved and against those they disapproved.

By this time, M.J. had a very full plate, for, in addition to teaching, administration and his municipal duties, he was trying to devote more attention to his family. Norah had given birth to their second child, Margaret Norah Coldwell, on May 4, 1921, and she was becoming old enough to want some of his time, along with Jack, who was six years older. Margaret had had a serious illness at the age of two that went under the vague name of "brain fever"; she had fully recovered, but that scare had made it all the more important to the busy politician that he must make time for family duties — and pleasures.

Still, the lure of politics proved too much. He joined the Progressives and helped nominate Dr. Hugh MacLean as the Progressive candidate for Regina in the 1921 federal election. He quickly became a member of the party's executive committee and chairman of its finance committee.[27] MacLean lost, but fifteen other Progressives were elected in the province, and the party formed the second-largest bloc in the House of Commons, with sixty-four members, among them Agnes Macphail, the first woman elected to the House of Commons. The Liberals, under Mackenzie King, had 116 seats, one short of a majority; the Conservatives, under Arthur Meighen, fifty. There were two new members who, despite their sympathies with the Progressives, would not join them — J.S. Woodsworth of Winnipeg Centre (against whom the charges of sedition had been permanently stayed) and William Irvine of Calgary East. They insisted on being called the "Labour Group." Irvine explained, "Mr. Woodsworth is the leader of our group, and I am the group."[28]

The Progressives should have been the official Opposition, but they refused to take the post, contending that they were sent to Parliament to cooperate in the passing of legislation beneficial to the country, rather than merely to oppose. This approach allowed Mackenzie King to pick off most of the key Progressives, including T.A. Crerar, with offers of cabinet posts or other appointments as time went by, and within five years, all that was left was the Ginger Group, mostly more radical Progressives from Alberta, who came into the CCF, rather than lapsing back into the Liberal party with their fellows. Crerar, in blunt terms, was suckered by King and eventually came to realize it. Many years later, when he was a senator and M.J. an MP, they talked about this.

Mr. Crerar was one of the few men who knew my first name, and he would call me up and say, "Major, can I come over and smoke a cigar with you?" And he would come over, and he always ended up by talking about Mackenzie King, and he'd say, "Major, he was a stinker."[29]

There were two strong strains to the radical movements then beginning to emerge in parts of Canada. One was the Christian Socialism of men like Rev. Salem Bland and J.S. Woodsworth, for whom politics was intended to be the practical expression of the social gospel by which they lived. Woodsworth embodied this in his "Grace Before Meat," which went: "We are thankful for these and all the good things of life. We recognize that they are part of our common heritage and come to us through the efforts of our brothers and sisters the world over. What we desire for ourselves, we wish for all. To this end may we take our share in the world's work and the world's struggles." The other strain was the American prairie populism of men like William Wise Wood, the American farmer who became head of the United Farmers of Alberta, and William Irvine, an undoubted socialist, but also a strong supporter of Social Credit monetary theories and "Co-operative Government," as opposed to party politics.

M.J. was not particularly comfortable with either approach. The political group that interested him most was the British Labour Party, he discovered. He took his family back to Devon on a visit in 1924 and, while there, made a thorough and sympathetic study of the policies of the Labour Party, which formed its first government, under Ramsay MacDonald, that year, but there was no comparable party in Canada.

When Crerar accepted a post in King's cabinet soon after the 1921 election, M.J., with other members of the Saskatchewan Progressive Association, voiced his disapproval and determined to run a candidate in Regina in the next federal election who would be committed to remaining independent of the Liberals. Not surprisingly, M.J., by now a popular civic politician and increasingly well-known intellectual leader, was selected, and he accepted with great reluctance. He believed that he was being pushed in two directions at once, neither of them attractive, and the Progressive nomination was the best way out. The Liberals offered him a nomination as either a Liberal Progressive or an Independent Liberal,[30] and offered him a $10,000 campaign chest to pay for "taxis and so forth." When M.J. pointed out that that was illegal, he was told not to worry about it.

The other pressure came from the left, from Jack Esselwein, the RCMP's

Communist stooge, who had become president of the Regina Trades and Labour Council on his way to a post as secretary of the Saskatchewan Communist Party. He would rise at almost every meeting where M.J. spoke to tell the crowd that M.J. was an idealist, but that "what was needed was a mass movement of the workers,"[31] not another politician, no matter how well motivated.

M.J. would not run either for the cash-heavy Liberals or the ideology-laden labour group. He noted, somewhat testily, that "if I was going to run, it would be as a Progressive." And that is what he did in 1925. He campaigned almost every hour of the night and day when he wasn't either teaching or involved in the ever-more-demanding business of the Saskatchewan Teachers' Alliance — he was elected vice-president of the Canadian Teachers' Federation at the annual meeting in Toronto in 1925, not long before the federal vote. In that vote, he went down to a miserable defeat, losing his deposit.

This was not a surprise to him. "When I was told I would lose my deposit, I replied that that might well be the case, but at least I will be running for something in which I believe."[32] M.J. campaigned for old age pensions, unemployment insurance and a railway to Hudson's Bay, to provide an alternative route for prairie grain.

Not long after his defeat, M.J. received a visit from Woodsworth, who was in town on a speaking tour. The older man hoped Coldwell was not too disappointed and that he would continue to work for progressive causes. M.J. replied that of course he would.[33]

The two men hit it off at once. They were quite different in their approaches to politics — M.J. was always a strong believer in organization, fund-raising and all the boring paraphernalia of getting out the vote, while Woodsworth was content to let the party, as well as himself, be fed by ravens, apparently. Still, they were both after the same thing — a complete reordering of the economy and politics — and they liked each other. M.J. took Woodsworth home to meet Norah, and thereafter, whenever Woodsworth was in Regina, if he could, he would visit the Coldwells.[34]

What he got out of this 1925 campaign, besides some experience and the meeting with Woodsworth, was a debt of about $800, which he had no way to repay, since he had spent all his own savings long before the vote. It was paid off for him by his electoral agent, George Thorne, a prominent Regina lawyer.[35]

The 1925 election resulted in a hung jury. King's Liberals were reduced to 99 seats, while the Conservatives held 116, but the 24 Progressives continued to back King, and the constitutional brouhaha that set off, the famed King-Byng controversy, led to another election in 1926.

This time, M.J. declined to run. As well as his duties as alderman and school principal, he was becoming more and more caught up in the teachers' federation, becoming president of the Saskatchewan Teachers' Alliance in 1924 and secretary-treasurer of the Canadian Teachers' Federation in 1928 — a job he held through 1934. He supported Charles Dunning, the Liberal candidate in Regina, in the 1926 vote, and then watched in dismay as the Liberals, sandbagged into introducing old age pensions by J.S. Woodsworth,[†] then abandoned every other promise, including one to bring in some form of unemployment insurance.

Federal politics were losing their attraction for M.J., and, in Saskatchewan, Jimmy Gardiner had taken over the Liberal machine, which he drove with zest and abandon over all the opposition, so that appeared to be out, as well. At the same time, M.J. was seen as an attractive young politician — he was still under forty — with backing across the political spectrum. He had a deep, attractive speaking voice and was becoming adept at radio talks, which were the new political medium of import. (He had almost nothing left of the Devon accent he grew up with, beyond the occasional broad "a.")

Radio has always been a powerful and persuasive medium in Canada and continues to be important even in an age of television, but at this time it was the overwhelming influence in a province where there were few organized entertainments and a deep and abiding interest in politics. M.J.'s skill before the microphone was key to the increasing acceptance of democratic socialism on the prairies. Unlike "Bible Bill" Aberhart, next door in Alberta, he never shouted, ranted or roared; rather, he delivered his message in straightforward language that appealed at once to thoughtful voters. Lorne Ingle, who knew, liked, and worked for both Coldwell and T.C. Douglas, contends:

> M.J. won more converts to democratic socialism, though he didn't often use that term, by convincing arguments, delivered in his well-modulated voice in weekly broadcasts listened to regularly by people

---

[†] King needed the votes of Woodsworth and A.A. Heaps, who had replaced Irvine as the Labourite Group, to survive a confidence vote in early 1926. Woodsworth extracted a written promise to introduce old age pensions within the year, even though they had not been mentioned in the Speech from the Throne; this promise was kept.

all over Saskatchewan, than were ever converted by the hilarious jokes that Tommy Douglas told at every meeting he addressed. Dr. James Mutchmore, Moderator of the United Church, once told me that he experienced a very different feeling among the people, in their attitude to one another, when he crossed the border from Manitoba into Saskatchewan. The Saskatchewan people seemed to have a much deeper sense of caring for one another. That, I am convinced, is one of the more important legacies that M.J. left to the province, and I think even Tommy Douglas would have agreed with me on that.[36]

While he never hesitated to embrace Socialism in his speeches, he was clearly open to any ideas that would improve the lot of ordinary people, and he was socially acceptable everywhere. When the federal government appointed three prominent men to represent Saskatchewan on the National Committee to Celebrate Canada's Diamond Jubilee in 1927, M.J. was named, along with George Edwards, President of the Saskatchewan Farmers Union, and Premier Jimmy Gardiner. M.J. was very proud of this appointment, which was to have some quite unintended repercussions.

We met in Ottawa, in March, where plans were laid for the celebration. I had the temerity to oppose the concentration of the celebration in Ottawa, and suggested that it should be nation-wide, and designed to pay tribute to the pioneers of our country, and to inspire the children with respect and love for Canada. After several speakers, including Agnes Macphail, had supported the nation-wide idea, a short recess was called. A lady sat down beside me, and said she had been most interested in the remarks that I had made. I told her that I thought there was too much "flunkeyism" in Ottawa, largely because the residence of the Governor General was situated there. She seemed very interested, and we were still discussing the matter when the Hon. Mr. Fielding[37] moved over, and, bowing to the lady, said, "Your Excellency, may I have a word with you when you are free?"

You can imagine my surprise when I found I had been unburdening myself to Lady Willingdon, the wife of the Governor General!

During my visit to Ottawa in March 1927, Mr. Robert Forke invited me to his office.[38] He told me that he had accepted the invitation to become Minister of Immigration because he wished to stop the corruption that was going on in that department. He told me that some Members of Parliament secured immigration permits for which they received contributions that amount to $200.00 per permit. Mr. Forke said that he felt that some of us who were critical of him should know of his determination to clear up the department. I regarded this, of course, as at least semi-confidential, not a matter for public comment.

However, when I returned to Regina, I was invited one evening to speak to the Sons of England Association. The topic was "Immigration." I assumed that this was a closed meeting and, in the discussion following my address, in answer to a question, I told them of how immigration permits had been misused to allow ineligible immigrants to enter the country. It transpired that this was not a closed meeting, and, the next morning, I read a fairly accurate report of my remarks in the local paper, under a headline suggesting, rightly, that I had levelled charges of corruption against some MPs. I sent Mr. Forke a copy of the newspaper, and received a letter stating that the information he had given me was confidential, and that I should not have related it at a public meeting.[39] The matter was raised in the House of Commons, and an Immigration Committee was established to look into the matter. After a good deal of controversy, I was called as a witness, but a lawyer friend informed me that I could ignore the summons, because no "caution money" had been forwarded with it. His opinion was that this was a loophole, of which I could avail myself, if I so desired. However, I was determined to "face the music" and appeared in Ottawa in May, 1928.

I was a bit overawed when I entered the Railway Committee Room and found every seat occupied. Before going down to the committee meeting, I had been reading in Mr. Woodsworth's room, on the sixth floor, when Tom Wayling, whom I had known in the old Progressive days as Mr. Crerar's secretary, and who was now in the Press Gallery, dropped in to see me. He told me that he thought I was in a tight box, because I had no documentary proof of my charges. He suggested that, when I was called at the committee, the statements I made in Regina would be read, and that if I said the story was an exaggeration, that would end it. But I could hardly do that.

Immediately after I was sworn, the Clerk produced the Regina Leader-Post and read the report. The chairman then asked me if this was an accurate report of what I had said. My reply was that it was substantially accurate. I was cross-examined, and asked to name Members of Parliament who had been cited to me by the Minister. I declined to do so, since the information had come to me through Mr. Forke, and was not the result of my own investigations. Thereupon, a member moved a motion that I should be compelled to name names, or face

Major Terrace, in Seaton, Devon. Except for the car, it looks much as it did when M.J. was born here, in No. 5 of six identical houses — second from the right. (WALTER STEWART)

M.J. as an infant.

M.J. about the time he began to go to school in Exeter.

Hele's School, which M.J. attended, is now part of the University of Exeter.
(WALTER STEWART)

Coldwell in 1909 (above), dressed for a debate. Doubts about his conservatism began to set in when he constantly lost to a socialist.

Norah Dunsford in costume for a performance of *The Mikado,* in 1910.

It was just not done to smile in a formal engagement picture
in 1910, but both M.J. and Norah appear pleased.

Before he became a Canadian, a socialist, and a pacifist, and while he was training to be a teacher, M.J. joined the "Territorials" (top), a militia outfit. That's M.J., with the pipe, standing at right, photographed probably in the summer of 1908.

Norah's photograph helped keep out the cold in Canada.

M.J. and Norah on the porch of their rented house in Sedley, Saskatchewan, 1911.

The Sedley school, en masse, in 1913. Norah, who taught the lower grades, is on the porch, at left, and M.J. is on the right.

The Coldwells (above) soon after the move to North Regina in 1914. They arrived the day war broke out.

A family portrait, taken after Jack had recovered from his childhood illness.

During a visit to Seaton in 1924, M.J. poses with his family, and Norah's sister, Mary Dunford. From left are M.J., Jack, Norah, Margaret, and Mary.

The Coldwells in Regina (above left), about the time M.J. first ran for city office. In 1932, Norah (above right) was clearly suffering from multiple sclerosis.

Candidate Coldwell in 1935, when he was first elected to Parliament.

a citation for contempt. I then named one name, as that of a man named by Mr.
Forke in our conversation. I learned afterwards that, had I volunteered a name,
rather than having it compelled from me, I would have lost the privilege that cov-
ered my evidence before the committee, and been subject to an action for slander.[40]

There were a number of results from this performance. One was that M.J.
was approached by a Saskatchewan MP, a lawyer, who wanted to know where
he had studied law, since the adroit way he had evaded the slander trap indicated that he must have done so. M.J. told him that he had never studied law
and owed his escape simply to telling the truth. A second was a change in the
law requiring the tabling of a report on the issuing of immigration permits
within fifteen days of the opening of every session of Parliament, while
absolutely nothing was done about the clear evidence of instances of corruption that had already taken place. A third was a demand from the
Regina School Board that M.J. pay back $80 of his salary for the five days
he had been absent from school in Ottawa. He argued, successfully, that,
as he had been summoned by subpoena to appear before Parliament, he
had no choice but to go. He kept the $80, but he had made an enemy of the
school board, with results that we shall see.

M.J. stepped back from politics, except at the municipal level, for the next
few years, until the crushing weight of the Great Depression forced him back
onto the hustings. In 1929, J.T.M. Anderson, a Conservative, won the
Saskatchewan election and promptly appointed M.J. as chairman of a three-
man provincial commission into the Saskatchewan public service. He took
the job on the understanding that no one would be discharged from the service while he was carrying out his commission. Despite this, two men were
given notice of dismissal. Coldwell promptly went to see Premier Anderson
and told him that if the men were fired, he would resign publicly. The premier explained that one of the men was "a Liberal spy," who had been taking
papers out of government offices to deliver to Jimmy Gardiner's organizers.
One of these documents was a list of members of the Ku Klux Klan who held
high positions in the Saskatchewan government.[41]

The Klan had been active in the province since early in the century,
spreading the gospel of hate, particularly against Catholics and immigrants.
Anderson had taken a strong stand against the KKK, but many of his supporters and political adherents had joined it. M.J. kept the man in his job and

later destroyed the list of KKK members, but he was considerably shaken by the knowledge that the Klan had managed to penetrate so far into the government and civil service. His even-handed report, in 1930, marked him as a man who could be trusted to work in a non-partisan way. Nearly forty years later, he would repeat very much the same sort of work, with equal skill, at the federal level, after his electoral defeat.

By mid-1929, the inability of both levels of government, federal and provincial, to deal with mounting problems on the farms, even before the depression struck, was beginning to make more and more westerners believe that that strange bird, J.S. Woodsworth, already one of the outstanding figures in the House of Commons, might have it right, and that a new approach to politics was a necessity. Clarence Fines, the assistant principal at M.J.'s school — who had been brought up a staunch Conservative like M.J. (he had won a public speaking contest for a speech in praise of Arthur Meighen)[42] but who quickly fell under M.J.'s spell — suggested the formation of a new political group to break the lock the old parties had on the electoral system. The two men cobbled together the Independent Labour Party, which was aimed, at first, simply at organizing for municipal elections to keep M.J. and Fines in their aldermanic posts. Before long, branches had been formed in Moose Jaw, Saskatoon and Melville. Coldwell gave political talks on the radio, usually on the subject of economic planning, and donations from listeners paid for the air time, with a little left over to help keep the party going.

Not that that mattered much; it would soon be absorbed into an entirely new political movement.

CHAPTER SIX

PLAN OR PERISH

The CCF is a federation of organizations whose purpose is the establishment in Canada of a Co-operative Commonwealth in which the principle regulating production, distribution and exchange will be the supplying of human needs and not the making of profits. — OPENING WORDS OF THE *REGINA MANIFESTO*, 1933

THE COLDWELL HOME IN REGINA, WHICH WAS SHIFTED DURING THIS PERIOD from the modest house on Athol Street, where Margaret was born, to a very fine home on Connaught Crescent, not far from the legislature, became the centre of intellectual activity of the political left in Regina. Along with the bank that held the mortgage, M.J. bought this home on what had now become a salary of $3,000 a year, until it was cut at the beginning of the depression. He paid $80 a month, principal and interest.[1] This home came to be a hive of socialism not only through M.J., but also through Norah, who had become an early and enthusiastic convert to her husband's views. He chaired and took part in a series of readings and debates at school and at the Regina Public Library that dealt with a number of issues, including tariffs, economics and politics. There were also meetings of the "People's Forum," on Sunday afternoons in the assembly room of City Hall. These were usually, but not always, addressed by socialism and agrarian-reform sympathizers. The new theory of Social Credit also got a hearing, and M.J. himself delivered a paper on the subject, even tackling the "A plus B" theory at the heart of the mystery. (This theory, first promulgated by Major Clifford H. Douglas, a reserve officer in the Royal Air Force in England, held that the capitalist system could not provide people with enough purchasing power to obtain the goods and service that they and their countrymen were producing. That was because the wages they received would always be less than the costs of production, because of profit margins, overhead, distribution and credit charges. To bring A — incomes — into balance with B — production costs — it was necessary for the government to provide the missing funds by way of a "social credit." The theory did not explain where this money was to come from.) M.J. wrote that while there were some obvious advantages in creating more money to expand the economy, the theory could only be applied by the kind of dictatorship that would never be welcome in Canada.[2] M.J. also organized a series of Saturday-evening meetings in his home, where all the latest developments in democratic socialism in Europe were discussed. For her part, Norah convened a similar salon, to discuss George Bernard Shaw's *An Intelligent Woman's Guide to Socialism and Capitalism*,[3] and works of that ilk. "Among ourselves," Coldwell wrote later, "we called this group, 'the Intelligent Women.'"[4] She also took over the chair of "Minnie Benson's Book Club," after that redoubtable socialist lady died. Finally, there was a "Peace Study Group," a group of Regina women who met monthly to discuss issues of war and disarmament. "They invited guest speakers from time to time, regardless of their political opinions."[5]

But Norah was increasingly dogged by a malaise that had been coming on for some time, which caused her considerable pain and left her with very little energy. In early 1930, at the age of forty-two, she took the train to Winnipeg, where, on the advice of the family physician, she consulted a specialist. He told her that she undoubtedly had multiple sclerosis, a malady for which there was, and is, no known cause or cure, and which attacks the brain, spinal cord and nerves, causing paralysis, numbness and, eventually, death. The couple's response to this devastating news was characteristic — they said nothing and went back to work for their political ideals as if nothing had changed. Norah could still walk, talk and look after herself and her children, so she went about her social and political duties as before, only grudgingly giving way, six years later, to the permanent confines of a wheelchair.

References to this tragedy are few and far between in M.J.'s *Memoirs* and *Reminiscences,* and beyond the occasional phrase about "my wife's illness" or "due to my wife's increasing disability" to explain why money was so short (because of the need to bring in hired help), the subject did not exist. Norah was not the clinging, kitchen-bound, aproned and servile companion as wives were envisioned in the women's magazines of the time; she was

M.J.'s friend, critic, debating partner and lover, as well as she was the mother of his children.

While she continued to be the central figure in M.J.'s life, she could not share the rigours of campaign travel with him, and her constant pain, increasing immobility and occasional black periods of depression undoubtedly affected him almost as much as they did her. But M.J. never gave any sign of it or sought any measure of sympathy from anyone; nor did Norah. After her return from Winnipeg, M.J. continued to undertake new responsibilities in political life as if nothing had happened.

One of the few references to Norah's condition comes in a section of his *Memoirs* where M.J. was writing mainly about prices.

My wife's health necessitated our having domestic help, at first on a part-time basis and later, in the depression when my earnings had been greatly reduced, to full-time. However, girls were placed in homes by the Relief Department at a wage of $5.00 a month. I took a girl but paid her $15.00 a month, with the understanding that she could attend school or business college, as she wished to do. This was a satisfactory arrangement, both to the girl and ourselves. We had, also, an occasional woman to help with the cleaning and laundry, for we had electric appliances for that purpose. Prices fell drastically. I remember buying eggs at three cents a dozen in 1934, creamery butter could be obtained, in three-pound blocks, for fifteen cents a pound, beef from ten to twelve cents a pound,[6] pork and lamb about the same, and good roasting chickens cost fifty to seventy-five cents apiece.[7]

Even before the depression struck, it was normal to have political allies stay with the family, rather than in a hotel, and 131 Connaught Crescent became a sort of home away from home for travelling socialists, Progressives and agrarian radicals. Scott Nearing, a Princeton professor who had been dismissed for his outspoken pacifism during the First World War, was a visitor, and Coldwell was later dismayed to find that he was a Communist. He had a lifelong dislike and distrust of Communists, because they were, essentially and always, anti-democratic, dogmatic and quite willing to do anything to further the cause; for M.J., the ends never justified the means. However, he did have one far-left visitor, a drunken expert on Canadian resources, who obviously fascinated him, despite the tut-tutting we can catch in the following passage. Note how the central figure loses the title "Mr.," partway through the narrative.

When I met Mr. J.T. Walton Newbolt, he had left the Communist Party and had become a member of the Labour Party and a member of the British House of Commons. Prior to his election, he had been a professor of economics and Manchester University, and the author of a number of books on international and domestic affairs. During his association with the Communist Party, he had been the British member of a governing body of the International Communist Movement and had visited Moscow on numerous occasions.

We had intended to entertain him in our Regina home, but, it so happened that, on the Saturday evening when he arrived, my close friends, Mr. and Mrs. A.D. Leslie[8] and their two daughters had arrived to spend the week-end with us. I therefore engaged a room for him at the King's Hotel, as my guest. I went down to meet him at the railway station. We had never met before, but I felt confident that I would be able to recognize our visitor. I watched the people leaving the station, but I saw no-one who resembled my idea of Mr. Newbolt. I was just about to leave when I saw a shabby, tall man carrying a battered brief-case, waiting in the rotunda. He perceived that I was waiting for someone and approached me, saying, "Are you by any chance looking for Mr. Newbolt?"

I replied that I was, and he introduced himself. I took him to the hotel and told him that I would call for him the next morning, to show him around the city and take him to lunch, and then to the People's Forum, which he was addressing that Sunday afternoon, but I was rather shocked because I thought that this shabby, unshaven individual was not a very creditable representative of the British Labour Movement. This was confirmed the next morning when, with my good friend, Mr. Norman MacLeod, the principal of the Scott Collegiate Institute, I went to the King's Hotel. We were told that Mr. Newbolt was in his room. We went up. We found him still in bed and wearing a very grimy suit of pyjamas. He said he did not want to go for a drive, that he had a cold and, therefore, he would meet us at the People's Forum in the City Hall, at 2:30 in the afternoon. He assured us he could find his way. He did. He gave an extraordinary address. He had a map of North America, and he told us of the great future Canada had if she developed her resources in the public interest. I thought I was fairly well-informed regarding Canadian resources, but his knowledge was more complete and detailed than anyone in that audience. He spoke of the great power resources in Labrador, at Hamilton Falls.[9] *He told us there were vast iron deposits in that area. He spoke of the highly mineralized areas right across Canada in the Canadian Shield, in northern Manitoba and northern Saskatchewan. He spoke of the possibility of oil in Western Canada, the source of which he traced to the Alberta tar sands. He had a comprehensive view of the lumber resources of British Columbia, and the possibilities of lumbering and the pulp and paper industry in other forest areas.*

After the meeting, I asked him how he had acquired such a comprehensive knowledge of Canadian resources. He told me that, as a member of the Comintern, his job had been to make as complete an economic survey of North American resources as possible. He had obtained reports of surveys, of explorations, from every conceivable source in North America. His outline made me, more than ever before, a convinced advocate of the need for public economic planning and the social ownership and development of our great resources in the public interest.

The next day, one of our supporters, Mrs. Hanway, telephoned me to say that Newbolt had not left for his next engagements because, he said, he had a cold. Mrs. Hanway told me that, after the meeting on Sunday evening, he had sought a bottle of whisky as a cure for his indisposition! Mrs. Hanway's husband secured this for him and, when she phoned me, she said that Newbolt had telephoned her home asking if her husband could provide him with another bottle of whisky. We came to the conclusion that we had an alcoholic on our hands. No more whisky was provided. From time to time in later years, I inquired about Newbolt from various Labour members of the British Parliament whom I met. Apparently, he gradually went down and, in spite of their admiration for his great qualities of mind, they were unable to do much for him. The last I heard was that he had died in poverty, alone, in a London garret.[10]

Many of the Coldwells' other visitors, men like Ted Garland, the Progressive, were more help than poor old Newbolt in advancing the cause of the Independent Labour Party on the Prairies. The underlying difficulty of the ILP, M.J.'s chosen vehicle at this time, stemmed from the fact that it was the farm vote, not the union vote, that really mattered in Saskatchewan. And the only effective farm organization on the left, the cumbersomely titled United Farmers of Canada (Saskatchewan Section) had specifically resolved not to play any direct part in politics at its 1929 convention in the spring.[11]

The farmers were keenly interested in politics and often embarrassed visiting MPs by quoting to them from Hansard to show that the statements they were making in Regina and Saskatoon were directly contradictory to the positions they had taken back in Ottawa, but they opposed party connections of every sort. Some members of the farm group thought the solution was to plunge into politics with a new, honest party, but others felt their only hope was to stay aloof from the melee and try to gain concessions from the rest that way. Of course, this was when the national economy was still booming, at least in the East; that was about to change.

In an attempt to break this log-jam, Clarence Fines, Coldwell and J.S. Woodsworth brought together a meeting they called the "Western Conference of Labour Political Parties" in the fall of 1929, just as the stock market crash that inaugurated the Great Depression was beginning to collapse the general economy, and not just the farm economy. In 1930, they met again, in Medicine Hat, Alberta, and in 1931, in Winnipeg. Fines, as president, worked busily to promote a union with the farmers' groups, to form an alliance that would bind labour and agriculture together for reform, and invitations were sent out to anyone who might be interested in creating a "new social order."[12]

When the next convention of the United Farmers of Canada (Saskatchewan Section) was held, a somewhat different feeling was in the air. While all the purveyors of received wisdom in Ottawa and Regina kept explaining that the best way to cure the evils of depression was to do nothing, hope for the best and wait for the miracle of capitalism to refloat the economy, these people were losing their farms, their livelihoods, their savings, everything. A diet of gopher, which is all that some of them had to feed their children, induced them to swallow their misgivings about getting into politics. At the 1930 convention, 600 rural delegates adopted, with only six contrary votes, a resolution to form their own political party. They also passed a "Charter of Liberty" to guide the process. It called for nationalization of the Canadian Pacific Railway, social ownership of currency and credit, and "nationalization of all land and resources as rapidly as possible."[13] These were all included in the platform of the Independent Labour Party and, indeed, all the groups who had been meeting annually under the umbrella of the Western Labour Political Parties.

Clarence Fines shot off an invitation to the farmers to meet with this group the next year (1932) when, at the invitation of the United Farmers of

Alberta, the convention of these groups was to be held in Calgary. Before that could come about, there were two other key developments. The first was a letter written by a fiery young preacher in Weyburn, Saskatchewan, named Tommy Douglas to J.S. Woodsworth in Ottawa. Douglas was impressed by some of the ideas Woodsworth had been expressing, and he was anxious to promote similar discussions in Saskatchewan. Woodsworth wrote back to tell him that there was an alderman in Regina, a fellow named Coldwell, president of the Independent Labour Party, who was working along the same lines, and perhaps they should get together. Tommy wrote to M.J. in April 1932. Here is M.J.'s account of what happened next:

Having nothing to do one Saturday afternoon, I took my car and my son Jack and we drove down to Weyburn, where I asked for the Baptist minister. I was shown a little house and I went there and knocked on the door, which was answered by a very attractive little lady, very young, who told me that if I went over to the little white church, I would find her husband in the library preparing his sermon. So I went over and saw Tommy Douglas for the first time. We talked about the Independent Labour Party, and Tommy agreed that he would try to form a branch of the Independent Labour Party there in the city.[14]

Thus was born one of the most effective political friendships in Canadian history. Tommy Douglas was twenty-eight at this time, M.J. forty-four; M.J. became a mentor, to the extent that anyone could act in that role towards someone as fiercely independent as Douglas. They would remain friends and allies until M.J.'s death forty-two years later. The most immediate result of that meeting was a mass rally at the Weyburn exhibition grounds, organized by Douglas and his allies, which M.J. addressed on behalf of the Independent Labour Party, in May 1932,[15] but meanwhile, elsewhere, things were hotting up.

The other key development that took place in this same time frame was the union of Coldwell's Independent Labour Party with the United Farmers of Canada (Saskatchewan Section), under George Hara Williams. First, the ILP met in downtown Regina, where Coldwell, re-elected president, told the delegates:

The Labour Party cannot adopt the suicidal policies of those who want to see conditions get so bad that people will be goaded to revolt.[16] *Nor must we join those who wish to patch up a thoroughly worn out economic system. Neither brute force nor blind optimism are acceptable... In the face of all things that beset us, we must plan or perish.*[17]

This was followed two days later by a united meeting with George Williams's increasingly militant farmers, who, now that they had opted to join the real political world, were looking for a suitable ally. Williams was the most likely choice to lead such a union, since his delegates far outnumbered Coldwell's ILP group. There were two barriers in the way. The first was a trip Williams had made to the Soviet Union not long before, which made a great many farmers uneasy — the collective farms of Russia were not their idea of the way to go. The second was that Coldwell, the public school principal, alderman and intellectual, was certainly going to have a wider electoral appeal than Williams, who was a wonderful organizer, but a prickly leader. He had been fired from the Canadian Farmers Union for trying to steer it into direct political action before it took that step itself.[18] Williams withdrew his name from nomination, and Coldwell became, by acclamation, the president of the new Farmer-Labour party.

Here is M.J.'s account of these events:

In 1931, I was out as much as I could be trying to organize locals of the party, and then the United Farmers of Canada decided they must go into politics, because they could get nowhere by making representations to the provincial or federal governments. It was then I came into closer contact with Mr. George Williams, and other leading figures of the U.F.C. It was hoped that somehow or other, we might co-operate, and in 1932, we began to hold meetings all over the province, and we arranged, as the Independent Labour Party, to hold a convention in Saskatoon in July, and so did they. We thought that by producing our own programs independently, we might find ways and means of co-operating, but they were more convinced that there should be a single movement that would embrace both farmer and labourer.

Shortly before the meeting in Saskatoon in July, I was asked if I would address a meeting in Govan. I drove up to Govan, and found Tom Johnston there, and some others who were active in the U.F.C., and they asked me to discuss the political situation, and what I thought should be done. Well, I gave the address and talked about planning the economy to serve the interests of the people, and they questioned me afterwards. I remember Tom Johnston questioning me very closely about socialism, and, while I didn't know it until later, it turned out that this meeting had been arranged to sort of look me over as the potential new leader of a political party in which they would take part. They had come to the conclusion that it would be unwise to choose the President of the U.F.C., George Williams, because he had been in Russia, returned and held meetings across the province, and while he had been critical of some of the things he had seen, he had not been really unenthusiastic about what they were doing in Russia. And of course he was plastered as a Communist, although he never was.

Evidently, they were satisfied with what I said that night so that when we met in Saskatoon, after considerable persuasion, which included my wife's remark that "You can't let these people down," I accepted the position of leader of the new Farmer-Labour Party in this province. When I accepted, it meant that I had to make a couple of decisions.

The first was that I had to decide whether I could spend the amount of time this new work would require and still remain an alderman of the city of Regina. I decided that I could not, and told my friends in Regina that, when my term expired in December 1932, I wouldn't seek re-election, and I didn't.

The second thing I had to do was to drop the position I had held since 1928 as Secretary-Treasurer of the Canadian Teachers' Federation.

These decisions had a very marked effect on my future, incidentally a financial effect, too, because I was getting $500 a year as an honorarium from the city of Regina, and a similar amount from the Canadian Teachers' Federation, so I was dropping my income by $1,000 a year at the same time that I was incurring a great many more expenses. I had to dip into my own resources all the time, to buy gasoline and cover other costs for the travel all around the province. The Farmer-Labour Party was not in a position to pay these, although the Canadian Teachers' Federation did. When I looked at the books of the political party at the end of that year (1932), it had $7.29 in balance on assets, and $2.49 petty cash. But that's pretty good; at least they weren't in debt.

One result of all this was that I could no longer pay $80 a month on our house, so I managed to get that negotiated down to $60, through the help of a friend. Another result was that I had to cash in all my life insurance policies at this time, just to meet current expenses. I never regretted it, because without taking on this new post I would never have had what was far more valuable, the friendship of thousands of people across the country.[19]

He began his new role with a solemn pledge to the delegates that this body would not betray their trust, as the Progressives had done when they drifted sideways into the welcoming embrace of the Liberals.[20] He also told them that he meant the party to be ruled by common sense, not ideology: "The task before us is difficult. We have to appeal not to the passions of the people but to their intellect. It can be done."[21]

Happily, he would not hold his new position long, because the new party was about to be swallowed.

Back in eastern Canada, a group of intellectuals, mostly academics, had formed the League for Social Reconstruction (LSR), in January 1932. The LSR was a sort of Fabian Society, with a dash of maple syrup, which wanted to point the way to social and economic planning, and to a more equitable division of the nation's wealth. The members included such distinguished intellectuals as Frank Scott of McGill, Frank Underhill of the University of Toronto, Graham Spry, long-time editor of the *Canadian Forum* (he had bought it from its bankrupt editor for one dollar), King Gordon, professor of Christian Ethics at United College in Montreal, and Eugene Forsey of Ottawa, union organizer and gadfly. Many of the young men had had some connection with Oxford or Cambridge, and a number of them had studied under John Maynard Keynes, the Cambridge economist.

The LSR had its beginnings in a discussion among Scott, Underhill and Percy Corbett, while walking up a mountainside in the Berkshires. Underhill wanted to initiate a third party in Canada that would not simply be swallowed by one of the main-line parties, as the Progressives had been, and the others agreed. Underhill and Scott, on their return to Canada, began corresponding with others whom they knew in Toronto and Montreal to get the process underway.[22] At the founding meeting in January 1932 in Toronto, J.S. Woodsworth was made honorary president; clearly, the member from Winnipeg North was not going to be swallowed by anyone. Frank Underhill, historian, political scientist and something of a grandstander (Frank Scott called him "the most Shavian of the Canadian Fabians"; same thing), announced that what they needed was not more high-sounding and woollen-headed proposals, but some ringing declaration of practical principles to focus attention on what they were doing and wanted to do.[23] A manifesto, no less. He wrote most of it himself, and the LSR adopted it as a policy statement. The central clause declared the LSR to be "working for the establishment in Canada of a social order in which the basic principle regulating production, distribution and service will be the public good rather than private profit."[24] This working document was presented to Woodsworth, in Ottawa, and he was obviously impressed.

In March 1932, Woodsworth rose in the House of Commons to propose the establishment in Canada of a "Co-operative Commonwealth" which reflected the same notion of a new social order:

> Whereas under our present arrangement, large numbers of our people are unemployed and without the means of earning a livelihood for themselves and their dependents;
>
> And whereas the prevalence of the present depression through-out the world indicates fundamental defects in the existing economic system;
>
> Be it therefore resolved that, in the opinion of this House, the Government should immediately take measures looking to the setting up of a co-operative commonwealth in which all natural resources and the socially-necessary machinery of production will be used in the interests of the people and not for the benefit of a few.[25]

The resolution, needless to say, was buried without ever coming to a vote, but its ideas went marching on. In May, the gaggle of parliamentarians on the left, who called themselves "the Co-operating Groups," met in William Irvine's office on the sixth floor of the House of Commons. They were a rather odd collection, people like Agnes Macphail, a militant farm spokesperson from Grey-Bruce in Ontario, representing the United Farmers of Ontario in Parliament; Ted Garland, one of the old Progressives, now part of the Ginger Group formed from the remnants of that movement; Humphrey Mitchell, a trade unionist; Henry Spencer, a Conservative of the variety later dubbed "Red Tory"; A.A. Heaps, who had gone to jail for his support of the unionists in the Winnipeg strike, and was now Woodsworth's fellow member from Winnipeg; William Irvine himself, a political evangelist and, in monetary matters, an enthusiastic supporter of Social Credit; and Angus MacInnis, then generally described as a Marxist socialist. The linchpin, of course, was J.S. Woodsworth, an extraordinarily charismatic figure who could persuade others to shelve — or split — their differences. He had prepared an agenda, which went through the meeting in an astonishingly short forty minutes[26] and which called for the creation of a new Commonwealth Party, with Woodsworth as temporary president. The party would be organized in Saskatchewan by M.J. Coldwell — who had been in touch with Woodsworth by letter — in Alberta by Robert Gardiner, president of the United Farmers of Alberta, and in Ontario by Agnes Macphail.

Thus, when the Western Labour Conference met at the Calgary Labour Temple on August 1, 1932, it had a pretty clear goal — to create a new political movement in Canada. The delegates included a fair cross-section of Canadians, except for the business community, who were not likely to be impressed, anyway. Grace MacInnis, J.S. Woodsworth's daughter and his biographer, listed them this way:

> There were fifteen farmers, twenty construction workers, two lawyers, six teachers, one miner, one professor, six housewives, three accountants, six railway workers, three journalists, two steam engineers, one hotel keeper, one retired minister, one merchant, one motion picture operator, three nurses, two union executives, twelve members of Parliament and the Legislature, nineteen unemployed men and women.[27]

Tommy Douglas wasn't there; he was away in Manitoba studying for his master's degree.

The convention lasted only one day, during which it gave itself a name, a president and a platform. The name was chosen from a grab bag that included "The Canadian Commonwealth Federation," which was Woodsworth's choice, "The National Party," favoured by Clarence Fines, "The United Workers' Federation," "The United Socialist Federation" and "The United Workers' Commonwealth." M.J. wanted the new body to be called "The Social Democratic Party."[28] Two delegates suggested "The Co-operative Commonwealth Federation," very close to Woodsworth's original choice, and one of them, John Fernstein of Regina, proposed that the words "Farmer-Labour-Socialist" should appear under the name. This proposal was adopted, and the new party was officially "The Co-operative Commonwealth Federation, Farmer-Labour-Socialist," but that didn't last long. It swiftly became the CCF (which, as a boy, I was solemnly assured stood for "Canadian Communist Fellowship").

The president was J.S. Woodsworth by acclamation. (One of the many ironies of the CCF, undoubtedly the most openly democratic party in the nation's history, was the number of times its leaders were chosen without significant opposition. On the other hand, it was perhaps not the most attractive post in Canada for anyone who wanted job security.) The program, which was drawn up by a committee chaired by M.J., was, by modern standards, terse — only eight pages long — and left no doubt as to what was proposed. To begin with, it called for "a planned system of the social economy for the production, distribution and exchange of all goods and services" and went on from there. Banking, credit and the financial system were to be socialized, along with the control of utilities and natural resources. There would be crop insurance, provided by government, along with insurance against illness, accident, old age and unemployment. Health services would be socialized, and workers would have tenure in their jobs, and farmers on their farms. All "co-operative enterprises" would be encouraged as "steps towards the achievement of the co-operative commonwealth," and the federal government would accept responsibility for the unemployed and "supply suitable work or adequate maintenance."[29]

The new party would be quite unlike anything that had gone before; it would be a federation, as Canada was a federation, and its members would belong to CCF clubs, organized wherever there was a need, demand or possibility to form a club, such as in farm organizations or trade union groups. The clubs would be directly affiliated to the central federation, although there would be a provincial organization, as well. The common thread for all of these was some degree of adherence to the principles already adopted by the group in Calgary. A somewhat ambitious program, to say the least, and it brought down roars of outrage from all the nation's purveyors of conventional wisdom, who saw it as a first step — nay, a milestone — along the road to Soviet Bolshevism. To keep the kettle boiling, the convention also set up a committee to prepare for another convention in Regina in 1933 to bring all these groups back together, along with any others who showed interest, to prepare for the new political age.

That was the now-famous Regina convention of August 1933, where 131 delegates assembled at Regina City Hall to have another go at the party manifesto, which Frank Underhill had reworked at his summer cottage in Muskoka and circulated to other LSR members for amendment and comment. Then the national executive of the new party — which included M.J. — went over it again before it was presented to the convention. That took place in Regina for the simplest of reasons: there was no money to pay expenses, and the Saskatchewan capital was close to the centre of the country. The delegates came by train, car and even by "Bennett buggies"; these were created by farmers who could no longer afford to run an automobile, so they removed the engines and hitched up a horse or a pair to pull the thing. A few hitchhiked. M.J. walked.

J.S. Woodsworth opened this three-day meeting with a speech that was obviously gleaned in large part from the LSR Manifesto, and that became the centre of debate over the duration of the convention. There was a good deal of controversy, as the delegates tried to position the party on the left of the political spectrum without falling over the edge. The Calgary convention had brought an unsurprising outpouring of editorial dislike and dismay. Anyone who wanted fundamental change in the economic system was either a "Red" or a "dupe of the Reds." The adoption of the manifesto was bound to increase this flow of rage.

In brief, this document denounced capitalism as cruel and unjust — an argument for which the evidence rang all around the nation at that time — and called for an entirely new approach based on social planning, public ownership of most of the important levers of power, including, finance, transportation and communications, along with nationalized health services, unemployment insurance, legal reform and fairer taxes.[30]

It embraced and expanded on all of the major points of the original LSR proposals, while adding a few new points of its own (the original eight became fourteen). One of these dealt with external affairs, which had been completely neglected in the first version. It called on Canada to back the League of Nations and the International Labour Organization, but contained a couple of caveats. The first was:

> But we believe that genuine international co-operation is incompatible with the capitalist regime which is in force in most countries, and that strenuous efforts are needed to rescue the League from its present condition of being mainly a League of capitalist Great Powers.[31]

and the second:

> Canada must refuse to be entangled in any more wars fought to make
> the world safe for capitalism.[32]

This last was a sentence that M.J., who was far more of an internationalist
than most of the delegates, backed with enthusiasm, but it would blow up in
his face a few years later.

Adopting the manifesto was no simple task, given the wide range of
views assembled in Regina. The delegates represented, besides the Farmer-
Labour Party of Saskatchewan and J.S. Woodsworth's Ginger Group, the
United Farmers of Alberta, the Socialist Party of Canada from British
Columbia, the Independent Labour Party from Manitoba, the Canadian
Labour Party, the Dominion Labour Party and the LSR. Only one union, the
Canadian Brotherhood of Railway Employees, was represented; this was by
a single delegate, A.R. Mosher, but the union declined to affiliate with the
new federation.[33]

There were many attempts to improve the work of the framers of the
program, one of which came from Ernest Winch, a B.C. Marxist, who
wanted the new party to embrace public nudism. Possibly the vision of J.S.
Woodsworth in the buff squelched this idea. William Irvine tried to shoe-
horn in Social Credit principles, which were becoming increasing popular
in his home province of Alberta, thanks to the regular radio broadcasts of
William Aberhart, but few delegates could understand the theory (any more
than did Aberhart; for him, it was a club as much as a philosophy). Many
of the farm delegates objected to the word "Socialism," which appeared
many times, but Woodsworth insisted that it remain in the document. The
B.C. delegation fought bitterly to delete the key sentence "We do not believe
in change by violence." They lost that battle, but won the addition of the
final sentence, quoted in the Introduction to this book, that began, "No
CCF government will rest content until it has eradicated capitalism." For
M.J., this sentence, which was never part of the documents he had been
working on for months, was "a millstone around the party's neck,"[34]
although that was not the reaction when it was read to the cheering convention in Regina. Coldwell swallowed whatever uneasy feelings he had, at
least for the time being.

Whatever its faults and failings, the *Regina Manifesto* was a clear battle cry, and M.J. took it up willingly and openly. He would discover that, on the hustings, it was a very tough sell.

There was a provincial election in Saskatchewan in June 1934, in which the Conservatives, who took the blame for much of the damage done by the Great Depression, did not take a single seat. The only opposition to the Liberals came from the Farmer-Labour (CCF) Party, as it was known, which returned five members. M.J. was not one of them; more ominously, George Williams was.

There were a great many reasons the fledgling party did so poorly, among them, lack of funds, the forthright hostility of the Roman Catholic Church and a Use-Lease proposal, which the party had inherited from the United Farmers of Canada. This was a plan to have the government, in effect, take over all the mortgages of farmers, in the country, and most homeowners, in the city. M.J. explained it this way:

The mortgage and trust companies would receive government bonds in lieu of the payments that were due to them on the farmer's land, or the worker's property in the city. The farmers would continue to occupy and till the soil, and they would pay as large a percentage as they could to the government. Meanwhile, the government would look after the mortgage and all the rest of it and these farmers and house-owners would occupy their land and their homes without any fear of being evicted. In other words, it was a system whereby land tenure would be on the basis of use rather than on the basis of individual ownership of the soil. That ownership would be vested in the government, but out of the control of mortgage companies, and removed from the danger of eviction. It would mean that they would continue to till the soil on these terms as long as they wished, and when they wanted to retire, or they died, the land could be continued to be on the Use-Lease system by their sons or their daughters, and they would have complete security of tenure.[35]

M.J. thought this new approach "very interesting," but the vast majority of his audience thought it was broccoli, and they said to hell with it. No one ever pointed out how close "Use-Lease" sounded to "useless," but the notion was in the air. It sounded like something George Williams had brought back from Russia, along with his postcards of the Kremlin, and even M.J.'s persuasive manner could not put it across. Williams was, in fact, asked about Farmer-Labour's farm policy at the Regina convention, but refused to elucidate. "We were reminded that we were from the East," Eugene Forsey explained,[36] and that was that.

This bizarre reform very nearly made it into the *Regina Manifesto*, but was blocked almost single-handedly by Agnes Macphail, the robust agrarian reformer from Ontario, who led that province's delegation from the United Farmers of Ontario. Macphail declared that preservation of the family farm was an absolute must with her group — and indeed of most farmers. If the resolution then on the floor passed, she said, she would leave and take the Ontario delegation with her.[37] As the Ontario delegation made up forty-five members, nearly one-third of the voting delegates, this was a potent threat, and the resolution died. However, the Farmer-Labour group felt bound to back the proposal anyway, as part of the program of the United Farmers of Canada, and did so in both the provincial election of 1934 and the federal election of 1935.

As if this clause was not enough to have hanging about the neck of the CCF, the difficulty was exacerbated by the Catholic Church's 1931 encyclical, *Quadragismo Anno*, which declared, among other things, that private property was a right "which the State cannot take away." The Archbishop of Regina, James Charles MacGuigan, weighed in with a declaration that all forms of socialism were contrary to the tenets of faith of the church.

M.J. ran in Regina, but spent much of his time travelling up and down the province, working for others. He was still carrying a heavy load as a school principal, and there was no question that the Board of Education, which was heavily Liberal in complexion, disliked M.J.'s uppity ways and didn't think schoolteachers should be involved in politics anyway, allowing him to take a leave of absence.

There were the money problems, as well, and Norah's increasing discomfort and disability. The result was that, by the time the election results were posted, M.J. was broke, exhausted and discouraged. His doctor told him to take some time off, or he would certainly experience a complete breakdown. A friend offered M.J. the use of a cabin by a lake in Alberta, and he decided to take it. On June 20, 1934, he wrote a personal letter to Frank Eliason, a friend and ally, in which he uncharacteristically poured out some of his discouragement:

I am feeling both tired and sick. I saw my doctor two weeks ago, and I know that when I see him again he will insist on a complete rest. I doubt whether I shall hang out till the end of the school term. The past several months have been a veritable nightmare of travel, meetings, school, articles and labour. Only the thought of effectiveness kept me going. Today the inevitable physical and mental reaction(s) are upon me. I shall go away to friends in Alberta as quickly as I can and stay there for a while...

...I have some obligations which must be met and have a deficit on the planes besides many out-of-pocket expenses in other directions. One cannot travel and sleep away from home night after night without innumerable expenses.

I shall not be in the legislature. The leader of the group should be, and so it seems to me that I should resign and make way for a new member to take my place. Moreover, I must relinquish either the leadership or my school; I cannot do both and my school has suffered sadly in the past four months. I regret that now keenly. I am thankful that I have not broken under the strain but I could not repeat it.

...In spite of all, I feel that we have laid a wonderful foundation for the future and the educational work must proceed immediately. By the time the Federal elections come the people will have been disillusioned regarding Saskatchewan Liberalism; hence there must be no let up in our educational activities. I am sorry, very sorry, for our younger supporters who will be bitterly disappointed. They form a wonderful nucleus and will one day put the Movement over.

In Regina, Booze, Boodle and Bigotry account for our defeat but, Frank, if the Movement wishes me to remain in politics I shall never seek election in Regina again. That means that the Movement will have to decide whether it can liberate me to fight in the country or not.

To you and all my other loyal friends I can only try to express a fraction of the appreciation I feel. My heart is very full and heavy today. Perhaps a holiday will lighten it again.

Good luck old man, and best regards.[38]

Soon after he wrote this, M.J. applied for and received a year's leave of absence from the board of education on health grounds — this was something the board could not refuse; he gathered up his family and drove to Alberta, to lick his wounds and consider his future.

CHAPTER SEVEN

P.S.: THE HORSE IS DEAD

On the way back home — this was on the 11th of November, a
nasty night, snowing and blowing — Jack, my son, was driving,
and I was sitting in the back seat, very tired and I suppose pretty
well asleep. And all of a sudden there was a crash bang! The car
stopped, and I found that, on the right-hand side of the car, the
fender had gone and the door was smashed, and there was glass
around. What had happened was that a grey horse stepped out
of the ditch, and the car had struck it on the side of the head and
killed it. And Wayne Miller, who was sitting in the front on that
right side, next to Jack, was picking bits of glass out of his face.

"Well, M.J.," he said, "not long ago I was with you when a jack
rabbit jumped up and smashed the windshield. This time, it's not
a jack rabbit, it's a horse." He added, "Thank God there are no
elephants in this country."   — M.J. COLDWELL, REMINISCENCES, 1972

SITTING BY THE SIDE OF JACKFISH LAKE, ALBERTA, IN THE AUTUMN OF 1934,
M.J. Coldwell had pretty well decided to give up politics. He had come to
Canada twenty-four years earlier and had now spent more time in this country than in the land of his birth, but he did not seem, to himself at least, to have
accomplished much. True, he had a lovely wife and two fine children, Jack,
now nineteen, and Margaret, thirteen. But his forays into the political arena
had received what could only be called mixed reviews. As an alderman in
Regina, he had done very well indeed, topping the polls almost every time out.
But his attempt to find a federal seat in 1925 as a Progressive had led to a
crushing defeat, and just a few months earlier he had been similarly spurned
in a provincial election, under the banner of the Farmer-Labour Party (CCF).

Study and experience had made of him a convinced socialist, and he was able to articulate his views with a good deal of vigour. Tommy Douglas, the quick-witted young Baptist preacher from Weyburn (who had also suffered an ignominious defeat in June), called him "one of the finest Christian gentlemen I have known," and paid him what for Tommy was a great compliment — he was a "flaming radical."

He was the most dynamic fellow I ever met. You see people were losing their homes, being put off their farms, going hungry — I went into a home north of Cedoux once where they had stewed gophers and coffee made of barley and nothing else. M.J. was outraged by these conditions. He and George Williams roused the prairies, became the centre of protest against these unnecessary *hardships of the people.* [emphasis in original] [1]

But the people, however hard-pressed, did not seem to be interested in radical solutions. Not surprisingly, as in other depressions, there was a small group who thought there was nothing to lose by breaking up the current system and remoulding it closer to their hearts' desire, which would certainly have been the effect of adopting the proposals of the *Regina Manifesto* on Canada's political economy. However, there was a much larger group concerned with holding on to what little they had, with keeping their heads down and their mouths shut.

Politics was a brutal game. The CCF was under attack from the left by Communists, who constantly tried to infiltrate the CCF clubs, take over their executives and then promptly shut the door on anyone who disagreed with them. The Communists and Trotskyists became experts at sitting; they would send a small group to a CCF club meeting and outsit everyone else. As others drifted off, the infiltrators would ram through resolutions that were likely to embarrass, if not destroy, the host club. In London, Ontario, where I grew up, solemn burghers who joined the CCF for its economic policies — they held pretty good social events, too — would find themselves at evening's end suddenly confronted with an invitation to join the comrades across the sea in the Soviet Union in a movement to crush the capitalist underfoot and otherwise turn the city over to the more rigorous forms of class warfare. It worked, sometimes, in some places. The CCF spent much of its energies in British Columbia, for example, in internal debate about whether it was better to try to regulate the hours and wages of the workers or usher in the New Dawn by more aggressive action, such as stringing up a few capitalists from the lampposts. In Ontario, the increasing infiltration of Communists led the United Farmers of Ontario, the heart and soul of the CCF in the province at the time, to march out in a body, led by Agnes Macphail.

This came about after a number of incidents, which included the London CCF council passing a resolution to join the Communists in defence of Rev. A.E. Smith, leader of the local Communist party, who had been charged with sedition. The provincial council had specifically rejected this course of action, but the London body had rammed through one of those end-of-the-meeting resolutions to join the protest, and that was that. Smith spent much of his time attacking the CCF and Woodsworth for various sins, and the party officialdom was not anxious to come to his defence (even though the charge of sedition was, like so many such charges at this time, based on airy nothing; if you were agin the government, you were seditious).

Agnes Macphail, as the provincial president, was horrified by the way the Communists had managed to take over CCF clubs (Woodsworth described them as "a happy hunting ground for cranks and Communists"), and she set out to chuck the left-wingers out of the party, because their views were nowhere near in accord with the *Manifesto*. She soon discovered that she could not do it. Because there were no individual memberships, the only way to get rid of a troublemaker, if his own affiliated organization would not reject him, was to expel the whole organization. In disgust, she took the United Farmers out of the CCF. J.S. Woodsworth stepped in, and the Ontario CCF was dissolved and reorganized, with individual memberships.[2] It was all to do over again. Ontario — and this is a point that is often missed in discussions of the CCF — was always the largest sector of the party, in terms of members and votes. In the 1935 federal election, for example, the CCF got 127,927 Ontario votes, almost twice as many as in Saskatchewan, although they did not produce any MPs. Canada's first-past-the-post electoral system made it almost impossible to elect a number of members commensurate with the ballots cast for the party, but that did not make it any the less important to the CCF as a whole. When Ontario was in trouble, the CCF was in trouble.

On the other side, the government was using its considerable powers to infiltrate and destroy any left-wing groups, including the CCF. Agents like Jack Esselwein, whom M.J. had run across several times as secretary of the

Trades and Labour Council in Regina, were able to act as *agents provocateurs* in a way that was quite illegal and not at all unpopular. It was not until much later that M.J. knew his real name — John Leopold of the RCMP.[3] This was a time when you didn't even have to be a Red to be investigated, rebuked and threatened; it was enough if you were not sufficiently anti-Red. In 1930, a peculiar group of idealists formed the Toronto chapter of the Fellowship of Reconciliation, which had taken on the awesome task of sorting out all international misunderstanding. They applied for a permit to hold a meeting at the Empire Theatre in Toronto, which was first promised and then withdrawn when the head of the city's Red Squad called on the manager and pointed out to him that these were dangerous people. A group of sixty-eight professors at the University of Toronto were foolhardy enough to write a letter to the Toronto newspapers in protest against this attack on free speech. That drew an editorial in the Toronto *Globe,* which wanted to know, "Why is the cause of a group of revolutionary agitators to be preferred to the welfare of a loyal, Christian nation?" The newspaper wanted the profs fired — so did the university chancellor, Sir William Mullock, but the board of regents balked.[4] The nation seemed to be running out of tolerance, crouching in fear before imagined demons, and anyone who represented democratic socialism could easily be smeared as a Bolshevik, Red and home-wrecker.

If the party seemed to be moving slowly elsewhere, the same was true in Saskatchewan, where M.J. was admired — but for himself, not his party. Jimmy Gardiner, the Liberal premier of Saskatchewan, offered M.J. a cabinet post (and then denied ever having made the offer), but Coldwell could not swallow the Liberal platform, to say nothing of the patronage that kept that party in power for so long in Saskatchewan.[5] The post he was offered, through Dr. Hugh MacLean, an old friend, now a Liberal, was the obvious one, minister of education. When Gardiner denied having made the offer, MacLean wrote him to remind him that he had gone straight from Gardiner's office to M.J.'s, as his envoy and for this purpose. Gardiner wrote back to acknowledge this. M.J. found this all very flattering, no doubt, but not of much practical use, given his low opinion of the Liberals and Gardiner.

To add to his problems, George Williams, despite an undertaking he had given M.J. not to fill the post of house leader in the legislature until M.J. got back from his recovery period, had taken on the job himself.[6] There was no place for M.J. in the provincial party, it seemed, even if he wanted it.

Then there were the financial problems, Norah's illness, the fact that M.J. was hardly able to spend any time with his family and his own electoral defeat. Why bother?

It was Norah who talked him around,[7] convinced him that a man with his abilities owed more to mankind than his work as a school principal, however valuable that might be, and as time went by, the serene surroundings and Norah's steadfastness worked their magic. Margaret Carman recalls:

My father said, No, I am not going to do this any more. And my mother said, "The people are counting on you. You must return." So he did. He was never sorry. He enjoyed political life. He just had to get over this hurdle.[8]

On June 3, 1935, the "On to Ottawa Trek" began in British Columbia, and it would help to reinvigorate — and re-enrage — M.J. That spring, some of the thousands of Canadians who had been shoved into labour camps to sweat out the depression earning twenty cents a day on public works projects kicked over the traces. They began to leave the camps in the B.C. interior and gather in Vancouver; from there, they would move eastward, gathering recruits as they went, until they could trek into Ottawa and lay their grievances before their rulers. After much brave speechifying, they piled onto boxcars and headed east.

Prime Minister R.B. Bennett, the millionaire corporate lawyer who was struggling, with little success, to cope with the economic chaos, decided to bring the Trek to a halt before it reached Ontario, much less Ottawa. On June 14, 1,400 Trekkers rolled into Regina, dismounted from their freight cars, formed into ranks of fours and marched over to the football stadium, their temporary headquarters. Their behaviour was without blemish, but that didn't keep them from being branded as Reds, gangsters and villains by the press and municipal officials.

M.J. joined 5,000 townsfolk who gathered to support the Trekkers and brought some of them home to have a meal or stay overnight. The outpouring of local sympathy simply proved to national leaders that civilization was tottering on its foundations. Squads of RCMP and special police were moved in to block the protestors' path to the east.

However, Premier Gardiner sent off a telegram to the national capital, suggesting that the federal government should at least hear what the Trekkers had to say, and eight of the Trek leaders went to Ottawa, where Prime Minister Bennett turned down all their demands, gave them a lecture on economics and reviled them personally. Bennett called Arthur Evans, the leading strike spokesman, a thief; Evans called the prime minister a liar.[9] The leaders went back west in a rage.

On June 28, when a group of Trekkers tried to proceed eastward by truck, they were stopped and five of them were arrested. This led to a mass rally on July 1, in Regina's Market Square, where the government decided the leaders of the protest should be arrested under an order-in-council that made it illegal to belong to any "unlawful association" — which was never defined; an unlawful association was anything the government said it was. The attempt to make the arrests provoked a riot, during which a plainclothes police officer was killed. The Trek was broken, and most of the protestors left the city to return to their camps. The police rounded up more than a hundred men, including all the strike leaders, but as none of these had taken part in the riot the charges were dropped. No one was charged under the order-in-council (which, it is to be hoped, would never have withstood a court challenge); twenty-eight were charged with rioting, and nine were eventually convicted.[10]

James Gray, a Canadian writing in the American magazine *The Nation*, argued that the only rational explanation for the government's actions in the Regina riot "is that Bennett, about to be booted into oblivion by an outraged people, was trying to escape from this fate by the dictatorship route."[11]

What M.J. saw was that a group of protestors had been smashed, and he strongly suspected that the riot itself was provoked by police, including his old nemesis, Jack Esselwein. Here is what he had to say about this in the House of Commons, and it is worth pausing to note that the first part of this could be applied to conditions in Canada today:

I well remember meeting that group of young men who came to Regina in an endeavour to concentrate public attention upon the difficulties which they faced. Now I know it has been said, and may be said again, that that was the result of a few men agitating among them. But you cannot agitate unless there is suitable soil in which the agitation may grow. I found them to be largely average Canadian boys who were not out to cause difficulty, but who were there in order to direct public attention to the difficulties under which they suffered. What I am afraid of is that the concentration in various cities of young men from the unemployment relief camps will lead to such a trouble in other parts of Canada. I submit to the ministers and the government that the requests which these young men are making for work and wages and the opportunity to live are natural requests, requests that deserve well of the government and of the Canadian people...

...I have been engaged in dealing with young people during the major portion of my life. One thing that has saddened me in the last few years is observing young men whom I knew as boys, with ability, initiative, ambition, unemployed for long periods of time and sinking down into deep hopelessness. I fear for the future of our country unless more comprehensive steps are taken than we are taking at the present time to solve this problem.

In Saskatchewan, they are given fifty cents a day for bed and board. That, of course, is totally inadequate and tends to breed grave dissatisfaction...

...As one of those who witnessed the coming of these young men to Regina a year ago, who knew that the intentions of the great mass of them when they came to that city were peaceful, that they desired only to compel public attention to their condition, I view this situation with the very gravest alarm.

Then I go a step further and say that I sometimes fear that the government and the departments which are handling these particular difficulties are not acting wisely or properly. From my own personal experience I believe that among the men who came to Regina were officers of the law who have not always acted in the interests of law and order. I, from my own personal knowledge and experience in connection with one of these police officers who gave evidence in connection with these young men, I know perfectly well that he was secretary of a Communistic organization and propagated Communism, although at that time he was in reality an officer of the Mounted Police. I say that not only on my responsibility as a member of parliament, but on his own sworn evidence, a copy of which I possess, given at an investigation a year ago.[12]

Strained but still moving forward, the CCF girded its loins to fight an election in mid-1935, and M.J. was now determined to re-enter the fray. If he ran federally, he could simply bypass the problem of the provincial leadership, which George Williams had successfully usurped. There had not been a federal vote since July 28, 1930, which meant that, under Canadian law and precedent, there had to be one in July 1935. M.J.'s leave of absence would cover this period, so he set about finding a suitable riding. It could not be in Regina — the two seats there were in firm Liberal hands and not likely to be shifted; besides, M.J. had already lost there twice. Clarence Fines had sent out feelers, and there were invitations from more than two dozen CCF associations for M.J. to run. Two of the best prospects were Maple Creek, where he had spent a summer as a guest lay preacher years earlier, and Rosetown-Biggar. He decided to run in Rosetown-Biggar for the very sound reason that he had made a number of speeches in the area and had always been well received. Moreover, scouting expeditions by others indicated that he would not only get the nomination, he could very well win the seat.

A local man, John Evans, had run in the riding before and rather wanted to be talked into running again. However, he wrote a letter asking M.J. to be the candidate and had the letter hand-delivered to Coldwell at Yorkton, where he was making a speech. Then, when the nominating meeting was held at Sovereign, in the middle of the riding, Evans turned up with a hopeful look on his face and a nominator at hand. M.J. assumed that he would step aside, but he didn't, and when Coldwell won by a substantial majority it appeared there might be some bad blood. Jack Douglas, who had been Evans's campaign manager, told Coldwell he didn't think much of his coming in from outside and muscling aside a local. M.J. produced the letter from Evans, and Douglas did a complete turnabout, becoming, and very effectively, too, M.J.'s campaign manager.[13]

It was a long, tedious process, but the riding was organized from top to bottom, with regional directors and poll committees, with at least three supporters in every poll responsible for getting out the vote. There was nothing to do but wait for the electoral writ. But it refused to come. Prime Minister Bennett, then sixty-five, had a mild heart attack in the spring of 1935,[14] and this was enough to bend the rules and extend his mandate, so that the election was finally called for October 14. This was going to be long after M.J.'s leave of absence had expired; accordingly, he applied to have it extended long enough to cover the election. If he lost, he would go back to school; if he won, that was another problem for another day.

The Regina School Board refused any extension of the leave and, while it was at it, got off a couple of cracks about the inadvisability of teachers messing about with politics, anyway. M.J. might have resigned, but he felt strongly that an important principle was involved, so he simply defied the board and was fired for not appearing at his school when classes began in September.

To show that there is some justice in this world after all, every one of the members of the Regina School Board who voted to turn down his request lost in the municipal elections that fall. A new board promptly reversed that decision and rehired M.J. By that time, he had been elected to Parliament, so he was able to resign, with dignity and having made the point for teachers all across the country.[15]

The election itself was part hilarious, part boring, part scary. One complicating factor was the increasing popularity of the Social Credit movement in neighbouring Alberta, where it won a smashing victory on August 22, just before the federal campaign got under way. "Bible Bill" Aberhart's new party won fifty-six of the legislature's sixty-three seats. The then-ruling party, the United Farmers, did not return a single member. It was natural for the Socreds to move into Saskatchewan, where the same appalling conditions prevailed, where, as in Alberta, there was an increasing conviction that there was nothing to lose by trying something new, and where the organizational methods honed to perfection by Social Credit members might be expected to pay off. The two parties were essentially competing for the same votes, and this was before the Socreds abandoned their entire program, with its attack on the "Fifty Big Shots" of the financial elite and its virulent dislike of the banks. The Social Credit of 1935 was a vastly different party from the arch-conservative encampment it became after the discovery of oil in the province. (Historian W.L. Morton later wrote of the Social Credit transformation, "Social Credit provided an easy and sweeping reform, without Socialism. The Albertans turned to it, and, aided by the war boom and the oil boom, achieved utopia. If it be objected that [William Aberhart] did not thereby achieve a new society, it must be admitted that he has attained a new complacency. If one must travel to nowhere, there is no more comfortable ride than on a tide of oil."[16])

Even without its monetary theory, Social Credit was a genuinely radical party, and until it took on overtones of anti-Semitism, its proposed reforms, including, in particular, its apparently undying hostility to the banks, were perfectly acceptable to many of the same people who plumped for the CCF. M.J. always believed it was an antidemocratic party, while Tommy Douglas thought Coldwell's approach too harsh, and wrote:

Throughout my meetings, I have consistently taken the stand that Mr. Aberhart has taken an economically unsound position but that he has endeavoured to give the debtor a fair break in his debt adjustment legislation,[17] and that when those who have supported Social Credit come to realize its inherent weakness they will find a more comfortable home in the ranks of the CCF.[18]

Social Credit won two of the twenty-one Saskatchewan seats in the 1935 federal election, the same as the CCF, while the Conservatives returned only a single candidate, and the Liberals, on their way to a massive majority nationally, took the other sixteen.[19] The two CCF victors were Tommy Douglas, in Weyburn, and M.J., in Rosetown; they were, in fact, the only two CCF candidates in the province.

M.J. knew he would never win a majority in the two largish towns that gave the riding its name — Rosetown and Biggar — but he could win it in the smaller centres and on the farms. This meant almost constant travel to meetings that sometimes foregathered half a dozen solemn agrarians in someone's field, a neighbourhood school or anywhere else that planks could be laid across chairs to provide seats and a couple of boxes stood on end to make a podium. To finance the process, there was always someone on hand to pass a hat or a tin bucket to collect coins. In this campaign, as in every campaign he fought from this time on, M.J. did not have the luxury of staying in his chosen riding to pile up votes. He was the provincial leader, as well as a candidate, and this meant that he spent most of his effort criss-crossing the province on behalf of others. Although it meant long periods away from his family, financial hardship and exhaustion, he never complained and, in some ways, enjoyed the gruelling pace. This is the place, I think, to show how campaigning worked in Saskatchewan in those days, through the stories M.J. told in various places in the *Reminiscences* taped in 1963 by his friend Sandy Nicholson.

I remember so well those tours of mine around the countryside staying at farm houses. We had no money to stay at hotels and indeed many of the hotels were closed, anyway. The hotel keepers could not maintain them. And always I was invited to some farm home. On one of these occasions, I was invited to stay at the home, not of a farmer, but a storekeeper, in Tisdale, a Mr. Lyons. Mr. Lyons and his wife had a daughter who was about sixteen or seventeen at that time, and her name was Molly. Well, they turned Molly out of her bed, and that is where I slept, while she went elsewhere in the house. Later on, the family moved back to Israel, and later still, in 1954, I was on a visit to Israel, at the home of the acting prime minister. There was a reception, and as people came in, a man stood at the door to announce them. I saw a stoutish lady come in, and the announcer said "Mrs. Bar-David." I had no idea who Mrs. Bar-David was, but she turned and said to the packed room, quite at the top of her voice, "Oh, I know Mr. Coldwell, he slept in my bed one night!" Of course, she hurriedly explained that she had not been in the bed at the time.

Incidentally, on that trip to Tisdale we had gone by plane. Because the roads were so dreadful, and time was so pressing, we flew in a small, single-engine aircraft when we could, and this was one of those occasions. The morning after my stay with the Lyons, we were to go on to Hudson Bay Junction, about eighty miles away, and then back to Tisdale, but we had not gone more than thirty miles when the engine began to kick up, and the pilot turned around to me and said, "I'm not going to risk going on to Hudson Bay Junction; if I find an open space, I'll come down."

We were losing height rapidly, but he did find an opening, and we came down near Crooked River, not far from the railway tracks. Well, I had to get over to the meeting, so we phoned and got a jigger that came out from Tisdale, and that is how I got to Hudson Bay Junction, riding on a jigger in the middle of a thunderstorm.

We had a very good meeting, although I was an hour late — the meeting was scheduled for two o'clock in the afternoon, but I didn't get there until three — and it was very late by the time we got back to Tisdale. While I was there, I ran into a cabinet minister in the provincial government, and he wanted to get down to Regina for a very important cabinet meeting, so he asked if he could have a ride in the airplane. There were really no roads you could travel on at that time in rural Saskatchewan, once it had started to rain heavily, so of course I said I would be delighted to give him a ride, since the aircraft was now running fine again. However, when he came out on Monday morning to where the plane was, he looked at the sky, which was very threatening, with heavy clouds, and he said, "No, I'm not going to risk this. You may get up, but I don't know about those clouds over there."

Well, we started out, just the pilot and myself, and we were buffeted in every direction, and soon we were completely lost, in very poor visibility, with clouds and rain; I was quite worried. The pilot wandered around for a while and then we came down close to the ground, and we saw a railway track, so we followed it, and then to our joy, we saw the name of a town, Nokomis. We knew where we were, and got back to Regina all right. I remember this trip because it emphasized that there was only one way to travel in Saskatchewan when it rained — by plane, if you could find one, because there had been a Liberal government in power for a good many years, and Jimmy Gardiner had been minister of highways, and his idea of transportation was to pile up the mud in the middle of the road and call it a highway!

We did a good deal of travel by car, in spite of the roads, and we would pass the hat for nickels and dimes at our meetings to help with the expenses. A dime was quite a good piece in the collection. I remember one meeting at Kamsack where one farmer went to put a dollar in the collection, and the chairman, a fine old gentleman, honest and sincere, insisted on giving him back ninety cents. A dollar was just too much.

I had a habit of keeping my pocket handkerchief in my right hip pocket, so I would have my pocket full of pennies and nickels and dimes, from the collections, swathed in this handkerchief. At a meeting at Coronach I was speaking on the platform, and on one of the planks where the audience sat I saw a woman called Mary Davis. Mary Davis was a very persistent letter writer to the Western Producer, and a bitter, bitter Liberal in those days. I thought, well, I would go after the Liberal party pretty hard, because she went after the CCF pretty hard, and so I did. I talked about all the scandals they were involved in, and all the money they had, whereas we, of course, didn't have any money. I had just got this out, when I suddenly had to sneeze, and I reached in and pulled out my handkerchief, and the whole floor was covered with nickels and dimes! To her credit, Mary Davis did not write to the Western Producer to denounce me as someone who doesn't tell the truth, because here I was complaining about having no money, and then strewing the floor with nickels and dimes.

There were times when I had difficulty to buy enough gas to get from one place to the next, let alone buy meals, but fortunately there was always someone in the district who would invite you back for lunch or dinner, and I made a great many friends in that way.

One of the families that gave us hospitality when I went to Biggar was the Jones family. Mr. Jones was a boiler-maker by trade and worked in the Canadian

National Railway shops, and there was always a room for me at his place. They kept a bed ready and left the door unlocked so that if I came along unexpectedly I could simply go upstairs, get into bed, and have a good night's rest. They used to say that they "always knew when M.J. arrived, because we slept down below and we could hear him snoring up above."

In those days, people were pretty well reduced to the same level economically, and we had no money to go anywhere, to do anything. And people helped one another as they had not done for a number of years, in creating simple pleasures. I think this was one of the strengths of the CCF in Saskatchewan and the neighbouring Social Credit party in the province of Alberta. We had our meetings in the evening, and very often after the meetings there would be something of a convivial little dance. People would bring along some food and we would make some coffee on the school stove, and there would be home-made cakes — they weren't very good, often, because we didn't have the currants, raisins or spices that often make a difference, but that was all right.

I must say I enjoyed the campaigning. I took my son Jack with me whenever I could, in my car. We cut down the seat of the car so that it made a bed, and you could sleep in it if there was no other accommodation.

You slept where you could, of course. At one place, I slept in a bunk, with the farmer and his wife in the top bunk and I occupied the bunk right below them; everything was very clean and nice, but somewhat primitive.

CHAPTER EIGHT

DAYS OF GLORY,
DAYS OF GRIEF

*Over the years I have encountered outstanding individuals
committed to social justice in different parts of the world. Few,
if any, shared M.J.'s rare combination of total integrity, innate
modesty and intellectual probity. His exemplary public personality
was the mirror image of the virtuous inner man.*

*Even during periods of stress, Coldwell was unvaryingly
courteous and considerate, incapable of pettiness or unkindness in
thought or deed. Never did I know him, even under the most trying
conditions, to utter an unkind word, express a vulgar thought or
tolerate a questionable act. Unlike some party intellectuals I was
later to meet, he was never doctrinaire, self-righteous, arrogant or
self-important.* — DAVID HEAPS, FORMER ASSISTANT TO M.J., 1997

B EFORE HE COULD DRAW A BREATH AFTER THE ELECTION, M.J. WAS PRE-
sented with a crisis by George Williams, his colleague and rival. Tommy Douglas, as we saw in the last chapter, did not rebuff the Socred backers in his
constituency as M.J. had. In the 1935 election, seventeen Social Crediters were
elected across the nation, because of the vagaries of our electoral system
(which remains unrevised and unrepentant). Social Credit won fifteen seats
in Alberta on 61,505 votes; the CCF gathered 54,491 votes in Saskatchewan
and two seats. The CCF had more than twice as many votes nationwide —
387,056 to 180,301 — and fewer than half as many seats — seven to seventeen.[1] (The Reconstruction Party, under H.H. Stevens, was even more
ill-used, returning a single member on 384,095 votes.) The rivalry between
Socreds and CCFers both before and during the election led to calls for

sanctions against anyone even suspected of co-operation, and George Williams reacted savagely when he found that Tommy Douglas was charged with this crime.

Douglas had been endorsed by Social Crediters at a meeting called in his riding without his approval or attendance, and no Social Credit candidate was nominated to run against him. As soon as he found out about it, he repudiated the endorsement — which he was required to do by the party bylaws. Nevertheless, Williams wanted M.J. to eject him and kept hounding the provincial leader on the subject; Coldwell refused, and then buried the issue in benign neglect.

George Williams and some members of the organization wanted me to issue a statement repudiating Tommy Douglas and this I refused to do. We had quite a warm executive meeting about this, and it ended in a rather unpleasant sort of atmosphere. I had to go on to Moose Jaw, for the beginning of a provincial campaign, and when I got there, waiting for me was a telegram from George Williams saying that he had received a lot of criticisms from various people in the province, and that he would turn these over to me, since I had been instrumental in keeping Douglas as a candidate. Well, as a matter of fact, I didn't get any of the objections that George said were in, and therefore I never had to reply to them. And from then on, of course, Tommy and I retained a very close association in the House until he left it to take over the leadership of the provincial party, which he led to its success in the 1944 election.[2]

In Ottawa, M.J. and Norah, who was increasingly crippled but still getting along gamely with a cane, moved into rooms on McLeod Street, not far from Parliament Hill. Margaret was at a boarding school in Regina, and Jack had a job there. Although he still gave his address as 131 Connaught Crescent in Regina in the *Parliamentary Guide*, M.J. was, for all practical purposes, permanently moved to Ottawa. There was never enough time to travel by rail back to either Regina or his riding in the short Parliamentary breaks, and in the longer ones, he had so many duties outside the House that he saw very little of Connaught Crescent.

When he came to write his mini-biography for the *Guide*, M.J. gave his religion as "Christian," where it was usually noted as "Anglican," "Presbyterian" or whatever. This was because he felt his Christianity was more important than whatever branch he belonged to, but when a few of his colleagues chivvied him on the subject years later, he adopted the usual rule — don't make unnecessary waves — and called himself an Anglican. In fact, his religion, while doubtless genuine, was simply part of his background, what he grew up with, an aspect of his sociability, rather than a spiritual guide. His daughter, Margaret, recalled that he was "not particularly religious";[3] it was certainly not the central force for him that it was for, say, Woodsworth.

Along the corridor of the sixth floor of the Centre Block of Parliament, ranging out from the men's washroom, were the offices of the seven CCFers who had been elected in the 1935 vote — "Socialist Alley," it was called. Besides J.S. Woodsworth, the party leader, they were: A.A. Heaps of Winnipeg and Angus MacInnis of Vancouver, both returning MPs; and four new ones — Grant MacNeil and J.S. Taylor from British Columbia, and M.J. Coldwell and T.C. Douglas from Saskatchewan. Tommy and M.J. shared the office closest to the biffy. By happy chance, the electors had served up some of the ablest of the party's stalwarts — the exception was Taylor, an enthusiast for astrology and numerology, whom even the kindly M.J. described as a "very queer duck, indeed."[4] Agnes Macphail had won again in Grey-Bruce, Ontario, but she ran as a "United Farmers of Ontario–Labour" candidate, not a CCF one, although the distinction soon blurred. She joined the CCF caucus, where she revered J.S. Woodsworth, fought with the sharp-tongued Angus MacInnis and took a while to warm up to M.J. Her biographers wrote:

> At first Agnes was not impressed by M.J. Coldwell: he seemed to her a shade too respectable, while Coldwell, for his part, looked slightly askance at Agnes' extravagant ways. But mutual respect and regard developed, as they sat in caucus and shared the round of Commons duties.[5]

Macphail, too, had an office in Socialist Alley, although she was not required to double up, like the men. (This doubling up meant that any time one member had a visit from a constituent or anyone else who wanted privacy, the other would have to wander up and down the corridors or adjourn for a cup of coffee until the meeting was over.) There were no party research facilities and only one paid national organizer, Ted Garland, who travelled the country by rail, coach class, sitting up at night to save the cost of a sleeper.

The MPs made use of the Commons' secretarial pool, but that was about all the help Parliament provided. Woodsworth's charming, brilliant daughter, Grace, acted as unofficial caucus secretary, kept the minutes and stuffed envelopes, as well as arranged speaking itineraries for the members. Angus MacInnis had very cleverly married her in 1932. M.J. did most of his own research or drew on figures gathered by the League for Social Reconstruction, whose 1935 book, *Social Planning for Canada,* became an important part of every CCF member's kit. The MPs were paid $4,000 a year and received a $2,000 tax-free expense allowance, as well as a railway pass. This was a boost in pay for both M.J. and Tommy, even though they were expected to — and did — kick back 5 per cent of their salary to the party every year, and twice that much in election years.

From the beginning, M.J. was seen as Woodsworth's lieutenant, and he took on many of the organizational duties that the leader had no time for or didn't believe were necessary. To provide links to the provincial parties and associations, he was made national secretary, adding that to all his other duties. In the summer of 1936, David Lewis returned to Canada from Britain, where he had been a Rhodes Scholar, and presented himself in Woodsworth's House of Commons office, eager to help in any way he could. Woodsworth introduced him to Coldwell, and he was soon seconded to work for M.J. as a part-time helper, while pursuing a legal career to survive. Lewis, brilliant, dynamic, tireless — and arrogant — was soon taking on more and more of the direction of the party, and the 1936 convention elected him to the National Council, which promptly elected him national secretary, on August 6, 1936.[6] He persuaded the senior partner in his legal firm to give him a lean-to at the back of some property he owned on Wellington Street, across from the Parliament buildings, and this lean-to, with a sand floor — a mud floor in wet weather — became the CCF national office; 124 Wellington Street, sand or mud and all, remained the official Ottawa headquarters for more than two years.[7]

Woodsworth's attitude towards these bread-and-butter matters was summarized in a letter he wrote to a Quebec follower, J.A. Martin, in 1932:

> If this is a genuine people's movement, it seems to me that the people themselves, all over the country, will have to take the matter up in their own localities. All we can do is to give a lead, then we must trust

there will come to the front individuals and groups, who will rally the people in their various neighbourhoods.[8]

Which was all very well, of course, but to Lewis, Coldwell, Douglas and others, it seemed useful to give the people a nudge now and then in the right direction, and this was likely to require organizers, secretaries and perhaps even the extravagance of a floor underfoot. David Lewis drew an interesting comparison between Coldwell and Woodsworth:

I felt that I worked *with* Coldwell but that I worked *for* Woodsworth. This was not because Woodsworth was more aloof or less thoughtful or less friendly. Indeed, I visited him in his office and he was always helpful and discussed matters as with an equal. Nor did I respect him more; I found Coldwell equally committed and equally intelligent, and in any case it is silly to make such comparisons between two exceptional men. It was simply that Woodsworth held a position in the movement which no one else could occupy. One respected and loved Coldwell, but one revered and worshipped Woodsworth.[9]

M.J. and Douglas became the agriculture experts of the caucus, which, since one of them was a preacher and the other a teacher, drew a good deal of scorn from Jimmy Gardiner, who had given up the premiership of Saskatchewan to become Mackenzie King's minister of agriculture. Gardiner, a successful farmer, as well as a politician, chided Douglas because he had never worked a farm. Tommy replied, "I can't lay an egg, either, but I know how to make an omelet."[10] The truth is that Douglas and Coldwell knew a tremendous amount about farm problems, spent a great deal of their time in farmers' homes, and they made a formidable pair. They had a good deal in common; both came from Britain to Canada and were drawn to socialism as a way to right some of the appalling wrongs they saw around them. They were both proselytizers, one as a preacher, the other as a teacher, although they had quite different styles. Douglas's humour was trenchant, an edged tool; M.J.'s was gentle, more often aimed at himself than anyone else. Once, when Tommy was debating Walter Tucker, a Liberal and the leader of the official Opposition in Saskatchewan, Tucker noted that his party had introduced mothers' allowances when Douglas was "just a little fellow."

Tommy shot back: "I am still a little fellow. Tucker is big enough to swallow me, but if he did, he would be the strangest man in the world, because he would have more brains in his stomach than he has in his head."[11] It was a good crack, but M.J. would never have said anything so personal or so cruel. He chuckled at Tommy's sallies, but never emulated them.

The two men had been at the centre of the move to join the farming and working classes in Saskatchewan into a single party, and they were the only two CCFers who went to Ottawa in that first election. Douglas looked up to Coldwell, the older man — when they went to Ottawa together, M.J. was forty-seven, Douglas thirty-two — much as M.J. looked up to Woodsworth, who was sixty-two. It was M.J. who urged Douglas to return to Saskatchewan and the provincial leadership, and he played an important role in both that event and the provincial election that made Tommy premier in 1944.

Tommy only shocked M.J. once, by telling an off-colour story on the platform. (M.J. was not averse to off-colour stories, only to such a public utterance.) Tommy was trying to illustrate the closeness of the two old-line parties, whose pretended hostility covered a common purpose, and gave this parallel:

When Noah first put the animals in the Ark, he told them that there was a shortage of room, so there could be no hanky-panky, and they all agreed. Then, when the storm was over and the animals were coming off the Ark, they came two by two, of course, until the cats came out, and there was a poppa cat, and a momma cat, and a whole litter of kittens. Noah was dumbfounded, and the poppa cat said, "I guess you thought we were fighting."

The first time Tommy told this story with M.J. on the platform, Coldwell announced that if Tommy ever did it again, he would leave the auditorium at once and let Douglas explain his exit to the crowd.[12]

In general, the two men seldom disagreed, and formed the core of a bloc of politicians that was far more effective than its numbers indicated. M.J. recalled those years with pride:

The opening of the new Parliament in February was rather a dull affair, because the country was in mourning for King George V. We organized our caucus, and started the session quite well. I made my maiden speech, and it was almost entirely on the wheat situation in the province of Saskatchewan, because wheat had been a tremendous problem on the prairies from 1930. Prime Minister Bennett had set up a Wheat Board to meet some of the difficulty, under John I. MacFarlane, which set a price for wheat, and that was very popular with the farmers. But then Mr. Mackenzie King took over, and Mr. Gardiner left Saskatchewan and came to Ottawa as the new Minister of Agriculture, and he appointed a man named Murray, who had been the manager of an Alberta grain company, a private company, to head the Wheat Board. This new fellow wanted to move us back to the old open market system, which the Liberals had advocated.[13] In my speech, I criticized the government very severely for deserting the idea of a national marketing system, and when I sat down, Mr. Bennett, who had been standing behind the curtain at the back of the chamber, came out and said this was the finest maiden speech he had ever heard in the House. That, of course, pleased me, and gave me a feeling of some security when I arose later to speak.

Mr. Woodsworth moved a resolution calling on the government of Canada and the people of Canada to establish a Co-operative Commonwealth based on our program in the Regina Manifesto.[14] This provoked a really interesting debate which lasted several days. Tommy Douglas made a very excellent speech — of course, he always made an excellent speech — and it went over quite well, but of course we got nowhere with it.

Tommy also played a very important role in the discussion of agricultural policy, and he said that appointing Murray to the Wheat Board was like expecting a weasel in a hen-house to hatch out chickens.

We worked with some of the Conservative members as well to try to help in these matters, and the question of wheat prices came up so often that some of the members of the House got fairly sick of hearing about it.

There were other problems that came to the fore, such as criticism of the King government in relation to its attitude to the Ethiopian War. Mussolini had invaded Ethiopia and the League of Nations had decided to impose oil sanctions to try to limit the supply of fuel for his mechanized divisions. Mr. King ordered our representative at the League of Nations, who had actually proposed the sanctions in the first place, to vote against them, and this caused a good deal of debate.[15] Mr. Woodsworth very ably criticized the government for deserting the League, which in our view was the only possible impediment to another Great War.

On the other hand, while we supported the League of Nations, Mr. Woodsworth was a great pacifist and he certainly dominated our thinking with regard to defence expenditures. All through this period, we opposed defence expenditures. We also opposed appropriations for the encouragement of cadet corps in our schools; this was something that Agnes Macphail felt very strongly about, and I supported her on a number of occasions.

Once, after I had done this, a Conservative from London, Ontario, a Colonel T.C. Betts, rose in his place and said he could not understand how a man who so obviously had had military experience and training and had risen to the rank of Major in the army could have made the kind of speech Major Coldwell had just made.

I rose and said, "Mr. Speaker, on a point of privilege, I would like to inform the Honourable Gentleman that the name Major was given to me when I was far too young to make an effective protest."[16]

Throughout this first session, the CCF members kept hammering away at social policy, farm policy and unemployment; the main effect was to place arguments for reform on the record, for later leverage. As the costs of relief spending grew, they were accompanied by a rich tradition, still with us, which holds that most of the money spent on welfare goes to ne'er-do-wells, welfare cheats and foreigners. The Ontario government of George S. Henry sent relief inspectors out to track down the rascals; one of them reported that in Hamilton, the supervisor of relief, one Sam Lawrence, was "a labour man...even a Red." He was committing the unpardonable sin of distributing relief "according to individual circumstances," rather than following guidelines that limited assistance to a risible amount. Being a Red, Sam had "foreign friends," who were "well stocked with all they asked for." While none of these things could be proven, who needed proof when everybody knew that foreigners living in Hamilton were getting allowances for family members "probably living in Central Europe"?[17] As in our own modern demonology, these unsubstantiated anecdotes were enough to convince a wide sector of the taxpaying populace that government support was simply thrown away, so there was very little sustained pressure for its expansion, except by the growing army of victims.

Aside from closing the relief camps, which had become a nuisance, and adding a little more cash to direct relief programs, the King government did very little throughout the depression. For King, charity was the cardinal Christian virtue, so there was no need to take government action until public agitation reached the point that his own political survival hung in the balance. The Liberal party had a medicare proposal in its platform in 1919 — it would be implemented in 1964 — that was the proper pace at which to introduce these radical changes.

The CCF role was to provide a constant prod and the threat of an alternative, but it was not a very concrete threat at this time. However, the party did keep up a constant barrage on the subject of the coming war in Europe — which King simply refused to recognize. When Germany violated the Versailles Treaty by marching into the Rhineland in 1936, he summed up official government policy this way:

> The attitude of the government is to do nothing itself and if possible to prevent anything occurring which will precipitate one additional factor into the all-important discussions which are now taking place in Europe.[18]

The first ten words might have made a suitable epitaph for King. Coldwell and Woodsworth went at the subject of impending hostilities from a shared vantage point in the beginning. Both made long speeches deploring the role of Canadian manufacturers in re-arming Germany and arming an expansive and aggressive Japan. M.J. opposed the Munich agreement and argued that the rise of fascism in Italy, Germany and Spain owed as much to the desire to sell arms as to the unwillingness of the major powers to allow the League of Nations to operate effectively.[19]

The CCF National Convention in Toronto, August 1936, called on the party to press for legislation that would allow Canada to remain neutral in any future war, even one involving Britain,[20] and Coldwell backed that resolution. There were some delegates, among them George Williams, who thought the party was foolish to oppose participation in *any* war, but they gained little headway.

However, because events in Europe pointed to the probable triumph of fascism, unless it was opposed soon and strenuously, Coldwell, Lewis and many other party members began to have second thoughts, and were eventually to do a complete about-turn. M.J. had spoken at a peace rally in Toronto, where he proudly proclaimed his son's willingness to go to jail, rather than enlist or accept conscription:

My son is twenty-one years old and physically fit in every respect...
I taught him that war is wrong, and this Christmas, when we were
discussing his future, he came to me voluntarily and said that I
could rely on one thing, and that was his determination to go to jail
before enlisting.[21]

In the House of Commons the next day, when defence expenditures were
being debated, Coldwell seconded an amendment that:

This House views with grave concern the startling increases of expen-
diture proposed by the government for purposes of national arma-
ment in contrast with the immediate provision for social security of
all sections of the Canadian people.[22]

These expenditures indicated that Canada was preparing for another war,
and Coldwell said, "I do not believe in war and I conscientiously object
to it."[23]

Wars were basically capitalist spasms, driven by arms sales, and he was
not willing to sacrifice his son to these economic interests. The *Regina Manifesto* had not made the CCF a pacifist party; it had, rather, insisted that
Canada stay out of any future *imperialist* wars, and those who, like Williams,
were increasingly dismayed by the tone of the statements made by Coldwell
and Woodsworth, had a point. (There was a tremendous amount of internal
party argument about whether the National Council, which was determining
policy in these matters, had the right to do so without consulting the provincial parties, which added to the furore, but made little difference in the end.)

But events overseas made the CCF position untenable in the eyes of most.
The party passed a resolution at its 1936 convention expressing sympathy
with the government of Spain, and another in 1937 — which passed without a single dissenting vote — calling for an end to the arms embargo then
in force, so that Spain could purchase arms to defend herself against the fascists. Obviously, there were wars and there were wars, and the press was quick
to seize on the issue. "Pacifists Now Ready to Fight Fascism," declared the
Regina *Leader-Post*, reporting that the CCF now championed the right of
individuals to go to Spain to fight, as long as it was on the right, which is to
say the left, side.[24]

In 1937, Japan invaded China, and the CCF again plumped for strict neutrality, combined with a call for a ban on shipments of nickel and steel to Japan. But in 1938, when the national convention made Coldwell national chairman, it was becoming clear that neutrality, for most Canadians, was no longer an option. Germany had marched into Austria, then the Sudetenland, then Czechoslovakia. A pogrom had been set in motion against Jews in Germany; friends, relatives and political allies of many prominent CCFers — not least, David Lewis, who came from Poland and had many relatives there — were now under direct attack. The CCF National Council shifted ground, and instead of opposing the government's defence expenditures because they were defence expenditures, MPs were instructed to oppose them because they were based on the wrong policy. No money should be spent to prepare Canadians to send an expeditionary force overseas; but it was all right to spend money to defend our own shores.[25]

Coldwell went much further and, in an interview with the party newspaper in Saskatchewan, made it clear that, if Britain declared war, Canada would have no choice but to join in:

Canada cannot decide whether she will go to war in the event of Great Britain going to war. Canada is part of the British Commonwealth of Nations and every part of the Commonwealth will be at war if Britain is at war.[26]

The boy from Devon was emerging clearly from behind the mask of the man from Regina. This was neither the official position of the party, nor of J.S. Woodsworth, who was still as opposed as ever to any policy that contemplated the idea of Canada taking part in any war. War was bad; war solved nothing. That was that. Canada should even make it clear to Great Britain that, if she joined in a war against Germany, Canada would deny her the use of the naval bases at Halifax, on the East Coast, and Esquimalt, on the West.[27]

Clearly, the party could not go on with its national chairman enunciating one set of policies, its leader another, the National Council a third, and some of the provincial councils — especially that of Saskatchewan, under George Williams — attempting to direct policy themselves.

M.J. wrote a letter to David Lewis, the national secretary, which explained that he was going to make a speech pointing out that Adolf Hitler was going to get what he demanded:

> This being so, the democratic nations should stand firmly against his aggression — if a war develops, no nation can be strictly neutral in a war against Fascism. J.S. would say that that is going a long way. It is, but I fear that if the present crisis develops, the issue will be clearer than we ever anticipated it would be.
>
> Chamberlain is anxious to avoid taking a stand in a situation where British imperial and class interests appear to be on the Fascist side. He may, however, be forced to take a stand by public opinion at home, by France or by Czechoslovakia. In that event, I take it that his interests would be in the direction of minimizing British assistance unless German planes raided British cities, when public opinion might force him to resign and make way for a coalition determined to end Hitlerism.
>
> In such a situation, the CCF would be divided probably four to two [i.e., in favour of war], and in the country in about the same proportion. We may, I think, conclude that Mackenzie King would call Parliament. A majority for various reasons would support a policy of support for Britain, allied to France and Russia, which would be opposed by a minority, some of whom will be against any association with Russia. In these circumstances, there would be many difficulties in the way of complete solidarity with Britain and her anti-Fascist allies. Should the situation grow blacker, our Movement will encounter serious internal difficulties to which we should be giving some consideration now. All this has worried me greatly during these past few days.[28]

This letter was all too prescient. Not only did events overseas develop as M.J. had seen them but so did the "serious internal difficulties" of the party. The matter came to a head soon after war broke out on September 3, 1939. Three days later, the National Council met to sort out what could be done about the conflicting party policies. A great deal has been written about that meeting and the debate in the House of Commons that followed. Woodsworth's principled stand against war was described most touchingly in the biography his daughter, Grace, wrote about him, in which she called this "His Finest

Hour." Coldwell put his recollections of what happened on the record in an extraordinary session with the Public Archives History Club in 1966.

On the Saturday, September 2, just before war broke out, I had a call from Mr. Mackenzie King — would I go in and see him in the afternoon? I went in to see him in the East Block and he said he was very alarmed and disturbed at what Hitler had done when he moved into Poland, but that he was still hopeful that Hitler would stop where he was, and he told me that Mussolini that very night was endeavouring to bring about some conference and negotiation which he hoped would bring the aggression to a stop. Mr. King was hopeful that this would happen. Of course, it didn't, and the next day we learned from the radio that Mr. Chamberlain had declared war.

Mr. King also asked me, if war did break out, what I thought the attitude of the CCF would be, because our leader was a pronounced pacifist, who had resigned his church in Winnipeg during the First World War to protest, and had taken a stand all through the years against war. I told Mr. King at that time that I thought that in all probability Mr. Woodsworth would pursue the same attitude, but that perhaps the rest of us, myself included, would feel that Hitler had to be stopped and that we were prepared to give support[29] to a war effort on the part of Canada.

On the outbreak of war, we had a National Council meeting[30] to decide our policy. Mr. Woodsworth stood firmly against our participation in the war and wanted us to oppose it in every respect. A group of us, myself included, thought that we had to support a declaration of war. The result was something of a compromise. We hoped that Mr. Woodsworth would fall in with that compromise (he didn't); that he would support the declaration of war and preparations in every way to assist in the defence of Canada while withholding our approval from the sending overseas of an expeditionary force at that time. That was the policy that I placed before the House on behalf of the national Movement,[31] when I made, I think, one of the most difficult speeches I ever made in my life, because we had a reverence for Mr. Woodsworth, of course, that was almost reverence for a saint. He wished to resign, but we persuaded him not to, and he remained our leader until he died. But from then on, we pursued two different attitudes towards the war.

The same day that Canada declared war I was approached by Mr. Arthur Slaght, a very prominent Liberal MP, to see if I and perhaps some others would support the formation of a national government to prosecute the war. I said that in no circumstances would we agree to a coalition. Many of our people thought that from then on we would have to more or less go underground as a movement. I never agreed with that. As a matter of fact, at the end of September, 1939, I undertook a national tour to explain our attitude and I found that it was well received, at least in western Canada, and in my own constituency.[32]

Although he didn't want it, didn't intend it, couldn't foresee it, the fact is that when J.S. Woodsworth sat down after making his dramatic statement in the House of Commons — "While we are urged to fight for freedom and democracy, it should be remembered that war is the very negation of both. The victor may win, but if he does, it is by adopting the self-same tactics which he condemns in his enemy"[33] — he had relinquished his leadership of the party. He went out as he came in, a man of steadfast integrity. A columnist in the Vancouver *Province* noted:

True to the principles he has so consistently advocated, this kindly, courageous man nailed his colours to the mast and sailed off on the lonely route where conscience is the only compass. There may be those who, at Mr. Woodsworth's own invitation, may call him a "dangerous criminal" or a "crazy crank." But there were many in that crowded House on Friday night who will not forget the sight of the veteran leader reciting his creed at the bitterest hours of his political career.[34]

Woodsworth spoke to Parliament only once more, four days later, when he attacked war profiteering and proposed that, before Canada should think once more of conscripting her young men to send them off to war, the nation should conscript wealth, including "bank accounts and property of every kind."[35]

Whether he wanted it or not, M.J. had inherited the mantle of leadership of the party. His admiration for Woodsworth never abated, but in a way Coldwell was in a much tougher position, and he handled it equally well. Both from principle and practicality, he could not simply take the high road and let the party make the best of it. He had to convince his own party, and the Canadian people, that the war must be fought and, at the same time, try to establish, right then, a position that was distinct from the mere "Ready, Aye

Ready" approach of the two old parties. That position was that the war had to be fought, but with two ends in mind, not just military victory. The first was that war profiteering must be blocked — a faint hope — the second that, after the war, a new kind of nation must be built.

J.S. Woodsworth had given the party a saint for its first leader — a rather hard act to follow — but the chance that Canadians would vote in large numbers for saintliness seemed remote. M.J.'s task was to bridge the gap between lofty principle and poll captains, to take the party forward on the more mundane level of envelope-stuffing, riding organization, pamphleteering and tubthumping, without abandoning the basic principles of democratic socialism that, in his view, made the whole process worthwhile. As we will see in the next chapter, it was never easy, but he made a very fair job of it.

PART IV

THE MAN FROM OTTAWA

When people sometimes say to me, "Don't you feel disappointed that you didn't achieve some higher place in the public life of Canada and the government?" my answer is No. I'm not disappointed because, after all, I was always more interested in bringing certain things to pass than I was in achieving place and power myself. — M.J. COLDWELL, *VANCOUVER SUN*, 1965

CHAPTER NINE

M.J. TAKES THE HELM

Coldwell was the leader of the CCF when it had its best chance of amounting to something in Canada. I think the CCF established its reputation under Coldwell as being a decent party, perhaps not to be trusted with government, but certainly to be trusted as an opposition. And it was a decent party. It had odd people in it, but Coldwell assured a sense of solidity and responsibility. That was why someone like the Liberal leader and long-term prime minister, Mackenzie King, seemed to esteem Coldwell so highly. Coldwell's virtue was that he could make Socialism seem like a decent and reasonable alternative. I see now what an enormous asset that was.

— DESMOND P. MORTON, HISTORIAN, 1994

THE CCF WENT INTO THE SECOND WORLD WAR DIVIDED, SADDLED WITH A war policy that was not easy to understand, much less explain (roughly, the policy said that Canada should mobilize for self-defence only, while standing firmly beside Britain in the battle to defeat Hitler, and that wealth should be conscripted before men — whatever that meant), and broke. True, it was growing in membership, with more than 20,000 adherents in CCF clubs and affiliates across the country; it boasted twenty-four members of provincial legislatures — including ten in Saskatchewan, where George Williams was now leader of the official Opposition — while 1,200 members of boards of education and municipal councils identified themselves as CCFers, and Regina, Winnipeg, Windsor and Toronto all had CCF mayors.[1] But from the inside, it was very much a Hollywood movie set, stronger on scenery than structure.

As well as the national organizer, Ted Garland, David Lewis was now on paid salary, and he hired — for five dollars a week — an assistant, Herb Dalton, who typed, filed and cleaned the office.[2] This was now expanded to two rooms, with floors and all, in a building on Wellington Street with a rent of thirty dollars a month. However, Woodsworth was opposed to almost all the changes initiated by Lewis and Coldwell, which smacked to him of undue centralization, as he wrote to M.J.:

> I recognize a good deal can be done at Ottawa, but at this stage of development it seems to me most of our energy should be put into local organization work, perhaps we members can perform the function of tying up the various territories and Provinces.[3]

Coldwell and Lewis simply worked around Woodsworth, assuring him that they would find the funds to finance the expanded Ottawa operation, while getting on with it. Not so easy. A quarter of a century later, M.J. gave an account of how close to bankruptcy the party was in 1939 and what he did about it.

One of our real difficulties immediately with the movement was the likelihood of our collapse on account of having no funds. Prior to the war we had little money, but when the war came we found that even these very small sources dried up. We had David Lewis as our National Secretary, to whom we were paying $150 a month, and we had E.J. Garland as our organizer, to whom we were obligated to the extent of $100 a month, but by the end of October or beginning of November (1939), I found that we had practically no prospects of raising funds whatsoever. I discussed it with David Lewis and some others and we decided that we would have to reduce. Mr. Lewis suggested he go back into his practice of law and let Mr. Garland continue as our national organizer. However, I sent out a letter to our executive, all of whom thought that if we could manage, we should keep both actively on our list, and, if not, we should try to retain Mr. Lewis.

The problem was solved for us at the end of December when an announcement was made that Mr. E.J. Garland had been appointed private secretary to the newly-appointed High Commissioner to Ireland and would be going to Dublin early in the new year. Mr. Lewis and I immediately sent a telegram to Mr. Garland, congratulating him. We hadn't heard of it before it happened, and we were all surprised that we hadn't, but we were very pleased that he had this appointment, because we knew he would fulfil this office well.

But we had no money, and it was suggested that I go down to Toronto and do something that I had never done before, and have never done since, which was to attempt to raise some money. I'm no money-raiser. I went down to Toronto and I saw Ted Joliffe (soon to become the Ontario leader) and one or two others and I collected a couple of hundred dollars. Ted suggested to me that Mr. J.E. Atkinson, the president of the Toronto Daily Star,[4] *had given the local organization a donation for their campaign and if I went to see him, perhaps I might get Mr. Atkinson to give me a small amount of money. Well, I went to see Mr. Atkinson. I didn't broach the subject to him, but he said to me, "I suppose you're short of funds."*

I said, "Yes, we're very short of funds. We have no money at all, as a matter of fact."

"You know," he said, "I always was in sympathy with the CCF, but, you know, Mr. Woodsworth put me outside the Movement altogether."

He called his secretary and said, "Bring me Mr. Woodsworth's letter, 1933." The secretary came in with it.

"Now," he said, "this is what happened. In 1933, when the CCF was formed, I got in touch with Mr. Woodsworth and asked him to come and see me. He did, and I told him that I was in sympathy with the new party and would like to support it but that I thought that with his colleagues he would have to arrange to establish a national office and launch a real campaign."

Mr. Woodsworth said that of course this was pretty difficult because of the shortage of money, and Mr. Atkinson said, "Well, I'll tell you what I'll do. I'll give you a cheque for $4,000 to start a national office."

Mr. Woodsworth said, "Let me think this over."

He went back home and then he wrote the letter which Mr. Atkinson read to me, and which went something like this:

Dear Mr. Atkinson;

I greatly appreciate your generous offer to help the CCF financially. I have just come back from a trip to western Canada. I was in northern Manitoba and northern Saskatchewan where I saw the supporters of the new party cutting cordwood and selling it for a dollar a cord and selling their eggs for fifteen and twenty cents a dozen and donating the proceeds

> to the CCF. Under the circumstances, I do not feel that I could accept a
> sum of money from an outsider.

And Atkinson said to me, "You see? An outsider!" And, he said, "I've never offered anything since. But you know, Mr. Coldwell, I greatly appreciate what you and your colleagues are doing. Here's my cheque for $500."

That's the one and only cheque that I ever received in my capacity as National Chairman or Leader of the CCF.[5]

This was an issue that would bedevil the CCF and its successor, the NDP, for decades. Was it all right to accept money from corporations, and if so, which corporations, and how much? Is it possible for a political party to become just a little bit pregnant? Any reader can make up his or her own mind, but it seems to me that Woodsworth was quite correct in refusing what was then a huge amount of money from a single corporate donor, and M.J. was quite correct to take the (much smaller) cheque and run.

M.J. had personal financial problems, as well, brought about by the sudden and unexpected dissolution of the House in mid-January 1940.

At about seven o'clock in the evening, Mr. [Jack] Pickersgill came up to my room and said, "Do you know where Mr. Woodsworth is, Coldwell?"

"No," I replied. "He's out somewhere."

"Well, I've been looking for him. I have a message for him from the Prime Minister."

"Oh, what is that?"

"Well," he said, "I'll give it to you and you can hand it on to Woodsworth. The House is dissolved."

Now this was a very serious thing for all of us because the sessional indemnity in those days was $3,600[6] and we were, all of us, flat broke. I had to go immediately to the bank and borrow money to pay the rent for my room — my wife was with me here in Ottawa — and I remember I had also been measured for a suit of clothes at Devlin's and I had to go to them and say, "Now, look. I said I would pay for this, but can you carry me for three or four months?" They said they would be very pleased to do so. Well, that was the position we were all in.[7]

I think we can call it the age of innocence when a senior politician is worried about whether he is going to be allowed to pay for a new suit on time, rather than where to bury the body or how to access his Swiss bank account. The reason no one was expecting an election was that Prime Minister Mackenzie King had given a solemn undertaking, when Parliament met in a short war session in September 1939, that it would meet again before he called an election. Then Mitch Hepburn, the obstreperous Ontario premier, rammed a resolution through the provincial house condemning the federal government's war record, and King seized on this as an excuse to go to the polls at once, "avoiding thereby all the contention of a pre-election session."[8] Parliament met simply to be told it would not meet again.

King won the snap election in a walk, without ever having to answer serious questions about the conduct of the war. M.J. and Woodsworth both campaigned vigorously, despite Woodsworth's failing health, but it was M.J. who performed on the free-time radio broadcasts that were provided for the first time by the Canadian Broadcasting Corporation. He used these with considerable effect in his rich baritone, very much more so than either King, who had taken voice coaching, but could not do much about a voice that sounded as if it had only broken in the last few weeks, and R.J. Manion, the new leader of the new National Conservative party, whose wooden delivery was considered so bad that the *Canadian Forum* claimed, "If you didn't hear him, you wouldn't believe us."[9]

M.J. hammered the government for its disdain for democracy — in calling the election as it did — for war profiteering, for its appalling record of inactivity during the depression — which the war was about to solve, almost entirely unaided by government action — but the results were preordained: a massive Liberal majority, with 181 of the 245 seats. The CCF came back with eight seats (one of them in Nova Scotia). It had barely budged its national vote — it was up to 393,230, about six thousand more than in 1935, but its percentage of the vote actually dropped, from 8.7 to 8.5 per cent[10] — and five of its eight MPs were centred in Saskatchewan, where M.J. won his re-election handily, despite spending little time in the riding. Once again, while it had most of its votes in Ontario, in electoral terms, the CCF was an agrarian, Western party.

Twelve years after its founding, Canada's only democratic socialist party was still a marginal force and seemed destined to remain so. The position appeared to be made much worse when J.S. Woodsworth was stricken during a meeting of the national executive. Here is M.J.'s recollection:

Then the election was held, at the end of March — March 26, 1940. We came back with eight members instead of the seven we had at the time of dissolution. A Speaker had to be elected first and Mr. Woodsworth supported the nomination of Mr. James Glenn, who was elected Speaker. This was the last speech that Mr. Woodsworth made in the House. It was Thursday. Friday, as was the custom, two members of the government party moved and seconded the Reply to the Address to the Speech from the Throne, and, on Saturday, we had a caucus in Room 216 with such members of the CCF who were there besides the Members of the House of Commons — two or three of them. We had a very pleasant meeting in the morning and we met at two in the afternoon. Mr. Woodsworth was sitting beside me, to my right. We had hardly begun our discussion when I felt his hand go on my knee, and he said to me, "Coldwell, I've had a stroke! I've had a stroke!"

I looked at him and could see nothing strange about him, but the people who saw me look at Mr. Woodsworth all looked at him and they could see that the right side of his face was contorted. He was carried up to my office. Dr. Gershaw, then a Liberal Member for Medicine Hat, came and pronounced that he had a very serious brain haemorrhage and would have to go to hospital. Of course, he never recovered from that. He was paralysed from then on until he died in March 1942. And so, because of his condition, I became immediately House Leader.[11]

M.J. took over the party, not as Woodsworth's lieutenant, but very much in his own name, especially on the crucial question of the CCF approach to the war effort.

Well, this was the period of the phoney war. Then, in April, came changes: Hitler moved, moved against France. One day late in May Mr. King sent me a note across the floor of the House in his characteristic hand-writing — "Coldwell, if you are not busy would you please come to my office now."

I went up to his office and I found Mr. Ernest Lapointe[12] *there. The two of them were just ghastly white and Mr. King said, "A terrible disaster has occurred. The French army has been entirely defeated, the British army has retreated, and the troops are now assembling on the sands and beaches at Dunkirk. It looks as though the whole British army will be captured and destroyed. We've got to do*

something. There is a danger of the imminent invasion of Britain. They are with-
out arms and," the prime minister said, "we have given instructions to Lindsay
and Valcartier arsenals and the armouries to send immediately to Halifax for
shipment to England all the old Ross rifles that were stored there from the First
World War. And, we're sending the anti-aircraft gun that we have at Halifax at
the same time. We will do anything we can to assist."

Well, that was the end of the phoney war. It had an effect, of course, on our
whole movement. Mr. Woodsworth never accepted the war. I saw him shortly
after this and he was very disturbed at the manner in which we were support-
ing the war effort. From then on, without exception, we supported all the war
expenditures and all the preparations that were made to send reinforcements
and equipment overseas to our troops and to our allies, with one reservation:
that under no circumstances would we support conscription of men for the
armed forces.[13]

At that meeting with King and Lapointe, Coldwell had changed his party's
war policy in an instant and had taken the reins of leadership completely away
from the ailing, but still alert, Woodsworth. It never seems to have occurred
to him that he had simply reached across and seized power; certainly, he
makes no mention of this aspect in any of his memoirs or reminiscences.
Gone was the notion that Canada should only prepare for war at home —
we would do everything we could to help Britain, short of invoking conscription. The change certainly reflected the feeling of the vast majority of
CCFers, including the national executive, but it was only discussed after Coldwell had committed himself to King.

M.J. went to see Woodsworth in March 1942, shortly before his death,
and found his views unchanged:

He thought that while Hitler was a menace and all the rest of it, no good could
ever come of war, and it would be much better if we were directing all our efforts
in the direction of trying to secure some kind of a negotiated peace — which, of
course, was quite impossible.[14]

In October 1941, six MPs, including M.J., were invited to go to Britain by
the British branch of the Parliamentary Association. They went via Baltimore
and Washington, where Senator Claude Pepper of Florida urged them to tell

Winston Churchill, if they got to see him, that "the Interventionist Group of the Congress of the United States would like to say that, while we are in favour of assisting Britain in any way, there is no possibility under any circumstances of the United States entering a shooting war." [15] Significantly, I think, Coldwell remembered the day this message was given to the MPs — October 21, 1941 — because "The 21st is Trafalgar Day in my vocabulary, in my memory." [16]

The MPs landed in Dorset, not far from M.J.'s Devon home, and M.J. paid a visit there. They toured the bombed areas of London, met Charles DeGaulle and his generals of the Free French army, as well as the heads of governments-in-exile of Poland and Czechoslovakia, and had a brief meeting with Winston Churchill at 10 Downing Street. At this meeting, Coldwell passed on the message from Washington, but the British prime minister made no comment except, "Well, we shall see. We shall see." [17]

The MPs also visited Canadian troops at Leatherhead, shortly after those same troops had booed Mackenzie King on a visit there (because they thought Canada was not doing enough in the war). M.J., like a good MP, also took advantage of this wartime visit to help out his constituency — he sold some Canadian flour. The Co-operative Movement in Saskatchewan had purchased a mill at Outlook, in M.J.'s riding, but did not have enough orders to keep it going full-time. Before he left for Britain, he was asked if he could do anything about this, and he said he would do his best. By chance, he was seated beside A.V. Alexander at a meeting of the Labour Party caucus in London, and Alexander just happened to be both the First Lord of the Admiralty and head of the Co-operative Movement in Britain. The result was an outpouring of orders for the mill.

Then M.J. went home and declared war on Japan. That, at least, is how he told it.

When we got back, it was agreed that I would take a non-political tour, to address service clubs as well as our own people across the country. I got as far as Biggar and I was there on the night of Saturday, December 6, 1941. The next day, we went up to the north part of the constituency, and we were there all day. When we drove back to Biggar that evening, as we came to the edge of town, there was a man standing there, in the middle of the road. He put up his hand as soon as he saw our car, and we stopped. He said, "Mr. Coldwell, will you please go to the telephone exchange at once. You are wanted urgently on the telephone."

So I went to the telephone booth and almost immediately a voice came on and said, "This is Walter Turnbull[18] speaking from Ottawa. The Prime Minister would like a word with you."

So on came Mackenzie King.

"Well, Coldwell," he said, "isn't this terrible news? A terrible disaster!"

"I don't understand you, Mr. King. What news and what disaster?"

"Where have you been all day?"

"I've been up in the north of my constituency."

"No telephones up there?"

"No," I said.

"No radio?"

"No."

"Well then," he said, "I must tell you that for the last five or six hours there have been broadcasts all over the radio networks telling us of the terrible disaster that happened this morning at Pearl Harbour. Virtually the whole American Pacific Fleet was wiped out by a Japanese attack this morning. The reason I am so anxious to get in touch with you is that we've had a cabinet meeting. The Americans have been very good to us all through the war. They've done everything they could, even to the extent of risking their own neutrality and you know," he said, "we'd like to be the first nation to stand beside them and declare war on Japan. In fact, we'd like to declare war before they can declare war, because they can't do that until tomorrow. Congress alone can declare war and they've got to wait for a meeting of Congress but, as far as we are concerned, if you'll agree, we can do this by Order-in-Council. We have an Order-in-Council drafted with a proclamation declaring war on Japan. I've been in touch with Mr. Manion and Mr. Blackmore.[19] They have both agreed and all I want now is your agreement and we'll issue the proclamation."

So I said, "Well, Mr. King, you know we've been critical of the export of scrap iron and concentrate to Japan for a long time. I'm quite sure that my colleagues will not object to my saying that this proclamation should be issued and we should declare war on Japan immediately."

The proclamation was issued immediately that evening, and I have sometimes said, "And so I declared war."[20]

Woodsworth was not consulted, nor indeed were any other CCFers; M.J. had assumed the right to speak for the party as representative of its majority opinion. He remained fiercely critical of the government on two grounds — first, on what he considered to be the massive giveaways to big industry as it geared up for the war effort, and second, on the violation of civil rights that went on in the name of patriotism. It was only the CCF — led by Angus MacInnis of Vancouver — who raised objections to the treatment of Japanese Canadians under the War Measures Act, and the jailing of hundreds of immigrants in other parts of Canada on suspicion of being "enemy aliens."

Despite these criticisms, M.J., and indeed the CCF, had become fervid patriots, and when Mackenzie King asked for a plebiscite to release him from his commitment not to enforce conscription on Canadians, the party, led by Coldwell, asked for a Yes vote. The party statement began:

> The CCF stands unitedly behind the forces of democracy in this world struggle. It recognizes that in the defeat of fascism lies the sole hope of humanity.[21]

At the National Convention that year, M.J. thundered, "Let our slogan be, total mobilization for total war, and nothing less."[22] He then went on to move an amendment to the government's legislation on conscription, which King accepted, and that is how conscription became law. This time, he had the full and previous support of the party in convention, and as David Lewis noted in his autobiography, "We had come full circle."[23]

Jack Coldwell, M.J.'s son, far from going to jail to avoid the draft, joined the RCAF and had a distinguished wartime career.

As the war drew on, the CCF, despite the small size of its parliamentary group, assumed a more and more important role as the critic and conscience of the House, especially on social issues. This was boosted in turn by the party's growing strength in the provinces, and the two strains reinforced each other. The Liberals were then pushed to take over CCF initiatives for fear of losing votes. By September 1943, the CCF had become the official Opposition in Ontario and, for the first time, led the Liberals in a national Gallup Poll — with 29 per cent support nationally to 28 per cent for the Liberals.[24] It was, at least for the time being, anything but a small regional group.

Reform was in the air. In England, Sir William Beveridge's white paper, entitled *Social Insurance and Allied Services,* was handed to the government in 1942. It proposed a postwar social security system that would cover every British citizen "from the cradle to the grave." It would be funded, in the main, from taxes, and it would provide a "social minimum" of income, health, housing and education for all.

The Swedes had already adopted a similar scheme, under a social democratic government, which threw in motherhood benefits, marital loans and subsidies for school lunches. There was even a tax on state construction expenditures to finance the acquisition of art for Swedish public buildings.[25]

A copy of the Beveridge report was brought to Canada in 1943, and Leonard Marsh, a social sciences professor at McGill University, was commissioned to prepare a document on "Social Security for Canada," which he did, recommending many of the same reforms. King used this to block what he called the "threat of defections from our own ranks in the House to the CCF."[26] Within weeks, the Advisory Council of the National Liberal Federation had met and drafted a fourteen-point program of reform, including improved pensions, unemployment insurance and a vastly increased government role in the economy. King told his diary, "I think I have cut the ground in large part from under the CCF."[27]

And so he had. In the 1945 election, the Liberals presented a platform full of social advances, and the Cockfield Brown advertising agency produced a series of pamphlets promising "womb to tomb" security. The Liberal slogan for the election was "A New Social Order for Canada," and the authors of the *Regina Manifesto* might have sued for breach of copyright. When this helped King win the election, he put the pamphlets away and forgot about them. The Family Allowance, introduced in 1944, was the only substantive reform made at this time, although the rest of the package was forced on successive governments over the next two decades, goaded by the CCF.

Gad Horowitz, the eminent political scientist, noted in a paper on "Conservatism, Liberalism and Socialism in Canada" that "Liberals depend on the CCF-NDP for innovations; the CCF-NDP depends on the Liberals for implementation of the innovations."[28]

The point to note about this in connection with M.J. was that it was all right by him. No doubt he would rather have led the nation, but as we saw in the quotation at the top of this section, he was far more concerned that the reforms be implemented than that he or his party get the credit.

King never understood this, never grasped why he could not assimilate Coldwell as he had swallowed Crerar and the Progressives. He made a new attempt to recruit M.J. into a coalition, and even offered M.J. a post, not merely in his cabinet, but as his deputy, and likely successor. Here is M.J.'s telling of this part of the story:

About the first week in April 1945, a very prominent gentleman came to see me. I knew that he was close to Mr. King. He came and sat down in my office and he said, "Now, Coldwell, general elections have got to come this summer. What's your forecast as to the result?"

"I don't know."

He said, "Do you think the government will be re-elected?"

"Well," I said, "I think that is very difficult to forecast, but I think the government will be in trouble. I think the government may be defeated."

"Do you think you're going to do very well?"

I said, "Yes, we're going to increase our membership quite substantially."

"Well," he said, "that's the general forecast. Now, provided that Mr. King didn't have a majority, would you be prepared to enter a coalition government with him?"

I said, "No, we have been opposed to coalitions throughout the war and before the war. I don't think my colleagues would agree to it and, as far as I personally am concerned, I would not agree to it and would not join a coalition government." He went away.

He came back two or three days later and he said to me, "I want to talk to you again about this idea of a coalition. If a coalition were formed and you were agreed to come into it, would it make any difference in your decision if you were assured by Mr. King personally that he would appoint you as his deputy in the Cabinet, with the possibility of your succeeding him when he retired?"

I said, No, it wouldn't make any difference at all — not at all.

Several years later, after Mr. King had retired and there was a dinner given for him in the Chateau, he alluded to this in his talk and said he had never approached me or anyone else regarding this situation, which was perfectly true. He hadn't. But the very next morning the gentleman who had approached me came to my office and said, "I just want to put myself right with you. The second time I came to see you I walked from Mr. King's office in the East Block to your office and made you the offer."[29]

Coldwell never told anyone, as far as the record shows, who made the approach to him; but other evidence shows quite clearly that it was Grant Dexter, then editor of the *Winnipeg Free Press* and a prominent Liberal strategist, as well as one of King's closest contacts.[30] Shortly before his death, King expressed his regrets that M.J. had not joined him. He said he would have been able to introduce reforms that had either been postponed or not introduced at all. The CCF had performed the valuable task of popularizing social reforms so that he could introduce them when the public was ready for them. M.J. replied that he could not join King.[31] Gad Horowitz commented, "The Liberals, says King, are too conservative because the left has not joined them. The left has not joined them, replies Coldwell, because they are too conservative."[32]

The main planks of the CCF social agenda (as opposed to the nationalization and social ownership planks) were all hammered into place about three decades after they first rang out in Regina City Hall in 1933. The process began when Tommy Douglas, at M.J.'s urging, returned to Saskatchewan in 1942. George Williams had enlisted in January 1941 and was overseas with the Princess Louise Dragoons. Most observers assumed that he would resign his position as leader of the official Opposition, but he did not. Instead, he mounted a new attack on Douglas, the man seen as his likely successor, on the grounds that the Social Credit support he had received in 1935 proved that he was not a man to be trusted.[33] Williams ran for the Saskatchewan leadership *in absentia,* at the 1942 provincial convention, promising to return to Canada if re-elected. M.J., in the meantime, had helped to move Clarence Fines into the provincial vice-presidency and, after some bitter infighting, and a good deal of organization by Fines, Douglas was chosen as leader of the Saskatchewan CCF in July 1942.

His election as premier in June 1944 — nine days after D-Day — changed politics forever in this country. For the first time, Canada had a democratic socialist party in power, and its record of achievement immediately put pressure on other governments, especially when it became clear that these social measures were not, after all, going to bankrupt the government or lead to the establishment of gulags in the Northwest Territories. With an overwhelming majority — forty-one CCF members to five Liberals — Douglas was able to move quickly. By the end of 1944, the government had stabilized farm debts, introduced free treatment for tuberculosis, cancer and mental illness, and provided free medical care for mothers on social assistance, the old and the blind. In mid-1945, there was a provincial government insurance corporation and, a year later, provincial automobile insurance.[34]

Rather than plunging the province into bankruptcy, the result that all the Right Thinking sort were sure would follow the CCF victory, Saskatchewan rang up twelve budget surpluses in a row, beginning with the 1945–46 fiscal year;[35] this was the prod that provoked reform in other provinces and in Ottawa. M.J., when he came to deal with this phenomenon, gave much more credit than most others would have to Mackenzie King, for the modest changes he made.

Now all through this period, we were very anxious about the postwar era. What was it going to be like? Economists and social scientists were in general agreement that when the war ended there would be a letdown; there would be a period probably of unemployment and depression somewhat analogous to the depression we saw before the war. Practically everybody believed this. Mr. C.D. Howe got busy and he was gathering together a shelf of projected works that could be used to ease this unemployment. We were talking about it in the House of Commons, urging the government to do something about it. All through the war we were anxious that the boys who had fought would not come back to the kind of conditions that the boys who fought the First World War encountered. They fought for democracy but democracy let them down, and we were determined we would try to get the government to consider something better than that.

In fact, I moved in the House on one occasion that we set aside as much as two billion dollars after the war to provide means of work for the men when they came back. We were very keen on the plan, which I think the government of the day must be praised for putting into effect — the plan of education for the veterans after the Second World War.[36] Well, those were the things we were working for. We wanted a national health plan.

The government of Saskatchewan had brought in a hospitalization plan; they had done something for senior citizens in the way of health services in that province; they had done a good deal to improve mothers' pensions and so on. We were plugging away at this, and towards the time when the next election was coming on in 1949, Mr. King introduced the hospital grants, he introduced the improvements in old age pensions, and he had already introduced the mothers' allowances.

And I am convinced of this — though I hold no brief for Mr. King, who had many characteristics that cannot be admired — but one day he said to me, "You know, Coldwell, I've always regretted that you didn't see your way clear when you were young to join the Liberal party. You might have been a great help to me in trying to bring into effect some of the things I've wanted to do."

And he went on to say this: "When I was elected Prime Minister in 1921, I faced the international situation, and a trade crisis that took up all my time. The things I intended to do for the working people of this country, I was never able to do. Of course, I had colleagues around me who were not favourable to some of the policies I hoped to put into effect."

Well, shortly before he retired in 1949, we saw these very interesting pieces of social legislation, and I've been convinced in my own mind that this was sort of a last attempt by Mackenzie King to do two or three of the things he had in mind when he became Prime Minister. I've always given him credit for probably wanting to do things that he wasn't able to do because the party he had around him would not be in favour of some of them.[37]

The portrait of King as a social reformer held back by his own party — Prometheus bound in velvet — may tell us more about the essential kindness of M.J. than it does about the machinations of one of the wiliest and most ruthless politicians Canada ever spawned. In any event, the response of the old-line parties to the increasing popularity of the socialists was clever, unscrupulous and successful. Enough of the CCF program would be embraced to convince the public that it could have the advantages of the promised reforms without electing CCFers, and at the same time the CCF was subjected to an extraordinary, and sometimes illegal, campaign of vilification, which continued as long as the party existed. In the next chapter, we shall see how this worked.

Chapter Ten

Millstones

Our role has been a difficult one. The press of Canada mainly take the ultra-American viewpoint, while an element in our movement are equally ultra-antagonistic to the United States. We have tried to be objective and realistic in our approach and decisions — in other words, we side with neither extreme. This is what creates opportunities for both the extreme right and the extreme left to attack us, so weak are we in numbers and publicity, that we are "ground between the upper and nether millstones."

— LETTER, M.J. COLDWELL, MARCH 1951

AT THE END OF THE SECOND WORLD WAR, M.J. WAS AT THE HEIGHT OF HIS powers. He was fifty-six years old, but looked younger, with clean-cut features and a steady, penetrating glance. He wore pince-nez, which heightened an uncanny resemblance to Woodrow Wilson, the former U.S. president. He was just over average height, and a love of good food was beginning to give him a hefty look. His daughter, Margaret, often teased him that he could remember meals he had been served years before, in detail, and loved to dwell on them.[1] He had an engaging smile that took something off the rather formal manners that were part of his background; despite his formality, he made friends easily and kept them loyally, whether they agreed on political matters or not. Tommy Douglas, in his reminiscences, recalled an example of this, played out in the House of Commons room he shared with M.J.:

Someone came in, a well-known Liberal, and started to berate Mr. M.A. McPherson, who had been an attorney-general in Saskatchewan, and who had run against Mr. Coldwell in 1934. Mr. Coldwell turned on him like a lion. He said, "Mr. McPherson is a political opponent, but he's one of the finest Christian gentlemen I've ever known and I will not allow anyone in this room to make comments like that about him. If this is all you have to say, will you please go away?"[2]

M.J. was, by now, a practised politician, but of a rather old-fashioned sort. He loved the craft of politics, believed very much in it, but eschewed the kind of deal-making that is so much deplored and so rigorously pursued in that craft. He smoked a pipe, but attended few smoke-filled rooms. To outsiders, he was a presentable, personable, honourable figure who made it difficult — but as we shall see, far from impossible — to demonize the CCF; to insiders, he was a patient, understanding leader, a skilled debater and superb parliamentarian, even if he lacked the thundering oratory of a William Aberhart, George Drew or that rising youngster from Saskatchewan, John Diefenbaker. Very few outsiders or insiders knew that after a long day in the House of Commons, he would spend several hours on party work, complete whatever speaking or writing engagements that had been arranged, and then return to the modest apartment on Bank Street where he and Norah lived and spend most of the night hours trying to massage some of the pain out of her cramped legs. The next day, grey with fatigue, he would repeat the process. When Margaret moved to Ottawa in 1943, she studied nursing and helped to relieve some of the burden with her newly acquired expertise. Not that M.J. ever thought of anything he did for Norah as a burden. Margaret recalls:

My parents had a bed-sitting room on MacLaren Street and I had a bedroom on the third floor. Meals were prepared in the dining room and it was a very congenial atmosphere. My mother had difficulty getting to the dining room and we finally got her a wheelchair. My father took us for many drives and, over the years, we were able to take my mother to an occasional movie. There was a lady at the Centre Theatre on Sparks Street who was very kind and helpful.

At the boarding school in Regina, I had attended small classes and liked it, so I was enrolled in the Ottawa Ladies College. Eventually, we moved into an apartment on Bank Street.[3] My mother could not walk by this time. I was a teenager and, as Dad was away a good deal of the time, we had a maid. I saw that my mother was dressed, washed, and helped her out of bed and into chairs from her wheelchair. I got her to bed at night, so really didn't have much social life, but I had many good friends and really didn't feel resentful. The various secretaries that my father had were most kind and would often come and lift my mother into the car for a drive. She loved to read, but her eyes gave her much trouble as time went on. She also loved the radio, especially the hockey broadcasts and the sportscasts from England. When I would come home at noon, she would be listening to "The Happy Gang."

My mother was unable to accompany my father to social functions, so I was most fortunate to be included at quite a few embassy functions and met many interesting people. I was my father's most ardent admirer. One winter's evening, we were on our way to the Dutch Embassy in tuxedo and evening dress when we got stuck in the snow. I got out and pushed and we arrived late for dinner.

My mother's condition continued to worsen and she began to have bad spasms in her legs. We spent many hours rubbing them during the day and night. When I went into nursing from 1940 to 1943, we had to hire a full-time housekeeper and someone to look after my mother. When I graduated and came home, I continued to do some hospital nursing but soon found I could not be up all night with my mother and continue nursing during the day.

I think my mother was a bit of a monarchist. When the King and Queen visited Canada in 1939 at the opening of Parliament, they made a special place for her wheelchair overlooking the Senate Chamber to that she could see them. She was thrilled. Shortly before my mother died in 1953, my father bought a television so that she could see the coronation of Elizabeth II.[4]

Norah continued to be the centre of M.J.'s life, despite her increasing incapacity. Again, Margaret remembers:

He would talk everything over with her, everything he did. He would practise his speeches with her and she would offer encouragement and criticism. He used to take her for long drives; he would bundle her up in a blanket and carry her out to the car, and they would drive all over the area.

The only thing she wanted that he could not provide was a house that looked out on the Gatineau hills, because it would remind her of home — she was raised in a house that looked over the hills of Somerset — but of course my father could never buy a house; he never knew when he was about to lose his job.[5]

Instead, the Coldwells, when they were able to move out of a boarding house, always lived in apartments, first at 612 Bank Street, then at 404 Laurier East, in Sandy Hill. Inevitably, her illness began to cost Norah some of her beauty as she became thinner and thinner, but it could not touch her spirit. M.J. called her "the Gibson Girl," because she was so striking, with long auburn hair and an air of self-possession. When paralysis robbed her of the use of her right hand, which meant that she could no longer use a pen, she learned to type with her left hand, so she could keep up the stream of correspondence that was so important to both of them. Later she lost the effective use of both hands. When her eyesight failed, she relied on the radio to keep informed. As she became more and more incapacitated, Margaret took on more of the burden of care, delaying her own marriage to do this. Margaret had met a quiet-spoken, handsome young man named Douglas Carman at a dinner party at Grace and Angus MacInnis's and they were soon in love, but, Margaret recalls, "People told me I could never get married, because there just wasn't the time."[6] Despite this problem, the marriage took place on September 29, 1951, and forty-eight years later, is as strong as ever. The Carmans have three children, who were great favourites with their grandfather.

During this period, M.J. offered on several occasions to give up politics, but Norah wouldn't hear of it; he was needed, and he must keep on; he must not let down those who counted on him.

Politically, the postwar period contained both good and bad news. The CCF was at last picking up real support in the labour movement. The first breakthrough came in September, 1943, when the Canadian Congress of Labour, at its annual convention, endorsed the CCF as the political arm of labour. In practical terms, this didn't amount to much, because Pat Conroy, the secretary-treasurer of the CCL, was wary of political interference in union business and kept a sharp curb on the amount of help the union central itself — as opposed to many of the individual unions and their members, who provided help, money and energy — could give the party. The next year, the

CCL formed its first political action committee, under the chairmanship of Charlie Millard of the United Steelworkers, but again, the impact was limited, for two reasons. One was the dislike and rivalry that existed between Millard and Conroy, who kept the CCL from putting much muscle behind the arrangement; and the other was the opposition of the increasingly virulent minority of Communists within a number of the major unions, such as the United Electrical Workers and Mine, Mill and Smelter Workers.[7] They not only resisted the activities of a committee dedicated to helping the CCF, but their activities allowed outside opponents to paint the party as the captive of communism. Still, the labour movement provided many of the foot soldiers and much of the money that enabled the party to keep going.

The CCF was moderating its policies under M.J., and by war's end was officially embracing the idea that Canada's economy was, and should remain, a "mixed economy" rather than the state-planned model envisioned by the *Regina Manifesto* (although that remained the official central party document, it was referred to more for spiritual uplift than practical policy). Ironically, this more moderate approach drew down on the party — precisely because it made it more electable — what Cameron Smith calls "the most vicious and concentrated campaign ever undertaken against a political party."[8] It lasted from 1944 until after the Korean War and the McCarthy era, more than a decade later, and in some measure dogged the CCF to the end of its days.

Supported by huge donations from chambers of commerce and boards of trade, and by most of Canada's largest corporations, including its banks and trust companies, the campaign portrayed the CCF as dictatorial (a wonderful irony at the time, for the CCF was the only political party in Canada that had open conventions; the Liberals' last political convention had taken place to elect Mackenzie King as leader in 1919), communistic and crooked. Typical was the intervention of Fred Gardiner, the reeve of Forest Hill, then an independent city within Toronto, who rumbled that "Socialistic rule in Canada would mean 'muscle men and gangsters' who understand mob organization and the handling of machine guns."[9]

In Ontario, the government of George Drew established a political police office on the second floor of a garage on Surrey Place, just down the street from Queen's Park. Ontario Provincial Police Captain William J. Osborne-Dempster was put in charge, provided with funds never authorized by the legislature and set to work as a political spy, using the code name "D.208."[10] He signed his reports to the deputy commissioner of the OPP, "Yours to command, D.208." The "Special Branch," as it was called, did not appear in the public accounts of Ontario, although that was a legal requirement. Osborne-Dempster set up files on all CCF members of the legislature and on anyone who levelled any sort of criticism against the government, free enterprise or international finance. These people were all seen as either Communists or the dupes of Communists, and they included not only Ted Joliffe, but B.K. Sandwell, editor of *Saturday Night*, Mitch Hepburn, the former premier, David Coll, a prominent Liberal senator.

Copies of reports purporting to link all these left-wingers with communism were fed, not only to the provincial Conservatives, but to two peculiar propagandists, Gladstone Murray and M.A. Sanderson. Murray, who had been general manager of the Canadian Broadcasting Corporation until 1943, when a House of Commons committee asked him to resign for failing to account for money he had received,[11] was employed by the Canadian Chamber of Commerce to mount an anti-socialist campaign. He received enthusiastic support from the heads of such companies as Imperial Oil, Noranda Mines, International Nickel and Massey-Harris, and he used the material from D.208 for propaganda pamphlets. Sanderson, known to intimates as "Buggsy," although his first name was actually Montague, was the manager of the Reliable Exterminator Company, but spent much of his time attacking socialism, because the resultant publicity helped his company. He used Osborne-Dempster's reports as the basis of a huge, crude advertisement directed at CCF candidates who ran in the 1944 municipal elections in Toronto. The ad, headed THIS IS THE SLATE TO RUB OUT ON NEW YEAR'S DAY, contained the flat assertion that all the CCFers were Communists, and since it was illegal at that time to be a Communist, the CCF candidates sued, successfully, for libel. A "special jury," which consisted entirely of businessmen, awarded the CCFers one dollar each in damages; in the meantime, all were defeated in the election.

Alvin Rowe, an OPP constable working under Osborne-Dempster, became more and more concerned about the activities of the Special Branch, which were clearly outside the law, and he took his worries to Agnes Macphail, who in turn took them to Ted Joliffe, the Ontario CCF leader. Joliffe consulted M.J., who advised him to use the materially carefully. Instead,

Joliffe, on May 24, 1945, in the middle of a provincial election campaign, went on the radio to charge that the Ontario government had set up a secret political police force, that Premier George Drew knew about it and sanctioned it, and that it was being used to harass the legitimate Opposition to the Conservatives, including Liberals and CCFers. He called the Special Branch George Drew's "Gestapo." Although Joliffe provided dates, incidents and facts drawn from the police files, the public simply would not believe that a Canadian government would engage in such activities. Premier Drew couldn't dismiss the charges out of hand, so he promised a royal commission to look into the matter, and denied all personal knowledge of either the Special Branch or its operatives. That got rid of it for the term of the election, which the Conservatives won handily.

In due course, Mr. Justice A.M. LeBel, formerly a prominent Liberal, was named as royal commissioner, and Joseph Sedgwick, a prominent Conservative, was named commission counsel. They were, by their terms of reference, not to look into the activities of the Special Branch, but merely to see whether Drew was personally responsible for its establishment. Drew claimed that Joliffe's entire charge was a "deliberate lie," and LeBel swallowed this whole. Drew said in evidence that he had never heard of D.208, had only infrequent and casual contact with Gladstone Murray, and never received any reports from the Special Branch, of which he knew nothing. LeBel swallowed this whole, too. He concluded that there was no direct link between Drew and the Special Branch, and therefore Joliffe's charges were groundless. A number of his other findings invite the adjective "fatheaded." For example, he found that Osborne-Dempster's role was not to make life difficult for the legitimate opposition, but to investigate communism, although Osborne-Dempster never once submitted a report on communism or the activities of Communists. LeBel also found that, while Osborne-Dempster's reports were frequently misleading and false, they were not intentionally so, and he ruled that it was "incredible" that big business — in the persons of Buggsy Sanderson and Gladstone Murray — would be in the business of purchasing palpable falsehoods. So, he ruled, it didn't happen. He found that the payments to Osborne-Dempster were illegal, but nothing was done about that then or ever. Gladstone Murray testified that he had never received the secret reports of D.208 or used them, and again Mr. Justice LeBel believed him.

The chief witness against the government, Constable Alvin Rowe, died in an airplane crash soon after the commission hearings, and the transcript of the hearings disappeared. Gone, vanished. No one seemed to find this odd. It was not until 1980, when David Lewis was writing his autobiography, that at least part of the truth about Drew's connection to the Special Branch came out. Lewis used two expert researchers, Dr. Alan Whitehorn and David Walden, to help him gather material for his memoirs, and they did a thorough search of the papers of both George Drew and Gladstone Murray. What they found in the correspondence of these two men was that Drew had a direct, personal and long-lasting relationship with Gladstone Murray, that the D.208 reports were indeed used in precisely the way that Alvin Rowe had said they were used and that, in other words, as Lewis wrote, "The head of the Ontario government had given false testimony under oath." [12]

The "Gestapo" broadcast by Ted Joliffe on May 25 had a severe and negative impact on the provincial election, ten days later — which saw the CCF plummet from official Opposition to third-party status. It also landed with a thud in the federal election, which took place June 10. The provincial Conservatives returned to power with sixty-six seats, while the Liberals became the official Opposition with eleven, and the CCF plunged from twenty-one to eight. [13] Federally, as well, the incident did inestimable harm, convincing many swing voters that the CCF was a party of desperation, which would use any tactic, including "deliberate lies," to crawl to power. Murray Beck, who wrote a definitive — and generally even-handed — volume on all the Canadian federal elections from Confederation on, noted that "the politically inept E.B. Joliffe" had hurt the CCF cause because "his charges that the Premier maintained his own private Gestapo backfired badly." [14]

So they did. But those charges happened to be perfectly true.

It is important to keep this material in mind when assessing the effectiveness or otherwise of M.J. Coldwell as leader of the CCF. The record shows that, during his federal leadership, the party fortunes moved up and down, but the expected breakthrough, while often promised, never came (see Table 1 in Appendix). What the record did not show, at least until recently, was that much of the damage was due, not to any inability on his part, but to the crude and illegal manipulation of the political system. The CCF was not merely outflanked by clever governments, it was dismantled and very nearly destroyed by the illegal actions of some of its political opponents.

Coldwell's *Memoirs*[15] reveal that Gladstone Murray, whose activities were so harmful to the CCF, was a drunken incompetent who had good reason to carry a personal animus against M.J.

When the Commons Committee on Broadcasting was established after the war, I was named to the committee. It was not long before Mr. Gladstone Murray invited me to have lunch with him. Apparently, he resented the placing of the CBC under the ministerial control of the Hon. C.D. Howe. He spent the lunch hour explaining to me his part — first, in the organization of the British Broadcasting Corporation, and then of his acceptance as General Manager of the CBC. He told me that when the war broke out, C.D. Howe immediately proposed the taking over of the duties of the Corporation as a wartime necessity. Gladstone Murray said that he regarded Mr. Howe as a dangerous man, who wished to use the Corporation for his own purposes and for his own ambitions. Although I had been critical of some of C.D. Howe's policies — particularly of his failure to implement Parliament's legislation in control of defence-contract profits — I nonetheless had a great deal of respect for him and found it quite difficult to believe Mr. Murray's charges.

I had, too, become acquainted with a member of the Broadcasting Board of Governors, Mr. Alan Plaunt, who had been one of the outstanding supporters of the old Radio League and of national broadcasting. Alan Plaunt was a friend of David Lewis — indeed, it was through David that I had met him. Although a very wealthy young man, he was a sympathizer and active supporter and contributor to the CCF. I told Alan Plaunt of the conversation I had had with Gladstone Murray. Alan then told me that he and Brooke Claxton had been largely instrumental in persuading Gladstone Murray to accept the management of the CBC some years earlier. Alan told me, however, that since then, he and Brooke Claxton had been compelled to revise their opinion of Mr. Murray and his reliability. Alan told me that, after the appointment was made by Canada,[16] the BBC was very glad to be relieved of Mr. Murray's services. Alan also told me of Mr. Murray's inability to participate in some conferences because of his addiction to liquor. Brooke Claxton confirmed this.

When the Broadcast Committee met, at Alan Plaunt's urging and with Brooke Claxton's assistance, we began to make inquiry into some of the activities of the CBC and of Mr. Murray's part in them... The Chairman of the Board [i.e., of Broadcast Governors] was Mr. René Morin of Montreal, who was unwilling to express any adverse opinions of Mr. Murray or of his reliability and activities in public, but he made it very clear when we sat in camera dealing with the suggestion that Mr. Murray should be removed from office, that he had come to the conclusion that Gladstone Murray was, in his words, "a liar!"

We discovered, too, from Mr. Leonard Brockington, who had been Chairman of the Board, that Mr. Murray was not a fit person to preside over the CBC. Mr. Brockington told me, for example, that on one occasion, Mr. Murray announced that Sir John Reith, Chairman of the BBC, was convening a meeting of Managers of the Broadcasting Corporations within the Commonwealth for a conference in London, and that he had decided to go. Mr. Brockington considered that this was such an important conference that he should go, too. On his arrival in London, he telephoned Sir John Reith, who told him he had not called any such conference. To placate Mr. Brockington, Mr. Murray arranged an elaborate dinner, to which he invited various outstanding Britishers. A bill of about $1,200 was paid for the dinner by the CBC as part of the expenses of a conference which never convened.

Other officials of the CBC told me personally of Gladstone Murray's drunkenness. Brooke Claxton and I were determined to remove him. This could have been accomplished easily but for the interference of C.D. Howe, who attended our in camera meeting at which Mr. Murray's dismissal was discussed, and urged us not to go to that extreme, but rather to demote him to another position. It was ironical that C.D. Howe, whom Mr. Murray had vilified in conversation with me, should have been instrumental in saving him from dismissal at this time.[17]

M.J. was not at his best in this kind of infighting. His approach to politics expected honourable behaviour on the other side, reasonable debate and shrewd argument, not vicious lies and propaganda made out of whole cloth. He left most of the infighting to David Lewis, the national secretary. This allowed the party's critics to portray Coldwell as merely the puppet of Lewis, the master manipulator. If not a master, Lewis certainly was a manipulator, and Carl Hamilton, who knew both men well, recalls that "David was running the party, on a day-to-day basis, while M.J. was more or less being the country squire, above the fray."[18]

There was a national paranoia about communism in Canada at this time, a good deal of which arose from the "Gouzenko Affair," which M.J. saw up close. Here is his account of it:

It was in September 1946 that I received a telephone call from Mr. King's office, asking me to see him at once, if possible. When I met him in the Prime Minister's Office in the East Block, he told me that he wished to communicate to me a matter which must be regarded for the time being as highly secretive. He then told me that one of the clerks at the Russian Embassy had sought protection and, indeed, political asylum from the Canadian government. The story he told me was that the official, Igor Gouzenko, a cipher clerk, had left the embassy and taken with him some papers that were at the moment being examined by Mr. Norman Robertson[19] and by the Mounted Police. He said that when Mr. Gouzenko left the embassy, he went to the Ottawa Journal, but the night editor was not interested in his story, and told him that he should go to the Mounted Police. He then went to the Justice Building, where the policeman at the desk told him that there was no-one in at the moment whom he could see, and Mr. Gouzenko, now very worried that the embassy would discover his absence, the absence of the papers he had taken, and of his wife and children, went to his apartment on Somerset Street, where he confided his fears to a Canadian friend in a neighbouring apartment.

On looking out the window, the friend told him that there were two men on a seat in the park opposite, and that he was suspicious that they were watching the apartment house. Sometime later, two embassy officials entered the apartment, and endeavoured to find Mr. Gouzenko, who was hiding at his neighbour's.

While they were ransacking his apartment, local policemen arrived to investigate. The intruders claimed diplomatic immunity, and were permitted to return to the embassy, while Mr. Gouzenko and his family were taken into police protection.

It transpired that the two men in the park were local detectives, for the officer at the Justice Building had been impressed enough by Mr. Gouzenko's story to communicate with the local police, with the suggestion that his apartment be watched. It was these two detectives who had followed the intruders and stopped their search of the Gouzenko apartment.

Mr. King told me that the next day, Mr. Gouzenko had been interrogated by the RCMP, and his story confirmed. Mr. King was very upset. He told me that Mr. Gouzenko had exposed serious espionage by Russian agents masquerading in various jobs at the Soviet Embassy. He said that Mr. Gouzenko had reported that secret information had been obtained from Canadian official circles, including members of the civil service and a Communist member of the House of Commons, Mr. Fred Rose. He said that not only were Canadian public servants involved, but that both the United States' and British civil services were implicated. He proposed to go to Washington to see President Truman, and then to Britain to see the Prime Minister and members of the United Kingdom cabinet.

I told him, of course, that the information he had given me would be entirely confidential and kept absolutely secret until he was prepared to release me from the promise, or make some public reference to the matter. I left him and Mr. King did visit Washington and London. I kept the matter to myself, not even following my usual practice of giving confidential information to my colleague, Angus MacInnis, whom I could trust completely, and to whom I imparted confidential information from time to time, lest anything should happen to me before I was allowed to discuss such information publicly.

I put the matter so completely out of my mind that it was not until I was returning from a conference at Houston, Texas, the following February, that I remembered it again. I had come from Houston to St. Louis, Missouri, where I had to change trains for Chicago, and thence home. It was just before noon. I intended to take my lunch on the train, but desired to quench my thirst at the lunch counter with a glass of orange juice. It so happened that in the next seat, a man was reading a St. Louis newspaper. I saw the headline, which stated that the Prime Minister of Canada had revealed an espionage plot. When my neighbour put his paper down, I asked if I might see it. It was, as I had guessed, an announcement that Mr. Mackenzie King had made regarding the Gouzenko revelations.

When I returned to Ottawa, I found there was considerable excitement, and that a number of arrests had been made before Mr. King made his statement to the country. The manner in which the arrests were made was subject to severe criticism in the country, and in the House of Commons. Mr. Louis St. Laurent was then the Minister of Justice, and I always think that he mistook the French methods of interrogation for our own methods of arrest — warning and questioning. The accused persons were held incommunicado; were not allowed to obtain legal advice, and were questioned by Mounted Police officers in a manner that was a violation of our ideas of human rights and Canadian justice. Much of the evidence obtained was, of course, subsequently used at several trials, and I have grave doubts regarding the results. One of those arrested was a Pilot Officer by the name of Poland, who refused to answer any questions without being *permitted to consult his lawyer. Doubtless, Poland was innocent, but it was his insistence on his legal rights that undoubtedly prevented his being brought to trial.*

Shortly before the public trials occurred, one of the accused, Mrs. Emma Woikin, who had worked as a stenographer in the External Affairs Department, came to my office with her brother, a Doukhobor, from Blaine Lake, Saskatchewan. She struck me as being a rather simple Doukhobor woman. I asked her if she had passed any papers, as alleged, to any Soviet agent. She said that she had. I asked her why had she done this? She said that she did it because she felt that Russia was good to the poor people. She told me that she married when she was young, that they lived on a Saskatchewan homestead during the Depression, that they had little food other than potatoes, that they suffered severely from cold in the winter, that she had a baby who died from malnutrition, and that her husband had also died from poor food and bitter cold. She herself was taken from the homestead, nursed back to health, and then enabled to take a stenographic course. Eventually, she obtained a job with the Canadian civil service and was engaged in the External Affairs Department, where she was recruited to do this work for the Communists. She was tried, found guilty, and sentenced to two years in jail. After she came out, I am told that sympathizers found her a new job, and that she was happily situated.

Another woman whom I knew slightly was Miss Kathleen Wilshire, a highly respected government employee, who was also sentenced to several years in prison. I had met her when she was a guest of Grace and Angus MacInnis at the House of Commons. Neither they nor I would have expected that this well-educated and likeable lady was implicated in espionage!

Others, too, were sentenced, although some of the papers they handed to the Russians were of no particular value to them, and, in one or two instances, were about to be declassified.

I have always regarded the manner in which these arrests were made, the holding of suspects incommunicado, without the usual warnings, were serious blots on the administration of justice and reflected badly on the minister who allowed it. Fred Rose, himself, was undoubtedly guilty, and was sentenced to jail and deportation thereafter. He returned to Poland.[20]

The Gouzenko Affair led to a royal commission, which indicated both that the Russians had indeed been spying on their allies for years and that the information passed in Canada was mostly passed free by sympathizers, who were, in the main, more naive than wicked venal. Kathleen Wilshire, whom M.J. mentioned and who actually worked in the British High Commission, was reluctant to claim $25 in expenses from her Russian contact for a trip to Montreal during which she turned over some papers dealing with the atomic bomb, information that was about to be published as the Smyth Report; she was sentenced to four years in penitentiary.[21]

Nonetheless, the revelations brought the Cold War to Canada with an abrupt shock, and opened the CCF to the charge that its members were secret fellow-travellers, if not actually in the pay of Josef Stalin.

Ironically, at the same time, the party was busy defending itself from attacks by Communists and their sympathizers from within, and its brisk defence against these intruders was seen, at one and the same time, as proof that the charges were true — else why were the Communists involved in the party in the first place? — and as a damaging reflection on the democratic structure of the party, since the invaders were, in the end, hustled unceremoniously out the door. The Liberals could and did combine with Communists; during the 1945 federal vote, the national director of the National Liberal Federation noted, "We're glad of co-operation; we're for co-operation, not coalition." David Lewis called this "an unholy alliance between the Liberals, who had no principles, and the Communists, who had no ethics."[22] No blame attached to the Liberals for these alliances, which involved deals in some ridings to help one another — or hurt the CCF, by refraining from putting forth a candidate who might split the vote — while any connection between the CCF and Communists was seen as proof that the party was, in the favourite cliché of the day, "in the pay of Moscow."

John Saywell and Walter Young, in a paper on the subject, pointed to the difficulty created by "the confusion that existed in the public mind between the CCF and Communist policy."

> It was difficult for the populace to ignore the words of R.B. Bennett when he said, "What do these so-called groups of socialists and Communists offer you? We know that throughout Canada this propaganda is being put forward by organizations from foreign lands that seek to destroy our institutions." The Attorney General of Ontario exhorted the churches to fight Communism and "its partner, atheism,"

as represented by men like Woodsworth, Heaps, Bland and A.E. Smith. The CCF, he pointed out, "is probably directed from Moscow."[23]

M.J.'s story of the expulsion of one member, Dorise Nielsen, provides an insight into what happened, and his somewhat naive approach to these events.

After the CCF was formed in 1932, we were, first of all, denounced by the Communist Party and its leader, Tim Buck, as "social fakers," and sometimes by the harsher term, "social fascists." To begin with, the Communist leaders were bitterly critical of anyone in any position of leadership in the new party, and I had been very active in organizing the Independent Labour Party, which brought me into constant conflict with the spokesmen for what was first known as the "Workers' Party," and which subsequently came to be known under its proper name — the Communist Party[24]...

...After the first onslaught, however, the tactics changed. The Communists endeavoured to infiltrate our movement and to urge the formation of a united front with them. This, we resolutely opposed, although some CCF supporters, particularly in Saskatchewan, were in favour of some sort of understanding with them. Mr. George Williams was for a time favourable to some co-operation, if not a united front. The CCF convention in Toronto in 1936 was faced with several resolutions in favour of a united front. Mr. Woodsworth opposed them vehemently, as did many others, including myself. Here and there, in various constituencies across Canada, we found Communists or fellow-travellers endeavouring to exert an influence. We invariably either cancelled their memberships, or refused to renew them.

One of the outstanding examples was a woman who lived in the Battlefords constituency, Mrs. Dorise Nielsen. Although I supported her expulsion from the executive, and from membership in the Saskatchewan provincial organization, I could have some sympathy with her bitter feelings against the society in which she lived. I had met her near her home at Spirit River, west of Prince Albert, when she was quite unknown. The area was desperately poor. She had come to Canada a few years before, from England, as a teacher, under the auspices of the Church of England's Maple Leaf Association. She had two children and when I met her, she was living in the direst of circumstances on a homestead. She was, however, a good neighbour, and when I met her first at a public meeting, she had just come from a confinement case near Spiritwood, where she had delivered a baby, and found nothing to wrap it in except the well-worn coat of the father. Gradually, she deservedly won the respect and confidence of her neighbours. She joined the CCF and became quite active, so that she was elected to the Provincial Executive.

In the district, there were a few members of the Communist Party and they obtained her support and, eventually, her membership. Because we insisted that anyone belonging to the CCF could not belong to any other political party, we had grounds for her expulsion. She appealed to the Provincial Convention in Saskatoon, but the convention upheld the ruling of the Provincial Council and Executive. Shortly before the federal election of 1940, Mrs. Nielsen was nominated in the Battlefords as a "Unity" candidate — a name which had become popular in northern Saskatchewan, and which often marked those who wanted to co-operate with the Communists. We felt certain that Mrs. Nielsen's nomination was largely the work of Communist organizers who had persuaded members of the Social Credit Party, the Conservatives, and a section of the CCF, that a Unity candidate could defeat the sitting Liberal. This, in fact, happened, and Mrs. Nielsen was elected. Although I disapproved of the Unity organization, I realized that, in her circumstances, she would not have the financial means to prepare for the opening of Parliament. I therefore wrote and told her that she was entitled to free transportation if she would apply to the Clerk of the House of Commons for a railroad pass, and that I had no doubt, now that she was a Member of Parliament, that almost any branch of one of the chartered banks would lend her a couple of hundred dollars to solve her immediate money problems. I saw her when she came to the House of Commons, and gave her some information regarding procedures. She seemed very grateful. She was given the same room in the Centre Block that Agnes Macphail, who was defeated in this same election, had occupied.

It was not long before I noted that she was visited by persons whom I knew to be Communists, and particularly Mr. A.A. MacLeod, who was afterwards a member of the Ontario legislature, and a key figure in the Canadian Communist Party. On one or two occasions when she needed help in the House, I gave her assistance, although, as time passed, I had less and less confidence in her motives. She was defeated in 1945, and after that, became active as one of the national organizers of the Communist Party, and in the United Front movements promoted by the Communists. She attended several conferences in Russia and, the last I heard of her, she was said to be teaching in China.[25]

M.J.'s natural kindness and instinctive helpfulness, in short, led him to extend a hand to a woman who was undoubtedly at heart a distinct liability, if not a danger, to his party. He couldn't win this one, because the Communists and their sympathizers had no compunction whatsoever about using the democratic processes of the party to gain and retain entry, while their own party was utterly impervious to the democratic approach. Since the Communists were not bound by any sense of honour, consistency or even ordinary truth, they had a distinct advantage in the public debate, and they never ceased to try — often with considerable success — to drive a wedge between the party leadership and its rank and file. In one of its self-swallowing acts, the Communists succeeded in backing the King Liberals and attacking the CCF for "playing into the hands of the reactionary forces" by criticizing King.[26] When M.J. reacted to this kind of gamesmanship by moving vigorously to quash the threat from the left, he was attacked as dictatorial; when he tried reason, he was dismissed as ineffective.

It was not going to get much better.

CHAPTER ELEVEN

MAN ABOUT THE HOUSE

I really honestly believe that he just had no unkindness in him.
If he ever expressed an unkind thought about anybody or used an
unkind word, he almost immediately withdrew it. I happen to be
a person who thinks that one should have unkindness in one on
occasion and that you don't really build a society and you don't
fight the forces of power in our society without occasionally having
to be unkind to it. So I'm not saying this is one of the characteristics
that had my unbounded admiration, but admiration it had. If you
spent an hour or two with M.J. you felt at peace with the world.
There were no enemies. There were no bastards. Everybody was
a decent human being.   — DAVID LEWIS, 1977

WHEN LORNE INGLE WENT TO OTTAWA TO WORK AS THE NATIONAL RESEARCH
director for the CCF, he prepared a set of figures for M.J. to use in the budget
debate, figures that showed that the government was about to bring in a set
of tax reductions that would be of enormously greater benefit to the rich than
the poor. Ingle recalls:

> I was sitting in the gallery in the House of Commons while M.J. deliv-
> ered his speech, feeling rather proud of myself, when a man came in
> and sat beside me, a member of the Press Gallery I knew. He said, "Are
> you the new research director?"
>   And I said, "Yes."
>   He said, "I suppose you helped with this speech?"
>   "Oh, yes," I said, and he said, "Well, I think you got hold of the
> wrong numbers." I had been working from the *estimates,* not the actual

budget spending, with the result that the figures M.J. was using in the House were wrong. The thrust of the argument was still the same, but the numbers were just plain wrong. I thought, "There goes my job." I scurried down and caught M.J. as he was coming out of the House and told him I had made this dreadful mistake.

He said, "Well, we'll just have to correct it, then, won't we?"

And he did, the next day, but he never from that day forward said another word to me about it.[1]

This anecdote says a good deal about Coldwell's style and abilities as a leader. He took responsibility on his own shoulders at once for Ingle's mistake (he told the House, "I am sorry I made an error in calculation, and I would like to correct it");[2] he never referred to the matter again, because he knew he didn't have to — Ingle would never make such a blunder again — and he made a correction at the first possible moment because of his respect, and fondness for, Parliament. Very few members would ever have caught the error; even fewer would have thought it significant, but to M.J., what was said in the House of Commons was never insignificant.

His love affair with the House began from the day he entered the place, and it never flagged. Towards the end of his career, he began to complain, as has practically every politician since Marcus Tullius Cicero turned in his toga, that things weren't the same as they had been in the good old days, when he was first elected, but even these criticisms were muted by this flat assertion: "Let it be said at once that, with all its failings, our parliamentary system is by far the best mankind has yet evolved for his own self-government."[3] His complaints were directed mainly at the qualifications, or lack thereof, of elected members — "Few Canadian Members of Parliament have made any preparation for their important work in the House of Commons" — and at "the diminution of influence and power of the private Member of Parliament and the increase in the authority of the Cabinet,"[4] a trend that has become very much more pronounced since he wrote these words.

Overall, however, he was an enthusiastic supporter of the political system in which he found himself — it was the economic system he attacked so vigorously — and he had no use for time-serving members who did not want to join in the battle:

In my first session one friendly old gentleman asked me if I wished to be re-elected when the time came? Of course, I answered "Yes."

"Well," said he, "Don't make any speeches and they'll have nothing on you!"[5]

Not make speeches? You might as well have told M.J. not to breathe. What made him so effective in the House was the respect he earned by his politeness, reasonableness and willingness to listen to other arguments, as well as his outstanding ability as an orator. Sometimes, his supporters wished he would be a little less reasonable and shout and wave his arms more. Donald MacDonald, who worked under Coldwell as a national organizer before moving to Toronto to take over the Ontario CCF leadership, remembers one occasion when they got their wish:

One day, some Liberal backbencher introduced a bill to name July 1 "Canada Day," rather than "Dominion Day," and there was a debate in the House. M.J. was very much in favour of making the change. Well, M.J. had been to a Speaker's reception and had had a couple of glasses of sherry, with the result that when he got back into the House for this evening debate, he was in exceptional form. He got going so well he had Liberal backbenchers standing and cheering as he recited the need to bring Canada into the modern world by making this sort of change, and in the end, the measure was adopted. After that, we used to joke with M.J. that if we really wanted him to get going, all we had to do was take him to a Speaker's reception and give him two sherries.[6]

Coldwell's normal debating style was measured, calm, occasionally humorous, but essentially serious and reflective. His sincerity shone through, and the thoughtfulness of his speeches, some of them carefully rehearsed with Norah, as well as their factual content, worked, over the years, to gain him friends even among those who disagreed with almost everything he said or stood for, from the arch-Tory Grattan O'Leary to Réal Caouette, the Créditiste leader, who called him "a great citizen" and "a great Canadian."[7]

An editorial in the *Stratford Beacon Herald,* which certainly never agreed with the CCF, nevertheless praised his way of going about his business:

Whatever one may think of Mr. Coldwell's political philosophy none can doubt his quite unusual gifts in gripping and holding the unflagging interest of his audience. On the occasion mentioned he spoke for well over one and one half hours without manuscript or reference note — his briefcase on the floor and his memory the unfailing source of an unbroken flow of eloquence. None of the ponderous pomposity of Mr. Mackenzie King is heard from Mr. Coldwell — no reading from voluminous documents…

…It was in his complete mastery of word and phrase, his warm but restrained declamations, his complete ease and his entire lack of affectation that he scored so instantly and so continuously with his hearers.[8]

Walter Young, who probably studied M.J. more closely than anyone else has ever done, traced this "acceptability," which he said was Coldwell's foremost trait, directly to his background:

His life was not an example of triumph over adversity, of burning passion to reform or to lead. It was, to that point, an example of above-average commitment, stronger than average dedication to goals, and a well-above-average sense of duty. He engaged himself thoroughly in the life of the community around him because he found such engagement satisfying and undoubtedly, the respect and admiration of others was necessary to his sense of worth. He clearly enjoyed the rewards of dedicated service as he enjoyed the company of those with power or influence. His willingness to serve coupled with the stern principles of a Conservative and High Anglican upbringing combined to produce a man who preferred to proselytize rather than antagonize, who, throughout his career, was never really partisan. His strong moral convictions were tempered by a tolerance that was, at bottom, a reflection of his desire to be respected by the leaders in the community. As a result, he never suffered from the sanctimoniousness or self-righteousness that afflicted so many of his CCF colleagues during the early years of that party's history.[9]

Another part of his appeal was his great sense of honour and responsibility. In the middle of a key by-election battle in North Grey, in February, 1945, a

Canadian soldier approached M.J. with the story that an entire unit of Canadian troops had dumped their military kits overboard while en route to Europe, to express their disapproval of conscription. Coldwell told the man that if he would supply the name of the unit and other corroborating details, he would look into the matter, but no such information was forthcoming. A few days later, a Conservative spokesman broke the story, which undoubtedly helped the Conservative candidate, Garfield Case, win the by-election. After the vote, an official investigation revealed that the number of Canadian soldiers who had chucked their kits overboard amounted to one.[10] In the short run, the Conservatives may have gained a seat, but M.J. did not want it at the cost of integrity.

He never became jaded or cynical, never lost the edge of outrage that made him so effective that even when the government in power refused to acknowledge the correctness of his arguments publicly, reform sometimes followed. One of the most important examples of this aspect of M.J.'s career concerns the case of J. Ludger Dionne, a Liberal MP. Dionne was a wealthy mill owner in Beauce County, Quebec, who approached the King government to grant him a special permit to import indentured labour from wartorn Poland in 1947. He wanted to bring in Polish girls to run the looms of his textile factory and, in his letter to cabinet, made no bones about the reason. He had 435 workers on staff, but they kept leaving because he paid them so poorly and treated them so badly. "The trouble seems to be," he explained, "that people have too much money to spend."[11]

He had the solution to that: bring in girls who couldn't leave, no matter how poor the pay. He would give them twenty-five cents an hour for a forty-four-hour week (the prevailing wage was fifty-four cents an hour), which he would generously raise to thirty cents an hour if they worked hard. In today's money, he was offering them $135 a week, rising to $162 a week. In case this did not prove attractive enough to keep them from wandering off, he wanted to bind them to two-year contracts. This was not legal, so to smooth the way, the cabinet passed an order-in-council on April 1, 1947, giving Dionne permission to break the law. In due course, one hundred "displaced persons" (today, we would call them refugees), all girls, were put to work in Dionne's satanic mills. Word got to M.J. through a Quebec contact, and he managed to get the matter raised as the subject of an emergency debate as "a question of urgent public importance,"[12] to wit, "the traditional policy of Parliament that indentured labour shall be completely prohibited."

The Liberal minister of labour, Humphrey Mitchell, tried to explain that the girls had been brought in because of a shortage of labour in the Beauce area and that they were to be paid "the prevailing rates in the district." That statement raised hoots of derision in the House. The opposition parties all joined the fray, and while the Liberals had the votes to defeat Coldwell's motion the subsequent public uproar throughout the nation spelled the ultimate end of indentured labour in Canada. M.J. lost, but he, and the nation, won.

Another and much more notorious case M.J. brought to light concerned the horses on the payroll of the Department of National Defence at Petawawa, Ontario. In mid-1952, Coldwell was passed an unexpurgated report of an audit of the Department of National Defence, which pointed to serious maladministration of funds. Among other things, it noted that there were, and had for some time been, a number of horses on the department's muster at Petawawa, although it was unclear whether this was a case of outright fraud or simply someone padding the books to get a larger budget. The result was an investigation, and the "Currie Report," as it was called, was released under the bludgeon of M.J.'s questions in December 1952,[13] but only in a carefully edited version. Again, Coldwell was able to tell the House about the cover-up, and the unsurprising result of that was that a young printer, who had retrieved a copy of the original report from the garbage, was apprehended, charged with theft, convicted and fined. Lorne Ingle managed to raise enough money secretly for a special fund to pay this fine and provide legal counsel for the young man.[14] The government of the day was embarrassed but unrepentant, and the horses on the payroll went into Canadian history. No one, except the printer, was ever punished.

Besides the respect and affection his personal conduct earned, M.J. was effective because of the way he handled the caucus and the party. He was a democrat, bred in the bone, but many a democrat finds, when placed in a position of power, that it is easier to make the key decisions himself and collect applause rather than try to engineer a consensus among wrangling factions. J.S. Woodsworth, who was certainly a democrat in principle, in fact seldom consulted either the party or the caucus until after he had made up his own mind, and once that was done, he was not likely to change. M.J. remarked on this in a conversation with Walter Young:

We'd go to J.S.'s office and J.S. would tell us what he was going to do and then go and do it. And then, of course, we had such tremendous respect for him we never contradicted, and we'd go right along with him as we did in defence matters and so on. Latterly, of course, against our better judgment, so to speak, but we always went along with him. He dominated us, there's no doubt about that.[15]

M.J. inherited a larger, more complex and more divided organization than Woodsworth led, but even given that difference, there was an enormous contrast in their approaches. Coldwell was essentially a consensus-builder, where Woodsworth was a visionary leader. Visionary leaders mount crusades, but they do not, not for long, anyway, lead democratic parties. One of the difficulties M.J. faced, which seems to be forgotten in most of the accounts of the era, was that the Liberal and Conservative parties had the luxury of paying absolutely no attention to democracy in their internal workings. King, as already noted, refused to have any party conventions and would not have heeded them in any event. The Conservatives were equally high-handed, and resolutions passed by the great unwashed were just so much scrap paper. It was the open conventions of the CCF that gradually forced the old parties to adopt a more democratic approach, and when that approach led to greater media attention, they reacted as if they had always operated that way. One federal Liberal convention I covered as a young reporter met its commitment to democratic free expression by providing the delegates with booths where they could enter and lay any complaints they wished to make about Liberal affairs into the receiving ear of a tape recorder. No indication ever came forward that any of the tapes had even been listened to, much less considered seriously.

M.J. was bound by party policy resolutions, even if he sometimes gave them his own interpretation, because he believed he ought to be. He said on a number of occasions that if, in his support for democratic socialism, he had to choose between democracy and socialism, he would opt for the former at once.[16] He also said, just as often, that in his view socialism was the only way to promote real democracy, even if the reverse was not necessarily true.

The active, some would say overactive, participation of CCF members was a great blessing and a dismal curse, as anyone who attended many CCF and/or NDP conventions will attest. Just when things are rolling along smoothly and it looks as if there is a chance to keep to the schedule for once, someone will rise in the aisle to lambaste the leadership for its wilful dereliction of duty, mischievous evasion of the paths of righteousness or other high crimes and misdemeanours. It can be intensely irritating, must be monumentally inefficient and carries all the inevitability of one of the longer Greek tragedies. The CCF came out of the federation of a series of farm and labour movements put together to give voice to protest. It would have been astonishing, and pointless for those who were intent on rebelling against a political and economic system that seemed callous, unresponsive and entirely beyond their control not to insist on mechanisms that would ensure participation and popular control of the party they created, even if that made ruling the party akin to trying to ride two bucking broncos at once.

M.J. knew this; as one of the architects of the CCF, he understood — as many of his colleagues sometimes failed to grasp — that party conventions were bound to be sloppy, disorganized, unpredictable and sometimes, it seemed, wantonly mad. He had endless patience with the process and never — almost never — complained about it.

Moreover, because David Lewis, as national secretary (and his influence continued almost unabated when he left that post in 1950) looked after much of the day-to-day party work and many of the internal brouhahas, M.J. was able to take a position above the fray, but not entirely out of it. Walter Young commented:

> The combination of Coldwell's statesmanship and David Lewis's political skills was a potent one for running the party... The arrangement was highly satisfactory for the members of the CCF. Their admiration and respect for Coldwell as the party flag-bearer provided a single and surprisingly strong bond of unity. Again, because he was so obviously respected by government and opposition alike, [and] was difficult to treat as a dangerous radical by the press and other critics, he brought to the party what many of its members so anxiously wanted: respect, respectability and a positive identity as a major force in Canadian politics.[17]

Similarly, in caucus, M.J. saw his job not so much as leading the charge and shaping the result as trying to gauge the temper of his fellow MPs and trying to match their views with his own. When he could not, the result was sharp, occasionally raucous debate, but the aim was to seek a consensus, not to impose the leader's will.

Stanley Knowles noted that a key change that helped this process came when the party decided to split the roles of party leader and chairman of the caucus:

> In Woodsworth's time he was always the Leader of the caucus…but, while M.J. was there, Angus MacInnis was in the chair. M.J. had full participation rights and he'd come in and argue his point of view very strongly, but he fitted much better into the situation where someone else was chairman.[18]

M.J. himself described his approach this way:

> *As leader I would very seldom introduce something in a manner that would indicate that I wanted the caucus to do something. I'd introduce the matter and leave it up to them to discuss it, and they discussed it all the way around, and very often I'd do this if I was a bit doubtful as to whether there was complete agreement on certain things, and I'd invite a group of them to my room… Everybody would express their views and at the end of the bull session I would usually say, "This is what I gather from what you have to say," and I would give what I considered to be the consensus. On a very difficult matter, I would actually write what I considered to be their consensus out, and when I rose in the House I would have that before me, and what I was actually doing was putting a consensus of the group before the House knowing that I was quite safe in doing it, because this is what they had more or less concluded.[19]*

M.J. considered that the caucus was bound in a general way by the resolutions passed at the national convention, but that it was up to the caucus to decide how to implement policies, roughly guided by the advice from the convention, the national executive or the National Council:

> *Conventions laid down policies, but we interpreted those policies in the light of the conditions in the House at the time when the matter rose.[20]*

One area in which M.J. tended to go his own way more than others was in foreign policy, because it was something he had studied all his political life.

As we have seen, he gradually shed his pacifism before the Second World War, as he saw increasing signs of the coming conflagration, and called, often and in vain, on the King government to take action, including action to block the shipment of strategic materials, especially steel, to the potential enemy, and action to shore up Canada's defensive posture. Throughout the war, he became an enthusiastic patriot, and while he kept up a drum roll of criticism of the government's giveaways to wartime profiteers his role was essentially that of a critic of the way in which the Liberals conducted the war and a cheerleader for the troops.

His first opportunity to make a direct contribution to policy formation came with his appointment to the Canadian delegation to San Francisco in 1945, when the United Nations was being designed. His comments on that process contain some details that have never been revealed before.

Now, there were five Members of Parliament in that delegation. The five were Mr. Mackenzie King, the Prime Minister, Mr. St. Laurent, who was not Minister of External Affairs[21] (Mr. King was that) but was Minister of Justice; Mrs. Cora Casselman, representing the women of Canada (she was the Member for Edmonton East); Gordon Graydon, the Chairman of the Progressive Conservative Opposition, and myself. We were the five. From time to time it has been suggested that Mr. John Diefenbaker[22] was on that delegation — he wasn't. Mr. Diefenbaker was in Vancouver when we were in San Francisco. Gordon Graydon said to me one morning, "M.J., Johnny Diefenbaker is up at Vancouver and would very much like to come down and take a look in at the Conference."

I said, "Why not?"

He said, "I can't get him a seat. There is nothing but the back rows of the gallery. That is not good enough for a Canadian Member of Parliament."

Standing beside me was Alex Macdonald, my secretary at the time.[23] Alec said to me, "Look, Mr. Coldwell, you have given me a lot of work to do, reports in preparation for the election that is coming. If Mr. Diefenbaker came down, he could get in with my ticket."

That's how he got in. And it used to irritate me from time to time to read that Mr. Diefenbaker at the Canadian Club would talk about how he was part of the delegation, and what irritates me more is that now the record reads in the Parliamentary Guide *that he "attended the United Nations Assembly at San Francisco, as advisor to the Progressive Conservative Representative on the*

Canadian Delegation."[24] *Well, the advisor to the Conservative Member was Mel Jack, who was secretary at that time to Mr. Graydon.*

One of the amusing stories that Mr. Diefenbaker tells of his visit is that he saw General Smuts write the Preamble to the Charter on the back of a package of cigarettes and he says he was always very sorry that he didn't rescue the package of cigarettes. Mr. Smuts didn't smoke!…

…Canada missed the boat at that Conference. We were looked upon as the leading middle nation. We'd been involved in the war but we had not suffered: we were wealthy, and able to produce the things the world needed. There was no doubt about it, the smaller nations looked upon Canada as the possibility of a leading nation in this particular group. But Herbert Evatt of Australia was a much more aggressive man; Mr. King was timid. Mr. Evatt usurped that position and became spokesman for the middle group.

In our delegation, we were very disturbed by the attitude of the Great Powers in several respects, particularly in their demand for unanimity before action could be taken to prevent aggression. That is known as the Veto. In fact, when Mr. King brought this back to us (because, you see, the Committee on Procedure consisted of the heads of all nations that were there, so Canada was represented by Mr. King), we said that we didn't want to agree to a charter in which there was this unanimity of the Great Powers. He went back to the Committee and urged them to change this. When he came back to us a second time, he said, "Well, I tried but failed. There can be no charter without this. The Soviet Union, because it feels that it is in a minority, ideologically, will not agree to a charter without the right of veto. The United States will not agree to a charter without the right of veto, because Congress will insist on the sole right to decide on future war, and the British are inclined to go along with the United States and Russia."

And so, we got the veto.

Canada was more active in setting up the Economic and Social Council. As a matter of fact, we take great credit for this for Canada. We had a brilliant group of advisors. We had Dana Wilgress sitting beside us. We had Louis Rasminsky, later the Governor of the Bank of Canada, sitting in with us. While we moved the amendments, they drafted them, and we did a great deal to strengthen the Economic and Social Council.[25]

M.J. had staked out his position on foreign policy in *Left Turn, Canada,* and it never changed:

No longer are famine in India, revolution in South America and agrarian depression in the Balkans matters of remote concern in the lives of Canadians. The effects of these events are speedily felt right here at home; tariff policies abroad throw Canadians out of work; planned marketing policies in Central Europe stimulate Canadian trade; war in Asia cuts us off from strategic materials; new methods of warfare bring Canada into imminent danger of invasion.[26]

This was not quite the same thing as the view reflected, in various degrees and at various times, in the resolutions passed at CCF national conventions. Often, these resolutions began as expressions of solidarity with international peace movements and carried a cargo of anti-Americanism in their subclauses. They were usually hammered into something softer on the way through. Coldwell was very much in favour of international peace movements, and played a prominent role both on committees for nuclear disarmament and the Canadian United Nations Association. But he regarded himself as a realist, and that meant, among other things, that he was much more mistrustful of the Soviets and much more inclined to support such U.S. initiatives as the North Atlantic Treaty Organization, despite its militancy, than many of his followers. He also felt that he really knew a little more about these matters, as Agnes Jean Groome, who wrote her history thesis on M.J. and foreign affairs,[27] noted:

> In the formative years, Coldwell was a prominent provincial leader respected by the party as one well versed in the theories and principles of Socialism. Gradually his role evolved from the local level to the national one. He was a scholar who kept up his reading. Increasingly, he represented the party at national and international conferences. He served on governmental committees and was a member of the Canadian delegation to San Francisco and to the General Assembly of the United Nations. He therefore became an expert on international affairs, and to him the CCF turned for guidance and direction. The result was that, more and more, he became the maker of policy.[28]

That policy did not always sit well with the party's left wing, especially as Coldwell moved the CCF into reluctant but clear support of the North

Atlantic Treaty Organization. In 1948, after a four-day debate in the National Council on international affairs, M.J. set out a position that was, at base, a "curse on both their houses" approach to the Cold War:

> The CCF believes that Canada should resist any attempt by the forces of Communism or those of monopoly capitalism, to dominate the world. For our part, we shall continue to fight against totalitarian dictatorship of every kind, whether it comes from the so-called Communist Left or from the Capitalist Right.
>
> We believe that Canada must participate in the defence of freedom and democracy everywhere, but we say that neither Communism nor totalitarian forces in any form, will be stopped by denunciation and war-like propaganda.[29]

Canada's role, according to a resolution adopted at the 1948 convention, was to serve as the leader of a "third force," made up of the nations of the British Commonwealth and Western Europe, to fill "the power vacuum between the United States and the Soviet Union."[30]

However, when the North Atlantic Treaty Organization was established in April 1949 and Canada immediately signed on, the "third force" approach came to nothing. Although all four of the Western provincial CCF bodies — Manitoba, Saskatchewan, Alberta and British Columbia — passed resolutions rejecting NATO, M.J. wanted Canada in, and threatened to resign if he didn't get his way.[31] The party went along. In the House of Commons, M.J. argued that, while the CCF still believed that economic development was the surest safeguard of peace, unfortunately, it was necessary to take other steps to preserve freedom:

> Some rearmament is essential in the present circumstances of the world situation. But it would be sheer folly to build up armaments at the expense of economic recovery. For economic well-being is the basis of peace, even though armaments may still be necessary to guard it.
>
> The CCF therefore urges our government to stand firm on this point...
>
> ...Because of failures to reach agreement in the United Nations

and the necessity for the prevention of further aggression and the maintenance of peace, the Western democracies have been compelled to consider regional security pacts…

…Contrary to much of the propaganda against the proposed Atlantic Treaty, the proposal is not an attempt on the part of so-called American imperialism to bring Western European democracies into an alliance with it to destroy the Soviet Union. It originates in the anxiety of the Western European democracies to persuade North America to support them in a defensive union.[32]

Coldwell had not become a friend of American capitalism, but like many others who had observed the aggressive expansion of the Soviet Union he preferred NATO to pious platitudes about peace, and he led his party accordingly. His frequent speeches warning of the dangers of Soviet expansion led to his harbouring key papers from the Czechoslovakian Embassy when the Communists staged a coup on February 25, 1948, and deposed Eduard Benes, then president of Czechoslovakia. This is how he told this story:

One gentleman whom I got to know very well was Frank Nemec, who was the Ambassador for Czechoslovakia. He had been president of the Railwaymen's Union in Czechoslovakia and had been a member of the Government in Exile, and was the ambassador here. When Mr. Benes came here, he saw that I had a nice interview with Benes and I got to know Mr. Masaryk[33] at the United Nations. I got to be very sympathetic to the Czechs.

On the fourteenth of February, 1948, Mr. Benes invited Mrs. Coldwell and me down to dinner and he also invited Stanley Knowles, Percy Wright and Angus MacInnis and their wives. But when the dinner was over, he said to me, "M.J., I wonder if you would step into my study with me? I'd like to talk to you for a few minutes."

So I went in and he said, "Now, the reason I want to talk to you is because I've had some very serious and disturbing news from Prague. Of course, it's come in a roundabout way, being smuggled out of the country, in a letter." The letter stated that elections were due in May, but they would not be held. It was quite obvious that the recent moves of the Communist Party in Czechoslovakia indicated that they were prepared for a coup, and a man whom Mr. Nemec regarded as a Communist had been sent from Prague shortly before this to spy on him.

J.S. Woodsworth is surrounded by the CCF members of Parliament in this famous 1937 portrait. From left are Tommy Douglas, Angus MacInnis, A.A. Heaps, Woodsworth, M.J., Grace MacInnis (wife of Angus, and the group's unpaid secretary), and Grant MacNeil. (KARSH, OTTAWA)

While speaking to a delegation of women in the 1940s, M.J., a strong supporter of women's rights, is supported by Agnes Macphail, Canada's first female MP (on his immediate right).

David Lewis, on M.J.'s right, was an admirer and staunch ally. The others are Angus MacInnis and Lucy Woodsworth, wife of the CCF leader, J.S. Woodsworth.

A longtime and convinced pacifist, M.J. became a firm supporter of the war, but always regretted the split with J.S. Woodsworth this caused. Here, he talks to troops during a 1941 visit to Prince Rupert, B.C.

As an international socialist, M.J. became a friend and admirer of Jawaharlal Nehru and his daughter, Indira Gandhi, during a visit to India on behalf of the United Nations.

M.J. played an important role as a Canadian delegate to the founding of the United Nations in San Francisco. Here, Prime Minister Mackenzie King leads the delegation, with M.J. second from his left. On King's right are two future prime ministers, Louis St. Laurent and, with his chin in his hand, Lester Pearson.

M.J. sent this picture of his beloved Norah to Beatrice Bramwell, her nurse in the final days, on the day of Norah's death, July 2, 1953.

M.J. is met at the train station in 1958 by his daughter Margaret Carman, her husband, Douglas Carman, and two of his grandchildren, John, left, and Jim.

M.J. at the final convention of the CCF in 1958. David Lewis is at the microphone. Montreal Mayor Sarto Fournier is to M.J.'s right, and Thérèse Casgrain to his left.

Officially retired, but still very active, M.J. is interviewed (above), in Lethbridge, Alberta, in 1964, by Jean Block, for the program *Woman's World*.

Tommy Douglas and M.J. (below) had been friends and allies for nearly forty years when this picture was taken in Tommy's parliamentary office in 1971.

Picnics in Gatineau Park were a family treat. At this one, in 1969, M.J. is with Beatrice Bramwell, his three grandsons (in foreground, from left, Jim, John, and Bill), Jack Dunsford (Norah's brother), and Margaret Carman. (DOUGLAS CARMAN)

One of the last photographs of M.J. and Norah together, taken the year she died.

And so he said to me, "I have in this embassy several suitcases of correspondence — telegrams, letters — that passed between the Czech Government in Exile in London and Moscow during the war, and these papers must not fall into the wrong hands. I want to put them somewhere where they will be safe."

I said, "Well, that's quite natural. What do you want to do with them?"

He said, "I want you to take charge of them."

"Well," I said, "I don't know if I can do that."

He said, "I wish you would."

I thought about it and replied, "Send them up to my office in the House of Commons."

"Oh, no," he said, "I wouldn't put them there. I want you to take them in your apartment."[34]

After some little discussion, I said, "All right. If ever it comes to a coup and you have to get out, I'll take them."

Within two weeks, one evening when I was at the House of Commons I was called to the telephone and found Mr. Nemec at the other end.

He said, "Have you heard the news tonight?"

"What is it?"

"The Communists have seized control of the government of Czechoslovakia. I'm getting out of the embassy. I've asked the city police to send a cordon of police, I've arranged for a van to move out my personal belongings, and I'm moving out tonight. But I've got to bring these papers to you."

So I said, "When will you come?"

"It will be quite late. It will be after midnight."

About two o'clock in the morning there was a buzz at the door of our apartment, and here was Mr. Nemec with his First Secretary and his chauffeur lugging six big suitcases up to my apartment. I stored them in the corner of my bedroom and there they remained for four months.[35]

Nemec took the papers back after he had been allowed to settle in Ottawa and opened a small business, then turned them over to the RCMP; they were thus kept out of the hands of the new regime.

Neither his party nor anyone else was ever told about this venture into individual policy-making by M.J., but his next foray in that area became very public, indeed. When North Korea, under Soviet control, invaded South Korea, under American control, on June 5, 1950, a debate broke out within the ranks of the CCF over what to do. South Korea was an unsavoury, corrupt dictatorship, and North Korea a totalitarian state; there was not much to choose between them. However, the Americans had managed to get a resolution through the United Nations Security Council during the temporary absence of the Soviets from that body condemning the invasion and authorizing a UN force to aid the South. The CCF National Council, after a bitter debate, passed a resolution supporting the UN action and sent it to the national convention for ratification. Before that convention had even met, M.J. made a speech in which he announced that the Council position was CCF policy and he heartily approved of it. In any other party, this would not even have raised an eyebrow; in the CCF, it infuriated the left wing, because, as David Lewis pointed out:

> Coldwell had failed to employ his usually unerring tactical sense and had opened himself to attack by not paying homage in his speech to the final authority of the delegates. The minority made the most of the opportunity; the contribution of the critics was particularly strident and unpleasant.[36]

In the event, the convention went along with M.J. and backed the Council resolution. In British Columbia, a bitter battle raged for years, when a group called the "Socialist Fellowship" made a determined effort to take over the provincial party and disaffiliate from the national party because "it was impossible to put forward Marxian ideas within the Movement."[37] The fellowship, which began as a rather vague experiment in favour of "scientific socialism" — M.J. hated both the term and the approach, for his socialism was anything but scientific; it was pragmatic, changeable, undogmatic — and evolved to become little more than a front for the Workers' Revolutionary Party, one of the many Marxian offshoots of the Communists. Like many of the future protest groups within the CCF and NDP, the Socialist Fellowship collected its own dues, published its own propaganda and insisted on its right to attack the party with vicious vigour while claiming the protection of the party constitution to keep members from being dismissed.

After years of skirmishing, Grant MacNeil, president of the British Columbia CCF, wrote a personal, and alarmed, letter to M.J. on March 4, 1951, in which he warned that "unless this situation is cleared up, the movement is through for many years in British Columbia."[38]

M.J. replied promptly:

You and I, and others, have given a good many years of our lives to the building up of a non-Communist democratic socialist movement in this country, and none of us can afford to allow any section of the movement to become a front for activities that will be acceptable to the Communist Party, whether it be Stalinist or Trotskyist.

Personally, I don't intend to remain either silent or inactive in the face of what I regard as a threat to liberty and freedom in Canada.[39]

An alarmed National Council passed a strong resolution that began, "The CCF cannot tolerate within itself another political organization for which its constitution makes no provision and over which it has no control," and ended — since it was not desirable to have Ottawa reaching over the shoulders of the local leadership to impose its will, with a hope that the province "will deal with this matter promptly and effectively."[40]

Under this prod, the B.C. executive dissolved the Socialist Fellowship, and an attempt to reverse this decision at a subsequent provincial convention was soundly defeated. Even so, organizational and educational work was bogged down for months, and meetings rang with denouncements and accusations.

Internal dissension was, and remained, the party's curse, and M.J. was never able to exorcise it. His own version of what he called "Canadian Socialism" had evolved into something that was much more a mix of public and private ownership than pure state socialism, and he was very much in favour of the co-operative movement and approach as a way to bring practical improvement to ordinary people. This put him into direct conflict not only with the "scientific socialists" in the movement, but with many party members who had more faith in state planning and public ownership than he did. His punishment was often that local CCF newspapers would refuse to publicize speeches in which he strayed from what the purists considered the straight and narrow path. He complained about this in a letter to Percy Wright, a friend and colleague in the CCF caucus:

Apparently, we have a section of our Movement which believes that State ownership is the best form of ownership. That is something I have always disagreed with...

...Perhaps it is because I am feeling very tired and worried that I am of the opinion that some people in our Movement are thinking in terms which are foreign to the basis of a Canadian form of Socialism. I noticed, of course, that my talk to the National Convention was not publicized in any of our papers. I now believe this was because they thought it wise to suppress it. If this sort of thing continues it will certainly mean that I shall refuse to speak for this Movement.[41]

It is fair to say, surely, that a party leader whose own party newspapers feel free to ignore his major speeches is having some problems, and so M.J. was. The CCF pace of progress during these years was painstaking, to put it mildly. The national office finally had an adequate home — on Metcalfe Street, about one kilometre from Parliament Hill — which was officially opened as "Woodsworth House" on January 25, 1947.

In the provinces, the party was making progress, especially in Nova Scotia, Ontario and Manitoba, to go with continued success in Saskatchewan. Alberta politics were changed forever with the discovery of oil at Leduc in 1947, and the CCF was never to make much headway either there or in Quebec, where, despite the election of Thérèse Casgrain as CCF leader, electoral success remained a cloudy chimera. In large part, this was because the Catholic Church maintained its ban on the party; in addition, Coldwell was anything but a sympathizer to the nationalist dreams of the majority of Quebecers, and he and Mme Casgrain remained cordial strangers to the end.

In the 1949 federal election, the CCF, despite much closer ties with and stronger support from the labour movement, suffered a bitter defeat. It went from twenty-eight to thirteen MPs, and went down from 15.6 per cent of the popular vote to 13.4 per cent.[42] Twenty-eight seats had seemed like a disappointment in 1945; now the party was reduced to less than half that, and the eighteen Saskatchewan seats had melted down to five. Although M.J. won in Rosetown-Biggar with a larger vote than ever, the election result was summarized in a single phrase by David Lewis — "All very depressing."[43]

The Liberals were still firmly in control of the nation, with Louis St. Laurent, for whom M.J. held little regard, in Mackenzie King's place. The 1949 election left the CCF as a Western party, at least on the electoral map, although it had a hefty vote in Ontario that the electoral system refused to translate into seats. The CCF got 306,551 votes in Ontario, which translated into one seat;

the Liberals got about three times the votes — and fifty-six seats. The CCF had more votes in Ontario than in Saskatchewan and British Columbia combined, but it was easily dismissed as a gaggle of discontented farmers. M.J. refused to consider proportional representation as the answer to this dilemma; he would play the game under the house rules, even if they made no sense.

Much had happened in the world since he assumed the leadership of the CCF, and after the 1948 International Socialist Conference in Copenhagen urged a new study of socialist approaches to such matters as public ownership, he opened the 1950 National CCF convention by asking the party to reconsider its "basic program" – that is, the *Regina Manifesto*, "in the light of new developments which have occurred in the past decade."[44] The Resolutions Committee then brought before the convention a document that, while reaffirming its faith in the *Manifesto,* instructed the National Council to "prepare a statement of the application of democratic socialist principles to Canada and the world today."[45]

The result was a bitter battle in which the party leadership was attacked for whoring after the bitch goddess Electoral Success, instead of remembering that the "main business of socialist parties is not to form governments but to change minds."[46] While the resolution passed, nothing much came of it, at least for the time being.

For M.J., the next four years were a constant struggle. At home, Norah was increasingly handicapped and in pain; she suffered a severe leg fracture because of the brittleness of her bones, from which it took her months to recover. In the country, M.J. was up against the effective capture of CCF programs by the Liberals, as and when required, and its own internal battles. There was even a shootout with Frank Underhill, the one-time stalwart, who attacked M.J. because he complained about the Liberals' cynical manoeuvres; Underhill dismissed this as "a silly performance."[47] Underhill was eventually removed from the board of the Woodsworth Foundation and became a Liberal.

Typically, the Liberals promised to consider a national health plan — which the party had first promised in 1919 — when the time was right. Health Minister Paul Martin explained that such an ambitious undertaking could not be adopted overnight, to which Coldwell replied, "It's been a long night — 34 years."[48]

When M.J. tried to get the old age pension raised from $25 to $50 a month, he was treated with derision; then the Liberals raised it when they thought the time was ripe.

In 1952, he began to have health problems of his own, and underwent a prostate operation, which slowed him, but only momentarily. He kept at the job, day and night, making speeches, answering letters, studying — he remained a great reader — and relaxing only occasionally, with Norah.

When the 1953 election was called, anyone could see that it would be crucial for the party and for Coldwell; if there was no breakthrough this time, when would it ever come?

Then Norah died. The news was brought to M.J. in the middle of the campaign, when he was touring in Saskatchewan. There was no particular crisis; Norah's heart, after twenty-three years of struggle with multiple sclerosis, simply gave out. Lorne Ingle, the lawyer who had worked as national research director for the party and then became national secretary when David Lewis returned to private practice in 1950, managed to locate M.J. by telephone, and he went home for the funeral. He insisted on going back to the electoral battle as soon as the funeral was over and Norah's ashes had been shipped to Regina for burial. Norah would have approved, but if anyone thought he was able to bury his sorrow in his work they were very much mistaken. M.J.'s daughter Margaret notes, "I always thought that some of the spirit and enthusiasm went out of my father at that point."[49]

Hardly surprising. Norah had been his love, support and strength for decades. Neither had ever had another serious romance. Their affection for each other, if anything, grew stronger during the years of Norah's torment, and when she died she left a void that mere politics could never fill. M.J. went on, because he had to, because, as Norah so frequently reminded him, people depended on him. But he was never again the same M.J.

Soon after this tragedy, M.J. wrote a letter to Vernon Boyle, his boyhood chum in Devon, with whom he had kept in constant touch by letter. Because it so perfectly captures the spirit of a man incapable of bitterness or pettiness, most of that letter is reproduced here:

At Winnipeg, July 26th

My Dear Vernon,
Your kind letter reached me yesterday. Fortunately, I am very busy

every day. I was at 8:30 a.m. service this morning but this afternoon will be occupied in visiting a Veterans' Hospital. Friends this evening. A rally here tomorrow and then a flight to Calgary — 1,000 miles west. Jack, my son, is flying here tomorrow from Montreal, 1,700 miles east of here!

Yes, my ways will have to be changed. I shall miss Norah greatly. She was deeply loved and respected. Illness seemed to bring out so much good in her.

I note what you say of retirement. I shall have to do so I think at the end of the next Parliament. I've saved nothing — medical expenses and care of Norah have taken all, but I'm not in debt. The children are well-off. Jack's salary, with further prospects, is $7,200 per annum (£2,400)[50] and Margaret's husband, a scientist, has $6,300 (£2,100) with prospects of increase. I do not have to think of them. If I retired now I am entitled to $3,000 (£1,000) per annum superannuation from Parliament and at 65 (next Dec. 2nd) to an additional $1,200 (£400) from the Teacher's Superannuation Fund in Saskatchewan. A further term in Parliament may, if the indemnity is increased, further increase my Parliamentary pension. Thus I can be quite comfortable henceforth...

...I gave up our large suite but I have taken a small one in the same building No. 105 Strathcona Apts., 404 Laurier E., Ottawa. I have a nice living-room, a small dinette, as we call them, modern kitchen and bathroom. I can get maid service, i.e. a woman will keep the apt. clean and tidy daily, see to the laundry and so on...

...Glad you are well, and blest with grandchildren, too.

I shall love to visit you next year.

With life-long affection,
Major

CHAPTER TWELVE

THE CCF STALLS

Unlike the Liberal and Conservative parties, the CCF needed as leader an individual whose personality, and therefore whose style of leadership, was consistent with the party's democratic norms. The leader of a democratic party cannot succeed if by his actions he threatens the participant rights of members and fails to reflect the consensus. On those occasions when Coldwell took a more authoritarian stance, he found himself at serious odds with his party. But, in the main, as a man who found deep satisfaction in serving the goals of his party, Coldwell was an ideal leader.

— WALTER YOUNG, UNPUBLISHED PAPER, 1976

COLDWELL NEEDED ALL HIS SKILLS AFTER THE 1953 ELECTION, FOR WHEN THE House reassembled, the CCF, far from making the hoped-for breakthrough at last, actually lost in its share of the popular vote — going down from 13.4 per cent in the 1949 election to 11.3 per cent — although the vagaries of the electoral system delivered it more seats — twenty-three, up ten from 1949. Again, these were clustered in the West; the CCF held twenty-one seats west of the Lakehead, one in Ontario and one in Nova Scotia. (Joe Noseworthy, who had originally vanquished the redoubtable Arthur Meighen in York South in a 1941 by-election, won re-election, and Clarie Gillis kept his seat in Cape Breton.) The Liberals, under Louis St. Laurent, who sailed through the campaign as "Uncle Louis," saying little, smiling much, had been returned for the fifth straight time. The Conservatives, under George Drew, were even more ill used than the CCF by the first-past-the-post system. They attracted 31 per cent of the vote, but received 19 per cent of the seats, while the CCF got just over 11 per cent of the vote and just under 9 per cent of the seats.[1]

Frank Underhill, in his role as gadfly, wondered why a reforming party such as the CCF did not come out in favour of proportional representation, and then answered his own question. He said it came from the party's "delusions of grandeur"; the British Labour Party had benefited from the first-past-the-post system, and the CCF, "in good, colonial tradition," followed that precedent.[2]

Coldwell once again won his seat handily, although he spent most of the election touring the nation on behalf of the party; his personal popularity was undiminished, but the party was going nowhere. The Conservatives promised to cut taxes; the Liberals had already done so. The CCF was certain to raise them, at least on the rich. Coldwell said little during the campaign about public ownership, beyond pledging to nationalize the steel industry, but instead promised specific social reforms, including a national health plan, increased social security benefits and large-scale construction of low-cost subsidized housing.[3] The national health plan was given top priority:

> We maintain that it may, in the long run, be just as essential to Canada's defence to have a nation of strong and healthy people as it is to have an air division in Europe.[4]

The defence note was struck because the Korean War was drawing to a close as the election ebbed; the armistice was signed on July 27, two weeks before the vote, and defence issues were on the minds of many voters. The war itself caused a deep split in the CCF, as we have already seen, and his statement was undoubtedly aimed more at reassuring possible swing voters than it was at the CCF rank and file. The party stalwarts would grumble, but in the end, they would remain loyal, in part because M.J. did not treat those who disagreed with him as foes to be vanquished, but as friends to be persuaded, if possible.

Betsy Bury of Saskatoon, who, as vice-president of the Saskatchewan CCF, spent some time driving M.J. to meetings across the province, recalls that he was very patient in explaining his views on controversial issues to people like herself, who thought he was wrong:

> I remember driving him out to Rosetown from Regina one time, and he spent about half the drive explaining why he couldn't accept our

provincial position, which was very much against NATO. That was the thing he was so good about; explaining and listening. A lot of people felt that he was a very formal man, and in some ways, he was; but underneath, he was a real sweetie.[5]

Sweetie or not, Coldwell headed a party which was still regarded by much of the nation as deluded at best, and dangerous at worst. The early 1950s were the time of Senator Joseph McCarthy's witch hunts in the United States, which had an inevitable spillover into Canada, as David Lewis noted:

McCarthyism has become a term synonymous with witch hunts and inquisitions and with disregard for the democratic process and individual rights. McCarthy's behaviour was so reprehensible that the Senate finally censured him in December 1954. In the meantime, however, he had damaged the reputation of many decent Americans and helped poison the political atmosphere of the North American continent. For Canadians also watched the antics of the Congressional Committees and were affected by them. Canadians never became as intolerant as their neighbours, but their resentment of Soviet actions in Eastern and Central Europe and their own experience with the spy-net exposed by Gouzenko prepared them to soak up the atmosphere of distrust and animosity towards unconventional ideas which the American investigators projected onto the television screens between 1948 and 1954.[6]

The CCF was constantly on the defensive once more against claims that it was somehow the stooge of the Soviets, and even M.J.'s steady anti-communism could not entirely bind the wounds. Dwight Eisenhower was the president of the United States, conservatism, albeit in a Liberal wrap, was dominant in Canada, and the election of 1953 reflected these trends. Thanks in part to the Korean War, Canada was going through a period of unparalleled prosperity, not a time to promote any kind of change, much less the radical reforms that seemed to be embodied in the CCF platform. In the provincial election in Ontario, where most of the votes and much of the organizational muscle came from, the CCF went, in the 1951 election, from twenty-one seats to two;[7] from official Opposition to negligibility, and this, too, affected both the morale and the capacity of the national party.

In addition to the outside hostility and internal struggles that were always part of the CCF baggage, there were two other factors that hurt the party — the Drew factor and the money factor. George Drew, who had moved from provincial to federal politics as leader of the Progressive Conservative Party in 1948, was one of the clear exceptions to the general rule that M.J. liked, and was liked by, his political opponents. Coldwell was unable to forgive Drew for the dishonesty of his attacks on the Ontario CCF in 1945 and his frequent snide references to what he claimed were the totalitarian ambitions of the CCF. In fact, it was with Drew that M.J. once — though not in the House of Commons, of course — nearly came to blows. Carl Hamilton, the national secretary of the party from 1958 to 1962, recalls the incident:

> Watson Kirkconnell, the President of Acadian University, was a tiny little man, a real right-winger who had written a book lambasting the Communists, in which he said that it bothered him that the CCF, for which he might otherwise have had some regard, unfortunately had some Communist leaders, and that kind of set the stage for a meeting at Acadia, where M.J. and Drew were on the same platform, debating these issues. Drew constantly referred to M.J. as a "National Socialist," which was the same as calling him a Fascist, and M.J. just rose up out of his seat with a clenched fist, and Drew got all het up, and Kirkconnell, who never weighed more than ninety pounds soaking wet, had to step between these two rather large men and calm things down.
>
> I never saw M.J. speak to Drew after that, but apparently he did, because when Russell Bell[8] and I went to see him not long before his death, he told us that, one day, he was walking up to the House and Drew came out of the Centre Block, walking the other way, and Drew said, "Coldwell, I was sorry to hear of your wife's death." They shook hands. They were never close but they did speak after that.[9]

During the 1953 campaign, Drew's bellicosity, as well as a rather bizarre alliance he formed with the Union Nationale under Maurice Duplessis, helped to convince the public that they were better off with Uncle Louis, who presented the same sort of father image as Eisenhower; a vote for the CCF might have let Drew slip up the middle, so they stuck with the Liberals. On the money front, a drop in CCF membership that began in 1949 meant that the party's national income from this source reached an apex, if you can call it that, of $25,000 in 1953,[10] the election year; there was very little money to run Woodsworth House, much less carry out the extensive and expensive business of organization across the country.

With all these handicaps and his own personal despair after Norah's death, it is a miracle that M.J. did as well as he did in 1953, but it was this election that seemed to most observers to mark the CCF as a perennial third party; always a bridesmaid, never the national bride.

Then came a personal repudiation of Coldwell over the question of German rearmament. In brief, M.J. was in favour of rearmament for West Germany, as a counterbalance to the growing belligerence of the Warsaw Pact, and a majority of his caucus, as well as the National Council, were opposed. For once, M.J. was unable to build a consensus of any sort, and when a vote was held on the issue in the House of Commons, only five CCF MPs supported his stand. Coldwell wrote:

I have not gotten over the feeling in my heart that this was a striking and public repudiation of my leadership in a very important field.[11]

The hurt was partly assuaged by a vote of confidence in his leadership passed unanimously by the caucus,[12] but David Lewis thought this incident did permanent damage:

That some of us gladly admitted to him that we had been wrong, as I remember doing myself, naturally gratified him, but I had the feeling that the German rearmament issue, which he considered a personal humiliation, took the starch out of him, especially as he saw the party slipping rather than making progress. A man who had always seemed cheerful, optimistic, and bouncing in a genteel way, became sombre; not morose or bitter — of this he was incapable — but resigned in spirit.[13]

With all respect to Lewis, there were quite a few starch-removing operations going on at this time, and it is far more likely that a combination of these affected Coldwell, rather than this single incident.

In any event, he bounced back in two major ways. The first was the battle over the trans-Canada pipeline, which began in 1952 and ran for four years, and recharged M.J. with indignation. He saw it, correctly, as part of a massive giveaway to foreign corporations, which was to get much worse as the years went by; he was not able to stop it, but he was certainly able to voice the protest that many Canadians felt but few could express so eloquently. That debate came to its climax in mid-1956, as we saw in Chapter 1, and it certainly gave M.J. a fillip, if only for the time being.

The second was in the redrafting at long last of a new declaration of principles for the party, to replace the *Regina Manifesto*. This was the process that had been set in motion, then set aside, in 1950 and that was finally taken seriously at a National Council meeting January 12–15, 1956. The party's leaders were agreed that the danger was that, if nothing happened to change the present direction, the CCF would become "a diminishing group, a small, well-respected, highly-thought-of minority, with increasingly less influence."[14] The words came from Tommy Douglas and the sentiment from everyone in the room, including M.J., who led the discussion. The upshot was the establishment of a committee, chaired by David Lewis, with Michel Chartrand, Morden Lazarus and Lorne Ingle as members, to report to the national convention in Winnipeg that August. This committee's report was, in turn, massaged by Coldwell, Lewis, Ingle and Donald MacDonald before being presented to the convention and passed as the *Winnipeg Declaration*.

It was the *Regina Manifesto*, in some ways — the goal was still the establishment of a co-operative commonwealth, established through democratic socialism — but the language was much less strident and menacing, and the approach to reform was quite different. Gone were the massive nationalizations and state-planning apparatus of the earlier document; the new declaration stated that a CCF government would apply public ownership only where it was necessary to break the stranglehold of private monopolies and facilitate social planning. Private business was welcomed and encouraged to make a healthy contribution to the development of the national economy.[15]

The *Winnipeg Declaration* was immediately attacked as a shift to the right to appease the newly united labour movement, which, under the Canadian Labour Congress (CLC) banner, was officially launched in April 1956. A fair enough criticism. The CLC was certain to become a major element in CCF circles, especially after Claude Jodoin, who was to become the president of the new body, had agreed with Lewis that the organization would commit itself to supporting the party. This was bound to be an element in the party's thinking, whether it offended purists or not. *Maclean's* magazine sniffed that with its new statement of principles, there was no reason for the party to exist any more; since *Maclean's* had never seen much need for the party up until then, this was a criticism most CCFers were probably willing to live with.

Times had changed; Canada in 1956 was a very different country from what it had been in 1933, and the *Regina Manifesto,* in this new world, was the equivalent of the party's having a large KICK ME sign painted on the leader's backside. The rolling, sonorous statements of the *Manifesto* were more quotable than they were persuasive. Anthony Crosland, a minister in the Labour cabinet in England, had recently published *The Future of Socialism,* which argued that public ownership was not a necessary adjunct to economic reform, because most large companies are run by their managers, not their owners; that Marx was passé; and that private profit, rather than a blight, was to be encouraged to increase tax revenues, which any socialist government would need to extend public programs and social planning.[16] Significantly, Crosland was a keynote speaker at the CCF convention.

The *Winnipeg Declaration* sounded more like Anthony Crosland than it did like J.S. Woodsworth, and unquestionably one reason it was treated with editorial scorn by the nation's media was that it made quite a lot of sense and made it more difficult to attack the reforming CCF as a gaggle of hotheads.

It is interesting to speculate — pointless, but interesting — what might have happened to the party had the principles enunciated in the *Winnipeg Declaration* been put in place when M.J. first proposed redrafting party principles, six years earlier.

As it was, the *Declaration* became somewhat moot, because by the time it was passed, a new party, about which M.J. would have mixed feelings, was on its way.

The seed was planted at the meeting of the National Council in January 1956 that led to the *Declaration,* when Tommy Douglas talked about forming "a new type of federation or the same type of federation enlarged for a genuine farmer-labour-socialist movement in Canada… I think that ought to be our aim."[17]

M.J. raised no objection; nor did anyone else. If the party wasn't going anywhere, it had to be re-formed or re-launched; that much was obvious to everyone involved in politics, inside or outside the CCF. Coldwell thought, hoped, it might be possible to work under the same name with a new organization, but if it was going to require a whole new party, he'd make no public objection to this. David Lewis, on the other hand, had no reservations whatsoever; he was an early and enthusiastic booster. True, in his talks with Claude Jodoin the previous July, the labour leader had promised to work for CLC support of the CCF, not a new party, but once the idea was on the floor Lewis seized on it:

> From then on I gave my attention and my support to the development of a political arrangement which would have the labour movement as its muscle and the CCF philosophy as its guiding spirit. For the first time I saw the possibility of building a successful social democratic movement in Canada along lines which had produced such movements in western and northern Europe as well as in Britain, Australia and New Zealand.[18]

M.J. never got around to the subject of the new party in either his *Memoirs* or *Reminiscences,* so it is a matter of conjecture what he thought as the pebble Douglas tossed into the debate in January 1956 set off ripples that became a tidal wave. He never once publicly expressed anything but wholehearted support for the new venture, although he had very little to do with it in the end. Clearly, at his age — he was sixty-seven when the National Council met — he would not be the leader of this party, and that was bound to be a matter of relief and regret at the same time.

At the August convention that adopted the *Winnipeg Declaration,* two resolutions were passed that welcomed the formation of the Canadian Labour Congress and embraced its legislative program, but nothing further happened until the way was cleared by the defeat of the Liberals, not once, but twice, and not by the CCF, but by the Diefenbaker Progressive Conservatives.

Diefenbaker, vaulting into the Conservative leadership in December, 1956, played both Louis St. Laurent and M.J. off the stage in the first election, on June 10, 1957, scattering bon mots, promises and charges with equal abandon across the land. This was Canada's first television election, and the camera loved Diefenbaker, with his broad gestures, rumbling voice and flawless timing. It was not a Conservative campaign but a Diefenbaker jubilee, and very few minutes of the free-time broadcasts allotted to the party were meted out to lesser lights; it was Diefenbaker who led the charge, from start to finish.

M.J. was all right on television; not great, but all right. He was uncomfortable with the medium at first. He and Lorne Ingle had a shouting match in an Ottawa television studio when Ingle insisted that he learn to use the Auto-Cue, so he would be looking into the camera and not down at the page while speaking. M.J. thought this unwise, since he would be dependent on someone else — the Auto-Cue operator — and he didn't like it. Ingle's insistence that he move with the times only made him more stubborn, and soon they were embroiled in a quarrel that the producer broke up by saying, "Mr. Ingle, I would like you to meet Mr. Coldwell. Mr. Coldwell, Mr. Ingle."[19] After that, M.J. learned to adapt to the new technology, but he was never the master of the sound bite that Diefenbaker was, and if much of what the Conservative leader said made little sense, carried little consistency, had very little acquaintance with the truth, well, that was another matter. Historian Denis Smith commented that Diefenbaker's sound bites were "not illuminating [but] often obscure, superficial, contradictory, or meaningless."[20] Nobody cared; Canadians were tired of the Liberals, anxious to punish Louis St. Laurent and his crew for their arrogance over the pipeline debate, and decided to hand their votes to Diefenbaker, who had played very little role in that donnybrook, because they calculated that the CCF, just as the CCF itself suspected, could not form a government.

There was another factor. On February 25, 1957, M.J. had a heart attack; not a serious one, in medical terms, although there is no such thing as a funny heart attack, but enough of a scare to convince him that he could not keep up the frenetic pace of a thirty-year-old in a sixty-nine-year-old body. Accordingly, he campaigned vigorously, but not all-out. Stanley Knowles took his place on many platforms in a cross-country tour. Knowles, although an effective speaker, was not in the same class as Coldwell.

The result was a minority Conservative (Diefenbaker) government, which was bound to last for only a very short time, and then the whole weary business would have to be done again. This led to what was probably the only occasion in his life where M.J. put his personal wants above the party — with disastrous results.

As a member of the Parliamentary Association, M.J. was slated to go to India on an extensive trip in the fall of 1957; those around him assumed that, in the circumstances, he would not go. Then, at a committee meeting in Ottawa in mid-September to plan the twenty-fifth anniversary celebrations for the party, Lorne Ingle, then national secretary, learned that Coldwell was determined to take the trip anyway. David Lewis, Stanley Knowles and Ingle himself all tried in vain to persuade him otherwise. Ingle wrote an agonized letter to Knowles, which said in part:

> I was absolutely flabbergasted that M.J. should take off on such a trip at one of the most crucial times that our movement has had for a long time. In the first place, this comes at a period which will see the culmination of our 25th anniversary activities and knocks into a cocked hat many of the plans we had for special radio and TV programmes, banquets, press conferences, etc. How can we make a big national whoop-de-doo about our 25th anniversary when the national leader is on a Cook's Tour of India is beyond me!
>
> The second thing, of course, and this may well be as important or more important than the first, is that he will be away for most of what could easily be the most important session of Parliament since the CCF was formed.[21]

Ingle wanted Knowles to intervene, but Knowles wrote back that, while "I share your view, and your concern," he himself was the alternative delegate if Coldwell didn't go, and it would put Knowles in an awkward position to tell M.J. to stay home while he went.[22]

So M.J. went. Had a fine time, too. He had been an early and outspoken advocate of Indian independence, and he was greeted with enthusiasm and red carpets everywhere. He met Jawaharlal Nehru, the Indian prime minister, and his daughter, Indira Gandhi, then serving as her father's aide.

The caucus was furious, the executive was furious, but M.J., for once, paid little heed. Unfortunately, he was away most of the latter part of 1957, and crucial matters were neglected, not only in Ottawa, but within his own riding. Lorne Ingle says:

> We couldn't persuade him and he did take off and neglected the party and his own riding. He would probably have saved his seat. That was the end of M.J.'s parliamentary career.[23]

Ingle, a fierce admirer of Coldwell, is obviously still a little sore over this incident, but there is no way of knowing whether, in fact, M.J. could have retained his constituency when John Diefenbaker, spouting fire, adjectives and Visions, went to the nation on March 31, 1958. He led an electoral sweep unlike anything Canada had seen up to that time: 208 of 265 House seats, clear majorities in every province but Newfoundland; the humiliation of the Liberals, who, under their new leader, Lester Pearson, came back with 49 seats; a complete wipeout of the Social Credit Party federally, and the reduction of the CCF to eight federal seats, all in Western Canada.[24]

M.J. lost to a Conservative, Clarence O. Cooper, in Rosetown-Biggar; he was defeated for the first time since 1934, when he had lost in Regina during a provincial election.[25] In 1957, when he had made only four visits to the riding during the campaign, he had won by 4,295 votes over Howard Ridell, the Conservative; in 1953, all four of those who ran against him lost their deposits.[26] Now he was beaten; not by much, but beaten nonetheless. He was shocked, hurt and surprised, but the Diefenbaker bandwagon rolled over people like Stanley Knowles as well; the only CCF survivor in Saskatchewan, Diefenbaker's home province, was Hazen Argue; as we will see in the next chapter, it might have been better had he lost, too. As usual, financial problems greatly hampered the CCF in this election; the national office spent just over $20,000 on this vote.[27]

M.J.'s campaign in 1958 cost less than $3,000; still, that was up sharply from the $802.04 he spent in his first successful run in the riding in 1935.[28] It wouldn't pay for taxis in a modern campaign.

One effect of the disaster was to remove M.J.'s major source of income, his MP's salary, at a stroke (fortunately, he was collecting the old age pension, then $55 a month, a parliamentary indemnity of about $3,000 annually, and $1,200 annually in pension payments from his teaching days); he was still going to need more money to live on, as we see in this revealing letter he wrote to Lorne Ingle, who had left his post as national secretary and gone out to work for the Douglas government in Regina. They were obviously back on their former good terms:

179 Carling Ave.,
Ottawa, Ont.
June 3rd 58

Dear Lorne;

Thank you for your kind letter. Of course I understand why you did not write before. You certainly have been fully occupied.

I am sorry you had a set-back to your plans.[29] You will I am certain recover from that though it means a summer of hard work and the foregoing of your presence at the convention. I am sorry about that also. We were all looking forward to your help and advice. Yes, you will have to postpone your plans to be active in the Regina CCF. I know precisely what you found in the organization. Regina and the Provincial organization have always been plagued with "fellow-travellers." I think they are more noisy than numerous. Unfortunately, some "key" people are among them. I used to get so disgusted with the international affairs panel at the annual provincial conventions that I vowed I would not participate in them. I did, however!

I am glad you find the federal statute set useful. I sent one to Frank Scott who finds it useful also. If there is anything else I have or can provide you with please let me know.

Following the election I had telegrams and many hundreds of letters expressing regret at my, frequently Stanley's, defeat. I was, of course, disappointed, but my last television address was quite unprepared and expressed just what I felt. I felt that through the years I had done and given my best. I had not let the Movement down. I am quite reconciled to it now. I feel that had I been elected with only the eight who were, I would have worked myself to death. It's a dreadful parliament. The Press Gallery, including people like Blakely,[30] are unanimous in this. Our little group is doing well. They shine in the setting!

Yes, I'm satisfied as I was from the outset that Stanley's decision to take the CLC position was the right one.[31] He is happy in it now. Had he decided to stay with us there is little he could do in comparison with the influence he can exert now. Then too, Stan's financial requirements as he stated them would have created difficulties. He wanted $10,000 & expenses — at first excluding his Parliamentary pension, though he finally agreed to have that counted in. He was $3,050 in arrears on April 1st, but by a special effort, we could have wiped those out. That meant raising $10,000 plus expenses in the current year.

I've had numerous letters asking me to reconsider my decision to retire from the leadership in July. When I undertook my column in the *Star* I said that I was retiring and that had some effect in securing the contract for a year. It is understood, and in fact so stated, that I can relinquish it by giving a month's warning. That I feel I would have to do if I yield to the representations that are being made to me. I understand the Movement's difficulty, emphasized of course by negotiations with the CLC, and if no other way can be found I suppose I shall have once again to put the CCF ahead of my own personal desires.

Immediately after the election, I was of course faced with the necessity of augmenting my income. I did not wish to give up my comfortable apartment & my good housekeeper and my little car. My Parliamentary superannuation was fortunately paid up but it amounts, less income tax deductions, to just enough to pay my rent, wages to my housekeeper and my telephone, light & perhaps my gasoline. What I have besides is insufficient to do the rest. So I have to do something & my writing is going to pay me quite sufficient[ly]. I've had some stiff medical and hospital bills in the past 18 months. Yesterday all my upper teeth were extracted. Next week the lowers are to come out. That's another postponed expense. So you see why I felt I had to retire and write! I wanted to retire anyway and I felt I could do something to augment my income and keep me occupied.

The postman has just delivered a registered letter containing a return ticket by Air to Britain in August! I was offered this as a holiday right after the election. I said I could not go until after the Convention. I should say it's from a well-to-do friend, or should I say "admirer" of my work? I shall appreciate a holiday in Britain this summer — a holiday I could not afford to take.

I hope you are all well and enjoying your nice new home in Regina. The children have settled down at school of course and no doubt are doing well.

My kindest regards to you all.

Sincerely,
M.J.

The reference to Stanley Knowles is a clear indicator both of how hard up the party was at this time — the prospect of having to put Knowles on the payroll at $10,000 a year was obviously a daunting one, and the party was trying to make him roll his parliamentary pension into the pot — and of the fact that the plans for forming a new party were well advanced. M.J. wanted to get out before that happened, preferably at the national convention just coming up. It was not to be.

CHAPTER THIRTEEN

ANOTHER NEW PARTY

We have some very able members in the Commons, but somehow
I have the impression that they have not caught the eye or the
imagination of the average voter. To some extent I think this stems
from a feeling that the NDP is not following a philosophy and set
of principles as the CCF did, at least in its early years. Perhaps the
elimination of the word "Socialism," so carefully and deliberately
done, has contributed to this feeling.

— M.J. COLDWELL, LETTER TO GRACE AND ANGUS MACINNIS, 1963

M.J. COULD SEE THE NEED FOR A NEW PARTY; THE CCF HAD RUN OUT OF steam, and so had he. He was overweight, beginning to have trouble with his eyes and his hearing, and sometimes he was quite querulous — an entirely new development that had to do with his health; he was suffering from emphysema. Still, it was hard to stand by, smiling, shaking hands, nodding, going along, as the CCF, founded with such high hopes three decades ago, disappeared down the drainpipe of history. The process, as we saw in the last chapter, had already been set in motion when Tommy Douglas spoke to the National Council in 1956. Stanley Knowles, defeated in Winnipeg North Centre in the July 1958 federal vote, was promptly elected an executive vice-president of the new Canadian Labour Congress, and as promptly put to work to bring the new party into being. The CLC convention that elected him at Winnipeg, in April 1958, passed a resolution introduced by Eamon Park of the Steelworkers calling on labour to "take part in the formation of a new political instrument."[1] Park told the delegates that the time had come for the trade union movement to depart from its traditional policy of merely supporting the CCF and to take the lead in establishing a new political voice in Canada.

A great many things were said at the convention, but a couple of them were merely whispered. This new body was, delegates were told repeatedly, not a labour party, but, like the CCF it was replacing, a grouping of farm, labour and other voices interested in the same goals.[2] What was not said was that Canada was now an urban nation, and the farm vote was not nearly as important as it had been in 1933, when the CCF was launched. (Canada's farm population was just over 31 per cent in the 1931 census, just over 11 per cent in 1961.)[3] In fact, the new party would be dependent on labour for much of its financing, manpower and expertise. M.J.'s private opinion was not entirely sanguine:

I've never been enthusiastic about a CCF-Labour alliance. It may work out, but labour has been for us a weak reed.[4]

A labour-linked party would go at the business of attaining office in a more energetic way than a Movement with a capital "M," such as the CCF. The CCF had never been able to advance beyond the role of national conscience and nag, except in Saskatchewan; organized labour had something more muscular in mind. That meant a softening of some of the old policy stances, and in particular, it meant much less emphasis on socialism, public ownership and national economic planning, and more emphasis on practical reforms.

In his memoirs, David Lewis argued indignantly that the CCF had always aimed for power:

There was never any doubt that the considerable educational efforts, the literature, and the meetings were intended to win support for the CCF as the political instrument of the people. From the first, the CCF was intended to be an electoral political party.[5]

Coldwell, as we have already seen, had a slightly different approach. The CCF should strive for power, but not at any price; in the balancing act that always takes place between the need to attain power to promote good policy and the need to trim policy to gain some lift towards power, he leaned more to a feeling that the party should form, and stick to, sound policies, and spend most of its effort trying to get the public to catch up. Among his papers, there

is a handwritten note, unaddressed and undated, on NDP letterhead, referring to his first meeting with J.S. Woodsworth, that sheds some light on this:

*It was not until after the General Election of 1925 that I became associated with
him. After my unsuccessful candidature for the Progressive Party in 1925, Mr.
Woodsworth came to see me. He knew that while I had been an Independent
member of the City Council since 1921, I had been assisting in the formation of
a branch of the Independent Labour Party. He said he hoped I had not been discouraged by the loss of my deposit in the recent election and that I would continue to work for the objectives for which the Independent Labour Party stood.
I told him I intended to do so.*

*He then remarked that he did not expect to see the economic and social poli-
cies for which he stood, enacted in his lifetime nor, though I was some years
younger, did he expect that I should, either. He realized that years of effort
would be necessary to educate public opinion and organize an effective Canadian political movement. To achieve this, he was prepared to dedicate his life
as an example and precept to others to do so.*[6]

Virtue on earth, rewards in the political hereafter. This is an old, old argument, not only in the CCF, but in any party that proposes social and economic change, a familiar tug of war between the purists, who insist the party
should not move from its foundations, nay, though the heavens fall, and those
who would like to come in out of the rain. There is no litmus test, and M.J.
never argued that the CCF was more virtuous than what became the New
Democratic Party, but it is hard to escape the feeling that he looked back a
little wistfully on what had been. He was not alone in this feeling; the CCF in
Saskatchewan remained the CCF-NDP until 1967.

Party insiders debate whether the 1958 disaster led directly to the foundation of the NDP or merely hastened the process. David Lewis, probably as
well informed an observer on this topic as anyone in Canada, leaned to the
latter view:

The new party would have been born even if the outcome of the
1958 election had been much better. What the result did influence
was the acceptance of the idea by many CCF members; there was less
opposition than there might have been had the party fared better.

But I have no doubt that both the CCF and the CLC leadership had reached the decision to combine efforts politically two years before the 1958 election.[7]

Even so, Coldwell would have been less than human not to have had some nostalgia for the old days and the old ways. For a time, he even hoped that the CCF would be reborn, with at least part of its old name intact, but that was never really in the cards.

Then, there was the Quebec factor. M.J. did not speak French, did not yearn to, and while he was in favour of the new emphasis on bilingualism, to him it meant that two languages should be accepted in official Canada, not that he should have to take on a new tongue at his age. Carl Hamilton, who served as national secretary from 1958 to 1962, while the new party was being born, puts it this way:

He would never learn French and could never see any reason why he should. At the very best, he was almost totally ignorant of Quebec, and at the very worst, prejudiced. I remember M.J. saying once, after somebody from Quebec had said something quite disagreeable in the House of Commons, "Well, that was the typical statement of a Quebec MP."[8]

The CCF had continued to flounder in Quebec, even after Coldwell and Frank Scott met with Archbishop Charbonneau in 1943 to explain the party's policies and he seemed receptive. A plenary meeting of Catholic bishops later that year issued a statement freeing their flocks to "support any political party upholding the basic Christian traditions of Canada,"[9] an indication that the hex had been removed. But the problem was not one of religious dictates, not anymore; it was a conflict between the aroused nationalism of Quebec and the national planning process envisioned in CCF programs.

Coldwell's view was that Quebec held a position in Canada as a province, an important province, but that was all; in today's language, he never believed in "special status." If the provinces were to be given the kinds of powers they constantly clamoured for, the necessary national planning would become impossible. At a time when most liberally minded Canadians were calling for the devolution of more responsibility to Quebec, he still held firmly, if in discreet silence, to the position he had taken in his book, *Left Turn, Canada*:

> Canada's constitutional problem is partly that, while the federal government holds the purse strings, its powers of action have been steadily whittled down by court decision; whereas the provincial governments, armed by the courts with larger powers, have been without the means of financing adequate social security measures and national economic development. But the problem, too, is one of overlapping jurisdictions, and one arising from the fact that certain powers of social welfare and economic planning, whose need could not have been foreseen by the Fathers of Confederation, when the Dominion was created in 1867, must now rest with the federal government if there is to be a prosperous Canada...
>
> ...The apportionment of powers between the provinces and the Dominion must be reviewed so that the federal Parliament may have complete authority to enact the necessary policy... If the Dominion assumed the necessary powers to deal with the grave social problems of unemployment relief, agricultural marketing, national health and other social security measures, the rights of minority groups could be protected by statute, writing into the law the rights of minority groups accepted at the time of Confederation. The fear that these minority groups may be restricted or interfered with explains to some extent the unwillingness of provinces to agree to a transfer of necessary power.[10]

The only "minority groups" whose rights were written into the British North America Act were, in effect, Catholics outside Quebec and Protestants inside, who were entitled to their own school systems; the rights, in fact, applied to religion, not language, but were generally seen the other way around.[11]

Quebec, in Coldwell's formulation, should be willing to cede more power to the central government in order that the nation as a whole could prosper; its "minority group," the French-speaking population of the province, could have legal protection to assuage their fears of absorption or discrimination. This was not a view likely to commend itself to Thérèse Casgrain, the new CCF leader in Quebec, much less to Claude Jodoin, president of the CLC.

M.J. began with the argument for a strong, centralized government to carry the mandate of social planning and economic reform, and fitted everything else into that; most of the people who were likely to support the new party in the province of Quebec began with the need to preserve and protect the status of their language and culture, and worked democratic socialism into that argument. The interesting, and politically useful — but historically bizarre — notion of Canada as the conjunction of two distinct, equal nations who came together to form a two-part federation in 1867, still lay ahead (Tommy Douglas would embrace *"deux nations"* in the 1962 election), but while M.J. never attacked that notion in public it clearly did not fit at all well into his own vision of a nation directed firmly from Ottawa.

David Heaps, the son of CCF pioneer A.A. Heaps, served as M.J.'s personal secretary in the 1940s and spent a good deal of time studying him in hopes of preparing a biography. He points out that the entire CCF hierarchy, not merely Coldwell, reflected a similar attitude:

On Quebec, I recall no written or public statements by Coldwell (or other CCF leaders) fifty years ago that displayed a real understanding or anticipation of Quebec problems and psychology. In 1944, he wrote a lengthy position paper on Quebec that exemplified the "progressive Anglo-Canadian" approach. He emphasized that Quebeckers, like Canadians elsewhere, were victimized by systemic social and economic exploitation; their problems were therefore analogous to those of all Canadians.

Coldwell recognized of course different language and religious traditions in Quebec, but paid little heed to their special significance. For him, progress and emancipation in Quebec were part of the larger national need for social and economic parity. He thought the CCF in Quebec had been unfairly stigmatized by irresponsible politicians who equated Socialism with Communism, and by clerics who mistakenly thought the CCF was an anti-religious secular party.

Coldwell, like his parliamentary colleagues, did not foresee the sectional, cultural, historical and psychological factors that later erupted. In those days, not a single CCF Member of Parliament spoke French or even thought of learning the language; and I believe no one at the CCF National office tolerably spoke the language.[12]

When the New Democratic Party was being formed, the Quiet Revolution was erupting; if we date it from the election of Jean Lesage in 1960, it almost exactly paralleled the formation of the new party. Quebec was being transformed, and M.J. had not caught up with the change, while many of those most involved in the launch of the NDP had. In these circumstances, and in view of his increasing age and infirmities, it is not surprising that, as the plans for the new party ripened, M.J. stepped back. The CCF National Convention, held in Montreal in July 1958, instructed the party executive and National Council to "enter into discussions with the Canadian Labour Congress" and other like-minded groups to pave the way for the new organization.[13]

M.J. was busy elsewhere; he got himself a job as a columnist with the *Toronto Star Weekly*, at fifty dollars a week, to help with expenses and keep himself busy. Beland Honderich, by now the publisher of the Toronto newspaper, personally recruited M.J. and promised that his writing would not be interfered with. Just kidding. A Coldwell column, advocating the national medicare scheme proposed by the CCF, was edited to add an editor's postscript, the effect of which was to make it look wrong. Coldwell had argued that the Liberal plan then under consideration would not cover sufferers from tuberculosis or the mentally ill; the *Star* editors contradicted this,[14] but in fact, M.J. was right and they were wrong.

The column did not last long — from April through October 1958 — but ranged over a number of topics, including the Trans Canada Pipeline deal, which still rankled, NORAD, Dwight Eisenhower and the Senate, all of which he attacked. He wrote favourably on the United Nations, the Canadian Teachers' Federation, a national transportation policy, and a proposal for a free trade agreement between Canada and the United States (not the one-sided arrangement that was actually formed in 1994). He took a trip to England and wrote a number of columns from there.

While he was thus engaged, a national committee for the new party was formed, with Knowles as chairman and Carl Hamilton as executive secretary. M.J. was down as "honorary member" on the CCF side, but, Hamilton recalls, "He wasn't around much; I don't ever recall him coming to one of our organizing meetings."[15]

M.J., in fact, spent three months in late 1958 and early 1959 on a fact-finding trip to India on behalf of the United Nations.

On his return to Canada, clearly, he had intended to fade out of the picture, but it became obvious that his presence as an interim leader would solve a number of difficulties. If he stepped down, whoever became national leader in his place would be seen as a strong contender for a similar post in the new party; since many of those who held posts of influence, including David Lewis, were determined to have Tommy Douglas in that role, that wouldn't do at all. M.J. had submitted his resignation, rather sadly, to the national executive two weeks after the election; it had been tabled.[16] He repeated the request to step down in his report to the national convention in Montreal. Lewis was instructed to form a committee "to approach Mr. Coldwell and urge him seriously to consider continuing in the role of National Leader."[17] This was done, and M.J. agreed, reluctantly. He was re-elected by acclamation.

No money went with the job, although M.J. could have done with some.

Now a nasty battle developed. Coldwell was the national leader, but he had no seat in the House of Commons. The eight-man CCF caucus elected a new House leader, Hazen Argue, who had been a boy wonder from Assiniboia (he was first elected in 1945, when he was only twenty-four), but was now anxious to reach beyond the status of a mere MP. As the only Saskatchewan survivor of the Diefenbaker sweep, he felt he was owed something.

Under his urging, the caucus began to push for his election as party leader at the 1960 convention, the one who was to act on the maturing plans for the new party. As usual, there were complications involved in the pushing and shoving. David Lewis, who was then the national president, but who always held what could only be called the David Lewis Office in the CCF, made it clear to the caucus that he did not want anyone to run against Tommy Douglas, the obvious candidate to lead the new party — although Douglas, the party's most successful politician, still firmly in control as premier of Saskatchewan, would not say openly whether he wanted the job or not. He was in the middle of the battle to establish medicare in Saskatchewan and was understandably reluctant to give any sign that he was about to bolt for Ottawa. He did not, in fact, agree to run until June 28, 1961, one month before the founding convention. He later made it clear that what had influenced him most in making his decision was M.J.:

Ever since 1941 he had said he hoped I would succeed him some day. And he felt very strongly that all the work he and Woodsworth had

done would come to naught unless someone could bring the various factions together in the new party and weld them into a fighting force.
It's not going to be easy.[18]

A split quickly developed between the parliamentary group and the party executive, with the former backing Argue and the latter bitterly opposed. Carl Hamilton, the national secretary, who had begun as a friend of Argue's, had, on further acquaintance, changed his mind. "Simply put," he says, "Argue was a totally conscienceless man."[19] At caucus meetings, which Hamilton attended in an ad hoc role, he made his distaste known. Not surprisingly, the caucus resented what they regarded as high-handed interference from outside, and they let it be known that if Argue was not named party leader they would not have him back as House leader.[20] M.J., alarmed and upset, said he could not possibly stay until the official launch of the new party unless the 1960 convention was unanimously in favour of such a role for him. When Argue made it clear that there would be no such unanimous vote, he refused to stand at all.

Carl Hamilton recalls:

The 1960 convention was very difficult. Hazen promoted the idea of my resigning as National Secretary and not being re-elected because of my open opposition to him. David and I wanted to leave the party leadership vacant, and we didn't know until the very last minute whether Hazen was willing to let it go at that. He wasn't.[21]

The executive proposed a solution: Argue could be named "parliamentary leader," something less than national leader but greater than House leader. Argue, with the caucus behind him, persuaded the national convention to bolt from the executive recommendation — a fairly frequent occurrence in the CCF — and Argue became national leader (House leader) on the books, but no one could make the party hierarchy like it. M.J. was out in the cold.

Later — far too late — David Lewis would see that much of the bitterness that developed was his fault:

I as president of the CCF was very much in the wrong in trying to get a unanimous vote for Tommy. It arose out of the tradition we had had

— no one had opposed Woodsworth, no one had opposed Coldwell. They were the Chosen.

I met with Hazen and tried to dissuade him from being a candidate. It was wrong. This attitude produced a bitterness around the Hazen-Douglas contest.[22]

When the party met again, in July 1961, it was to give itself a name — the New Democratic Party — a leader, Tommy Douglas, and a just-left-of-centre program that did not once use the word "socialism," causing the *Ottawa Journal* to break into verse:

Oh no! We never mention it;
Its name is never heard.
Our lips are forbid to speak
That once familiar word,
Socialism.[23]

As for the leadership, that was a walkover for Douglas, who won by a vote of 1,391 to 380 over Argue on the first ballot. John Courtney, a Saskatchewan political scientist, described the tussle as:

A contest between a small, belligerent, but quite powerless caucus, most of whose members supported their leader, and the extra-parliamentary party professionals in support of an extraordinarily successful provincial premier. There was never any doubt who would win.[24]

After the vote, Argue had his picture taken with his arm around Tommy, while he told the party, "No matter what my role in the years ahead, I shall speak for you, I shall work for you, I shall never let you down."[25]

Six months later, he indicated the depth of his commitment by bolting to the Liberals, and at a press conference in Regina — after an uneventful meeting with the Saskatchewan Provincial Council and a friendly visit to Tommy Douglas at his home — he tore up his party card. The NDP, he declared, was "under the heel of the unions," which made it, rather than a democratic party of reform, "a dark and sinister threat to democratic government in Canada."[26]

The party had had no notion this thunderbolt was coming. Carl Hamilton was one of those who could scarcely believe what was happening:

> The first we knew of it was when Norman DePoe, the CBC fellow, telephoned from Regina. He had been covering the Provincial Council, and he had apparently had a word with Hazen, who tipped him that he was about to hold a press conference and bolt the party. Most people didn't believe it, simply couldn't take it in. I suppose we should have known better; he really was a terrible fellow.[27]

To the immense satisfaction of Hamilton, among others, Hazen Argue came to a very sticky end. Re-elected in Assiniboia in 1962, he was defeated a year later, then transmogrified into a senator by Lester Pearson in 1966. He was so unpopular in Saskatchewan that news of his appointment had to be held up until after a by-election, because of reports that the Liberals would lose if it were known.[28] Sandy Nicholson, M.J.'s friend, complained:

> Never in history has any person been appointed to the Canadian Senate whose main qualifications were that he betrayed the thousands of hard-working people who trusted him.[29]

In a rather strange exorcism, the NDP national office banned any photographs of Argue from its walls, so that, while every other man and woman who has held the post of national leader is on display, Argue is not. Not the kind of person the party wants to claim, anyway. He became secretary of state for agriculture, and then in 1989 he was charged with misuse of Senate funds, which he had diverted from various accounts into a boodle bag to support the (unsuccessful) bid of his wife, Jean, for a Liberal nomination in an Ottawa riding. The charges were eventually withdrawn on compassionate grounds when it was discovered that he was dying of cancer. He died on October 2, 1991.[30]

M.J. made no reference whatever to Argue in his own memoirs, though the incident must have hurt, since it deprived him of what might have been a pleasant interlude as elder statesman in the party councils. He became, by unanimous consent, "honorary chairman" of the NDP, a courtesy title that did not include an invitation, as he well understood, to voice his views on party policies in public.

However, he did express some private concerns about the new party in a letter to his old friends, Angus and Grace MacInnis, in late 1963. By this time, there had been another federal election, in which the freshly minted New Democratic Party came back with nineteen seats, up from the eight in the last CCF caucus, but still a disappointment. The great labour alliance did not produce the expected results; the NDP was the fourth party in the House, behind the Conservatives (116), Liberals (99) and Social Credit (30, of whom 26 were Quebec Créditistes). The good news was that the NDP had gathered more than a million votes for the first time, although its proportion of the popular vote, 13.4 per cent, was just about where the CCF had been in 1949.[31]

The bad news was that Tommy Douglas had been badly beaten in a Regina riding (he got back into the House of Commons when Erhart Regier resigned his seat in Burnaby-Coquitlam to make room), and that exit polls indicated that more members of organized labour voted for the Conservatives and Liberals than for the NDP.[32] (The proportions were 38 per cent Liberal, 25 per cent Conservative, 23 per cent NDP and 14 per cent other.)

Another election on April 8, 1963, did not improve things much for the NDP. This time, the Liberals got to form a minority government, with 129 seats, while the Tories got 95, the Socreds 24 and the NDP 17, 2 seats fewer; its share of the popular vote was virtually the same, 13.1 per cent.[33]

M.J. might have been forgiven for wondering what all the fuss was about if the new party was to remain clad in the same bridesmaid's clothes as the old one and carry the same bedraggled nosegay, with the blooms marked "socialism" pruned away. However, he refrained from any such comment and, even in private, confined himself to wondering mildly whether the changes were all to the good. The quote at the beginning of this chapter carries this comment; the same letter to Grace and Angus MacInnis then went on to return to his belief that an unwarranted differentiation was being made between Quebec and other provinces:

Certainly we have been pushed into a difficult position in regard to Quebec. I felt in 1961 at the Founding Convention, in trying to placate our Quebec friends, we were joining those who aimed to foist a form of bilingualism and biculturalism upon Canada that was never contemplated by the Confederation founders. As an advocate of social and economic planning, I find it difficult to follow a course which tends to recognize Quebec's, or any other province's, right to control its own resources for its sole benefit. Lesage's and [Premier W.A.C.] Bennett's tax control demands are quite impossible if Canada is to flourish as a nation. I never liked the elimination of the words "national" and "nation" from the NDP official literature.[34] However, perhaps these are minor matters one can tolerate in the hope that more sensible counsels will eventually prevail.[35]

To some, this letter will simply show that M.J. had not moved far enough or fast enough to keep up with national political evolution, especially when it came to Quebec; to others, that he retained a solid core of principle that would not be remoulded by changes in fashion. In either view, he was not the right person to lead the NDP.

Still, it was done; the CCF was gone (except in letterheads in Saskatchewan); no doubt it would all work out in God's own way in God's good time; it was time to move on.

Part V

After the Limelight

CHAPTER FOURTEEN

"A DEAR AND LOVELY MAN"

*My father was finally defeated in the Diefenbaker sweep of 1958.
After the election, he met Lester Pearson on Carling Avenue. Mr.
Pearson said, "You are lucky, I have to go on!" After his defeat, he
received many accolades from friends and strangers. In reaction, he
said to me, "I do not understand, I am a very ordinary man, really."*
— MARGARET CARMAN, 1998

ON JANUARY 15, 1962, THE *OTTAWA CITIZEN* CARRIED A STORY ON PAGE 3,
headlined "Coldwell Receives Praise, Bonds." It was accompanied by a handsome photograph of M.J. with Walter Gordon, Liberal, J.M. Macdonnell, Progressive Conservative, and Blair Fraser, then Editor of *Maclean's* magazine,
who was supposedly a political eunuch, but who was in fact a lifelong Liberal. The photograph was meant to tell us in what high esteem M.J. was held
by persons of every political persuasion, and it did; it was also meant to show
that he was in fine fettle, and in a way, that was right. He was certainly in better fettle when the picture was taken than he had been a few hours earlier,
because the occasion was a luncheon gathering in his honour at the Chateau
Laurier Hotel, where he received a nosegay of accolades from several friends
and colleagues, which was nice, and $9,000 in Canada Savings Bonds, which
was nicer still.

When Coldwell agreed to stay on as national leader of the CCF until the
new party could be formed, he had to give up his column in the *Star Weekly*
and the money that went with it. When the Argue imbroglio caused him to
back out entirely, he was virtually abandoned by the party. It is true that, at
the founding convention of the New Democratic Party, he was named "honorary chairman," but the post carried neither cash nor clout. Lorne Ingle says:

We treated him very badly. I had no idea, and most people had no idea, how poorly fixed he was. He had nothing but a couple of small pensions; and he had spent nearly every spare penny he had on Norah's treatment. He was penniless, but you never knew it, because he dressed well; he always managed to look sharp. You could see that Stanley Knowles was hard up, but you couldn't see that M.J. was.

Of course, the party had no money, either. I don't know how we would have been able to help him. But we certainly should have tried to do more than we did.[1]

Ironically, the man who rode to the rescue was Frank Underhill, the erstwhile CCF gadfly, now turned Liberal, who agreed to serve as chairman of a committee to raise a fund to help M.J. David Lewis, when the proposal was put to him, responded, "It's not a bad idea, as long as I don't have to have anything to do with it."[2] (Lewis and Underhill shared a cordial dislike; the two men did not speak to each other, not even at the Coldwell luncheon.) The result was a passing of the hat among supporters of all the parties, and a presentation made to M.J. in Ottawa on January 13, 1962. He was expecting bouquets; he got bonds and he was obviously taken aback, but not too much to accept the bonds.

At the luncheon, Frank Underhill called him "the greatest member of Parliament in my lifetime," and Walter Gordon, who was soon to be a member of the Liberal cabinet of Lester Pearson, thanked M.J. for representing "courage, principle and dignity in public life."[3]

In his speech, Coldwell, typically, did not talk much about himself, but about Parliament, and declared, "If I were asked to pick 265 of our finest citizens, I could not do better than point to the House of Commons."[4] A view that might have drawn some smirks even then.

More money came in after the luncheon publicity, and he ended with a modest nest egg of just over $16,000; he put most of it aside and spent the rest on a trip to England and Europe to visit old friends and make new ones.

He was now living in a small apartment at 179 Carling Avenue, where he had moved from the Glebe district in 1964. He was helped, and cosseted, by a housekeeper, Beatrice Bramwell, who came in every day and served him devotedly. (She died not long after M.J.) The best portrait available of M.J. at this time comes from his youngest grandson, William Mackay Carman, who wrote an essay called "My Grandpa" in 1993:

It has been almost 20 years since my grandfather passed away, but my memories of him are still very vivid. Perhaps that is because I do not want to forget.

Grandpa taught me how to play cards. Every Sunday after dinner (usually roast beef and Yorkshire pudding), Grandpa, Beatrice (his housekeeper, who was like a grandmother to me), my eldest brother, Jim, and I would sit down to a game of cards. Be it hearts, cribbage or Michigan rummy, I would sit across the table and watch him, sitting in his favourite armchair, studying his cards and smoking his pipe. In bridge, we were always partners. Every time I would play a hand, he would tell me when I was about to make a mistake; when he played a hand, he would explain every move. This method had two results; I quickly learned how to play bridge and we usually won the game!

Family dinner on Sunday was traditional. When I was very young, we would visit Grandpa and Beatrice in the Glebe. I can still remember that house [that is, apartment], its antique furniture and chiming grandfather clock. In the apartment below, there lived an elderly lady who always had a bowl of chips, peanuts or candy when we would visit her.

When Grandpa moved to his apartment [that is, the one on Carling Avenue, which was smaller], he and Beatrice would visit our house on Sundays. Occasionally, at dinner, Grandpa would talk of some memorable event in the far-distant past (so it seemed to me). He would often conclude by recalling, to everyone's amusement but no one's surprise, exactly what he had for dinner that day.

In the summer, Grandpa would stay with us while Beatrice was on vacation. We would sometimes have our lunch together outside, usually ending up in a two-handed game of cribbage. On the weekends, when my Dad was at home, we would all go sailing on Lake Deschênes or walking in Gatineau Park. I recall one afternoon in our backyard when I was ten or eleven telling Grandpa how I wanted him to see me graduate from university. He smiled and said that he wished he could, but didn't think he would. In 1983, when I did graduate, I couldn't help wishing that he was there.

I was too young really to understand his national stature, but I did get some hints of it when meeting such people as Tommy Douglas, David Lewis, Stanley Knowles, and Grace MacInnis. I remember sitting with him and watching the national election returns come in one year; I remember him at the NDP leadership convention that elected David Lewis;[5] I remember him going away to receive doctorates from far-off universities.

Now, I am often reminded of his contributions to my country and the way in which he has influenced and continues to inspire the lives of many people. The name M.J. Coldwell seems to surface at unusual and totally unexpected times. At a party a few years back, I heard him referred to as a "saint," and recently, I was introduced to someone who proudly declared that he was from Rosetown, "the home of M.J. Coldwell." (I gently corrected him on this.)

I was thirteen years old in the summer of 1974 when my grandfather died. The news of his death arrived while my parents and I were on summer vacation at a favourite resort in the Muskoka region of Northern [sic] Ontario. I vividly remember loading up the van and driving home through the night to Ottawa. I don't think I slept too much that night.

The last time I saw him was the Sunday before we left. As we were saying goodbye in the back hall of our house, he took a five dollar bill out of his wallet and, without anybody noticing, put the money in my hand and said, "This is a little something for you, on your trip. But don't spend it all at once." He patted me on the shoulder, turned, and walked out the back door. I will never forget that image.[6]

M.J.'s active career in politics was finished, although he carried honorary titles in the NDP, as honorary national leader, then honorary president, and finally, after 1971, as president emeritus. However, as his grandson saw, he was still very much interested, and one of his favourite occupations was to receive visits from people like Carl Hamilton, Lorne Ingle, Cliff Scotton and others who were still very much engaged. He read, played cards, walked and talked. He also wrote, although not for the *Star*.

In April, 1962, he was approached by Norman Robertson, then under-secretary of state for external affairs, with an offer of a fellowship at Queen's University in Kingston, but he turned it down:

I didn't want to leave Ottawa, and the honorarium they offered, from the Skelton Foundation, was $9,000 a year, and I felt that if I accepted $9,000, I would want to do $9,000 worth of work and I didn't wish to assume such a responsibility.[7]

That November, he was offered a fellowship at Carleton University in Ottawa, paying $1,000 a year — and this he accepted. It would allow him to work on his memoirs, talk to students and conduct occasional seminars. It seems that he did at least $9,000 worth of other work at Carleton, because the memoirs were only well begun in the eighteen months he spent there.

In early 1963, he fired off a sharp note to the Anglican Church of Canada, of which he was still a member, via the *Canadian Churchman*. He had been outraged by an editorial in the magazine that attacked "the spiritual bankruptcy of political parties."

M.J. wrote that "having had a long association with members of the House of Commons of all parties, I say that a general condemnation [that] they are deserving only of contempt is undeserved and unjustifiable." Then he went on to complain that it was, in fact, the Anglican Church that was lacking in principles, or at least worthy principles, and he cited an instance. The primate of Canada, Archbishop Howard H. Clark, had said that, on the question of nuclear arms, "Canada is, of course, bound to honour her treaty obligations." M.J. wrote:

To me, the Archbishop's pronouncement in favour of Canada's acceptance of the frightful instruments of mass destruction was almost the last straw. In what direction should one turn for religious leadership — to the Pope, to the Quakers, or to the Unitarians, all of whom have spoken, it seems to me, with a common religious motivation in their outspoken condemnation of nuclear arms and of those who are endeavouring to inflict them upon mankind?...

...The Anglican Church is no longer, if it ever were, the church of the common people.[8]

M.J. also travelled a good deal, happily with someone else picking up the expenses in most cases. He went back to India, this time at the behest of the United Nations, as chairman of the UN Mission to Evaluate Community Development, in 1958–59. He also served as guest lecturer at the University of Jerusalem, toured NATO bases as an observer for Canada, returned to Exeter to deliver a paper and maintain his membership in the Exeter University Club, and attended a number of conferences on nuclear disarmament.

For several years after his defeat, friendly editorials suggested that he ought to be appointed to the Senate, and in a move unprecedented in Canadian history Liberal and Conservative senators actually joined in requesting that Prime Minister Lester Pearson appoint Coldwell to the Red Chamber. A number of his friends and supporters immediately announced that, as a avowed foe of the Senate and all its works, he would of course refuse such an appointment, but that was far from certain. When he spoke to members of the Public Archives History Club in 1966, he was willing to allow that it might have been an appropriate gesture to signal acceptance of his role in politics. The money would certainly have come in handy, and it was far easier for a lot of others who weren't in his financial straits to refuse on his behalf than it might have been for M.J. himself. In the event, no appointment was forthcoming, so he was spared having to explain it. (Thérèse Casgrain accepted a Senate appointment in October 1970 and served with distinction.)

In 1964, Pearson, who had always been an admirer, appointed him to the Privy Council, a post traditionally reserved for cabinet ministers, leaders of the Opposition, premiers and, occasionally, members of the Royal Family. Later that same year, to M.J.'s intense pleasure, both for the activity and the income, Pearson appointed him to the House of Commons "Advisory Committee to Study Curtailment of Election Expenses," along with Art Smith, a former Conservative MP, two Liberals — Alphonse Barbeau and Gordon Dryden — and Norman Ward, a political scientist from Saskatoon. The committee came to be called the Barbeau Committee, after the Montreal lawyer who was its chairman. The last time anyone had looked at this subject had been in 1920, when amendments were made to the Dominion Elections Act; and since these amendments, while they did establish some rules to govern election spending, thoughtfully left out any mechanism for enforcing the law,[9] it could be said that reform was overdue.

Norman Ward later wrote about this collaboration:

The committee was a congenial one, but opinions within it ranged from a firm belief that the state should assume all campaign expenses to a broad scepticism that anything worthwhile could be done at all on specific matters. Since we were anxious to produce a unanimous report, and one that would be acceptable to the House of Commons, whose members would be among those most immediately affected, finding formulae on which to agree was not always easy. Often M.J. was the one who broke a log jam; and when we came to a recommendation about which he felt strongly, he would cannily remind us that he was the one who had made a major concession on a previous paragraph, and thus perchance entitled to some consideration on this one.[10]

The other committee members, who did not know M.J. well, were impressed by his gallantry towards Judy LaMarsh, the cabinet minister who was to receive the report, at a private dinner in Hull, Quebec. Ward wrote:

At the dinner, held in a celebrated Hull bistro, Miss LaMarsh was in splendidly indiscreet form and, as one of two women among five men, much in her element. What the ladies' presence (the other was my wife, Betty) did to M.J. was bring out an old-world courtliness we had not observed before in our deliberations, a wonderful mixture of unabashed admiration and deference that had to be seen to be comprehended. Betty was so charmed that when we said goodbye after the next day's meeting, he received a healthy kiss on the cheek. He blushed.[11]

This committee represented the first serious attempt to approach the subject of election expenses in Canada, and its report, tabled on October 11, 1966, was not exactly a radical document. It recommended a series of measures, including, for the first time, formal registration of the national parties and mechanisms to make sure their official agents complied with the law. There were no restrictions on the amount of money that could be contributed by individuals, corporations, unions or other entities, but candidates were to have limits on their spending; for example, each candidate would be limited to spending ten cents per elector on broadcast or print media. The report came with a couple of good ideas that died aborning. One was a prohibition on the publication of public opinion polls during the campaign period; another was the establishment of a registry of election and political finance, separate from the chief electoral officer, to report directly to the House of Commons on the enforcement of the legislation.[12]

Then, there was a sound idea that did make it into law, a provision, for the first time, that the party leader or his representative be required to endorse each party candidate. This provision, which gave the leader of any recognized party an effective veto over the nomination process in any riding, was used for the first time in 1974, when Conservative Leader Robert Stanfield refused to endorse the nomination of Leonard Jones in Moncton, because of Jones's unwillingness to accept the party platform's proposal on bilingualism.[13]

The commission's report might never have seen the light of day, since neither of the old-line parties was anxious to change the old ways, except that the federal election of 1972 produced a minority Liberal government in which the NDP held the balance of power. As part of the price exacted for support, the Election Expenses Act was introduced on June 22, 1973, and finally became law on August 1, 1974, nearly ten years after the process had been set in motion and eight years after Coldwell et al. had submitted their report. For the first time, the law established spending limits, required the official registration of national parties, reimbursed candidates for their spending, under guidelines, and provided for enforcement of its own provisions. The law was far from perfect, but it was a vast improvement and a credit, eventually, to its authors, including M.J.

This assignment involved another trip to the United Kingdom, to examine the approach taken there, and M.J. enjoyed that very much.

Then, in December, 1966, scarcely two months after this job was concluded, Coldwell was appointed to the Royal Commission on Security, a three-year project that kept him occupied — and, more important, paid — for three more years. (It is a nice irony that M.J. owed much of his financial security in his later years to Liberal-government appointments.) The other members of the commission were Yves Pratte, chairman of Air Canada, who also served as commission chairman, and Maxwell Mackenzie, a Montreal businessman. The study was set up as the result of revelations from the Munsinger inquiry and the Victor Spencer case. Gerda Munsinger, a divorcee from Munich, who earned a livelihood by being friendly to strangers, had been involved with Pierre Sévigny, associate minister of national defence, at the same time she was involved with members of the Montreal underworld. She had also, apparently, been on chummy terms with George Hees, Diefenbaker's ebullient trade minister. The RCMP had informed Justice Minister E.D. Fulton, who in turn informed Diefenbaker on December 7, 1960. Diefenbaker called in Sévigny, ignored his indignant denials and ordered him to end the affair. Nothing was done about the matter, and it lay in the RCMP files for six years, until the Tories were attacking the Pearson government over the case of George Victor Spencer in March, 1966.[14] Spencer had been dismissed from government service on security grounds, without a hearing. In the heat of that debate, the Liberal justice minister blurted out the name of Gerda Munsinger (he gave it first as "Monsigneur," which confused everybody for a few days), as proof that the Tories were not above reproach in the security line. A fine time was had by all, as the joined cases displayed more of the elements of comic opera than spy thriller. One highlight was a limerick contest conducted by *Maclean's* magazine. The winning entry read:

There was a young lady from Munich
Whose bosom distended her tunic;
Her main undertaking
Was cabinet making
In fashions bilingue et unique.[15]

A judicial inquiry under Mr. Justice Wishart Spence managed to whitewash the Liberals, outrage the Tories and confuse most of the nation, but it also made clear that the RCMP were, to say the least, neither apt nor adequate custodians of national security. (Two members of the RCMP's Security and Intelligence Directorate, "the Red Squad," descended on the home of a Winnipeg youth because he had written a letter to the newspapers complaining that Santa Claus was a Communist, because he wore a red suit and gave things away.)[16] Prime Minister Pearson, angry and embarrassed, took the traditional way out and set up the royal commission to which M.J. was named, and which took thousands of pages of testimony — all in camera. That commission eventually produced a report in June, 1969.[17] The report very sensibly recommended the establishment of a body of civil servants, trained for the work, to take over the job of guarding national security from the RCMP. It dealt with the manifest incompetence of the Mounties very gently, noting that the investigations of the Red Squad "seem sometimes to be conducted with a certain lack of tact and imagination."[18] (At one point, the boys in red blew up a barn in Quebec because they had a report that separatists were planning to hold a meeting there, which seems fairly imaginative.) With rather less sense, the report also said that homosexuals "should not normally be granted clearance to higher levels" within the civil service, because they might represent a blackmail, and thus a security, risk.[19]

One sidelight of the commission's investigations, which was kept rigorously suppressed, was that it turned up an extensive report that the Mounties had assembled on M.J. himself, as a potential subversive.[20]

The report was commissioned by Lester Pearson, but turned in to the new prime minister, Pierre Elliott Trudeau, who gave it the back of his hand. The RCMP's Security and Intelligence Directorate were the best people to handle these matters,[21] Trudeau said in defiance of all the evidence. It was not until 1985, after more RCMP embarrassments, that the Canadian Security Intelligence Services Act established a separate civilian-controlled intelligence service, very much along the lines that Coldwell and his colleagues had contemplated sixteen years earlier.

In 1967, while he was still serving on this commission, M.J. was made a companion of the Order of Canada, which made him proud and his daughter, Margaret, even prouder. By the time this second government contract was finished, in June, 1969, M.J. was eighty years old. He was suffering from emphysema, diminished eyesight and heart problems, but he remained cheerful and kept up his friendships with an increasingly smaller circle, as age diminished their number.

He made a few speeches and, as Canada grew closer and closer to the United States, warned, as he had always warned, against the danger that Canada's economy would be swallowed up by that of its larger neighbour. Walter Gordon's *Royal Commission on Canada's Economic Prospects* in 1958 and the report authored by Revenue Minister Herb Gray in 1972 called *Foreign Direct Investment in Canada* both warned against the aggressive invasion of U.S. capital onto Canadian soil and expressed an uneasiness that M.J. had been reflecting for years. There was very little said in these reports that hadn't been implicit in M.J.'s arguments during the pipeline debates from 1952 to 1956, although his solution, government ownership, was not likely to appeal to either Gordon or Gray. Theirs were reports of Liberals to Liberal governments, not that that made much difference. The Gordon Report was almost entirely ignored, in legislative terms, while the Gray Report resulted in the establishment of a foreign investment review agency to approve or refuse applications from foreign (read, mainly American firms) to take over Canadian companies. The agency's theme song appeared to have been stolen from the script of *Oklahoma:* "I'm Just a Girl Who Can't Say No." The CCF under M.J. had taken an increasingly strong stand in favour of Canadian control of the Canadian economy — always translated as "anti-Americanism" — and so did the NDP, but neither party was ever notably successful in persuading successive governments to do anything much of substance in this area.

Happily, Coldwell received a number of honorary awards from universities, which always cited his exemplary parliamentary record. The citation from the one he was awarded by St. Francis Xavier University in Nova Scotia in 1972 is worth recording for its inclusion of a wider scope. It honoured him for:

> His work in the councils of his city…his immense contribution to the Commonwealth, for his call to equal sacrifice in war as well as co-operation in peace, for being one of the first to sound the alarm at a time when few of us could see that the independence and sovereignty of this federation of ours would be threatened by the very foreign capital that we then so eagerly welcomed, and for accepting our collective ingratitude at that time with the courage and grace that belongs only to those who know their cause is just.[22]

He spent a good deal of time in the early 1970s tape-recording his reminiscences with Clifford Scotton and Carl Wenaas. He also exchanged a number of letters with Walter Young, his chosen biographer, but he never had the energy to return to the task of completing his own memoirs or even editing the parts that had been done, which is a great pity. His financial affairs were in much better order, thanks both to improvements in parliamentary pensions and his government assignments, and he moved into a nicer apartment at 330 Metcalfe Street, very close to the NDP headquarters and not far from Parliament Hill.

One of his last trips was back to Regina in 1973, when Ed Whelan, a long-time CCF supporter and member of the legislative assembly, drove him around many of his old haunts in the city. Whelan remembers:

> I took him up to the corner of Pasqua and Sherwood Drive, where his first house in North Regina stood, but it had been knocked down years ago. He said, "Well, they like the place anyway; see, they've cut the lawn." Every corner we turned brought back another memory. He was getting on, certainly, and his hearing was failing, and so was his eyesight, but he seemed in good spirits.
>
> The highlight, I guess you could call it, was when I took him up to the school on Coldwell Road. The school was designed so that you could open up four classes, and speak to them all at once. "What am I going to say to them?" he asked me, and I said, "Don't worry, they'll have plenty of questions." And they did; very good questions, about Canadian politics and history and all sorts of things. The bell rang for luncheon, and they stayed right there and went on asking questions. They were a very bright bunch, and they all had a wonderful time. Well, when it was over, we came back out to my car and he got in and sort of put his head down, and I wondered if he was tired, or something. And then I looked across and I could see he was crying, very softly, to himself. I didn't say anything, and just drove away.[23]

M.J.'s final years were marked by some physical discomfort due to deteriorating health, but a good deal of contentment as well. There had been one troubling family upset in the 1960s when his son, Jack, went through a messy divorce, the effect of which was to make it hard for M.J. to see his other two grandchildren, Jack's son and daughter, who remained with their mother, Helen. She was very bitter toward all members of the Coldwell family. In general, however, he was at last fairly comfortable financially, and in personal terms serene. He was content that he had accomplished more than he had ever expected and, more important, that he had never "let anyone down," which had been so important to Norah. His relationship with Margaret, her husband, Doug, and their three children, was a source of great comfort to all of them. They travelled together often, once going out to the Coldwell Park Picnic Site south of Saskatoon, where they had their picture taken together, looking very pleased with themselves and each other.

As we learned in his grandson's essay, his fatal heart attack took place when his daughter and her family were away, on August 25, 1974. He was rushed to Civic Hospital when his housekeeper, Beatrice Bramwell, gave the alarm, but suffered a second attack a few hours later — he had given strict instructions that no "heroic measures" were to be taken in the event of another heart episode,[24] and he was pronounced dead shortly before 6:00 p.m. that same day.

It was not a sad event, for reasons outlined by Norman Ward in his tribute to Coldwell:

An M.J. slow and infirm, with failing sight, is hard to reconcile with the lovely MP of the opposition benches who became so familiar to the country in the 1940s and 1950s. None who loved him would have wanted to have him continue to waste away, and his death at 85 is no ordinary cause for mourning. Much will be written of his adroitness and persistence as a politician; I hope it is not overlooked that he was a dear and lovely man.[25]

CHAPTER FIFTEEN

THE DRAWBACKS
OF DECENCY

*Possibly in this day and age the gentlemanly style may be less
dramatic, and therefore less likely to capture the imagination of
the public. The advantage of a reasoned, more gentle style is that you
may win respect among your parliamentary peers and professional
politicians; the disadvantage may be that you don't electrify the
public as much.* — ALAN WHITEHORN, POLITICAL SCIENTIST, 1993

M.J.'S DEATH BROUGHT AN OUTPOURING OF EPITAPHS, MANY OF THEM
from men who for decades had opposed almost everything he stood for, but
who were forced into reluctant admiration of his integrity, steadfastness and
decency. A memorial service in Ottawa, conducted jointly by his two old
friends, Stanley Knowles and Tommy Douglas, and attended by hundreds of
friends and admirers, along with a few non-admirers like John Diefenbaker,
was followed by cremation. The ashes were to be shipped to Regina for burial next to Norah, after another memorial service in the Saskatchewan capital on September 10, 1974. Stanley Knowles took on responsibility for all the
details. Knowles, a lifelong worrywart, checked with the undertaker shortly
before the ceremony and discovered to his dismay that the ashes had gone
missing, swallowed somewhere in the maw of the post office. A frantic search
located them, and the ceremony went forward as planned. Knowles's biographer, Susan Mann Trofimenkoff, commented that the incident would have
amused M.J.[1]

The tributes that poured in ranged from the banal — the *Ottawa Citizen*
assured its readers, solemnly and wrongly, that M.J. had frequently turned
down an appointment to the Senate, to the soaring.

Tommy Douglas's remarks are worth quoting, in part:

We have lost a great friend. And yet with this feeling of ineffable sad-
ness there is a second emotion which I feel and that is one of thank-
fulness, to have had the privilege as many of you have had, of knowing
this man, of working with him, of associating with him, has meant
that we have had the rare privilege of walking with greatness.[2]

One discordant note was struck not long after his death when his son,
Jack, now in financial difficulties, took M.J.'s Order of Canada medal to an
auctioneer to sell. The auctioneer telephoned Tommy Douglas, and, outraged,
he began calling around to keep this precious memento from becoming just
another sales item. Finally, Alvin Hewitt, a wealthy Saskatchewan farmer,
bought it back for the family for $7,500.[3]

History will make her own decision about Coldwell's position in Canada's
political development, but a quarter-century after his death, it is possible to
see how he functioned as the essential link between the early radicalism of
J.S. Woodsworth and the far more pragmatic — some would say prosaic —
approach of the modern political party that is the NDP. He was thrust
into the leadership by circumstance; no other obvious replacement for
Woodsworth existed. He was not ambitious, never lusted for power, never
bent himself to pick it up.

Perhaps, in a way, that was a weakness. He lit no fiery beacons, stormed
no barricades, hurled no thunderbolts. A superb orator, he did not have the
stage presence of a Trudeau or a Diefenbaker any more than he had their
hypocrisy. Politically, he was a left-of-centre reformer, who changed his views,
modified his stances, but never betrayed his old friends or his old principles.
He believed in a form of democratic socialism that began centred on public
ownership as the principle means of production and segued into something
like "public ownership if necessary, but not necessarily public ownership." A
firm supporter of Canadian farmers, and especially Prairie farmers, he never
wavered in his enthusiasm for the Canadian Wheat Board and marketing
boards in general, but he rapidly cooled to the early notion of lease-owner-
ship as a method of holding farmland. He was a staunch monarchist, but a
stauncher Canadian nationalist, and indeed felt the two went very well
together. His position on Canadian federalism — that the central government

should have enough power to legislate on many matters, such as health and social policy, that had been given to the provinces by the BNA Act — was equally unwavering, and that certainly put him out of step with modern views on Quebec; he was sorry, but not repentant, and simply kept his counsel on this to avoid embarrassing the NDP when it adopted a policy that gave him grave unease.

He was never able to lead his party into power or even into the position of official Opposition; but he was able to harass, embarrass and nag successive governments into passing legislation of benefit to all Canadians. Charles Lynch, a Southam columnist and High Tory, wrote of him that:

> Coldwell's real monuments will be found in the massive system of social security now in place, and the swing towards a governed, regulated economy, and acceptance of public ownership of such massive instruments as Canadian National, Air Canada and the CBC. For so humble a man, he made a massive mark.[4]

Some may note the irony that M.J. made socialism respectable just in time for his own party to disown it as a practical approach to politics. Today, many of the achievements of his era are being rapidly unravelled by a new generation that has little patience with state ownership, public control or anything that does not contribute to the bottom line. Canadian National and Air Canada, both cited by Lynch, are now private companies, with majority ownership in the United States, and the CBC is in a state of disrepair, if not dissolution. The social security M.J. helped to put in place is being treated to the death by a thousand cuts in the name of economic advancement; we are told that Canada can afford to spend billions on corporate subsidies, but we must withdraw funding from medicare. It is hard to know whether M.J. would have laughed or cried; most probably, he would simply have dug in and set forth his arguments once again. Medicare would have saved him and his family untold thousands of dollars in the treatment of Norah's disease; he never even raised the subject in his long battle for a national health system. Now that system is being undermined, taken apart, remoulded into a two-tier system, closer to the American private system — perhaps it was all in vain.

And yet, and yet. There is a growing impatience with the destruction around us, the beginnings of a sense that we went wrong, somehow, in our efforts to construct a society driven by nothing more satisfactory than self-interest. In this setting, it seems that M.J. has quite a lot to say to modern Canadians, both about the way in which a nation should be governed and about the way in which a life should be lived.

If he did not achieve power, he did set an example of what could be done by persuasion, reason and common sense. It is in his personal attributes, as much as in anything he did on the public scene, that M.J. deserves the attention of Canadians today, whether they are democratic socialists or follow any other or no political creed.

We have had greater leaders than M.J.; we have had none who were better.

With that in mind, it seems suitable to end this survey of his life by quoting something that his daughter, Margaret, wrote about M.J. soon after his death:

How Do I Remember My Father

I remember his all-prevailing love surrounding me like his warm hand holding mine on a cold prairie day as he walked out in the frosty air without his gloves.

I remember him lying on the floor by my bed one night when I was ill and getting up periodically to see if I was all right.

I remember as a child being told by my mother to pull his coat-tail after a meeting when it was time to go home.

I remember his inability to strike a bargain and his frustration with mechanical gadgets.

I remember his abhorrence of snobbery and social-climbing.

I remember his pain at my mother's long illness and how he said there would never be another woman in his life.

I remember him carrying her in and out of the car and going for long drives in the country to see the hills and rivers my mother loved.

I remember the sleepless nights he spent trying to give her comfort.

I remember the important speeches he made, and beforehand he would read them to my mother. She would make suggested changes, and often it was done.

I remember his joy in good food and his laughter at a good joke.

I remember his joy in his grandchildren and his concern for them.

I remember my feeling of awe and pride when an auditorium of people gave him a standing ovation.

I remember his amazement and feeling of humility at the time of his defeat for Parliament in 1958, when he received messages from so many admirers.

I remember his pride in being Canadian and his belief in our Democratic Constitution, copied from the British in the land of his birth.

I remember the stories of warm hospitality shown him by the prairie folk (whom he thought were the salt of the earth) in their homes during campaigns.

I remember his interest in young people and his faith that the future would be safe in their hands.

I remember with what pride he received the Order of Canada.

He loved people.

Margaret Carman
September 3, 1974

APPENDIX

CCF FEDERAL ELECTION RESULTS
1935–1958

Year	CCF Vote	Seats	Percentage of Vote	Percentage of Seats
1935	387,056	7	8.7	2.9
1940	393,230	8	8.5	3.3
1945	816,259	28	15.6	11.4
1949	782,410	13	13.4	5.0
1953	636,310	23	11.3	8.7
1957	707,659	25	10.7	9.4
1958	692,398	8	9.5	3.0

Source: Adapted from J. Murray Beck, *The Pendulum of Power: Canada's Federal Elections,* Scarborough: Prentice-Hall, 1968, various pages.

Some Key Dates

1883 Fabian Society founded in England.

1886 *Das Kapital* published in English.

1887 APRIL 4: Elizabeth Farrant marries James Henry Coldwell, butcher, of Seaton, Devon.

1888 Edward Bellamy's *Looking Backward* published.

   DECEMBER 2: Major James William Coldwell born at Seaton, Devon, England, son of James Henry Coldwell and Elizabeth Farrant.

1893 Independent Labour Party founded in England.

   FEBRUARY 18: M.J. enrolled at the Infants' School, Seaton.

1900 ILP founds the Labour Representation Committee.

1901 JANUARY 22: Queen Victoria dies, Edward VII succeeds.

   SEPTEMBER: M.J. enrols at Hele's School, Exeter.

1904 SEPTEMBER: After graduation from Hele's, M.J. enters the part-time teachers' training program at Prince Albert Royal Memorial College, Exeter.

1905 SEPTEMBER 1: Saskatchewan and Alberta become provinces.

1906 The Labour Representation Committee becomes the Labour Party, under Keir Hardie.

1907 J.S. Woodsworth appointed superintendent of All People's Mission in Winnipeg.

   SEPTEMBER: M.J. enters full-time teacher training at Prince Albert Memorial School, Exeter. Meets Norah Gertrude Dunsford.

1909 JULY: M.J. passes final exams in Exeter.

1910 FEBRUARY 9: M.J. sails from Liverpool for Canada, on the *Grampian*.

   FEBRUARY 19: M.J. arrives in Halifax.

   FEBRUARY 26: M.J. reaches Edmonton.

FEBRUARY 29: M.J. takes up first teaching job at New Norway, Alberta, for $660 a year.

MAY 6: King Edward VII dies.

1911 Tommy Douglas is brought to Canada as a boy.

JUNE: M.J. visits Jack Dunsford, Norah's brother, in Saskatoon; visit leads to appointment to Sedley.

AUGUST 15: Trip to Sedley to open school.

SEPTEMBER 21: Borden Conservatives win the "Reciprocity" election.

1912 JULY 1: Storm strikes Regina; M.J. leaves for England.

JULY 22: M.J. marries Norah Dunsford of Bridgwater, Somerset, at Wembdon Church, Bridgwater.

AUGUST 2: M.J. and Norah sail for Canada on the *Victorian*.

SEPTEMBER: M.J. and Norah take up posts in Sedley, Saskatchewan.

1913 Salem Bland, Methodist preacher in Toronto, calls for "a new party, a party that will have what no present party commands — moral enthusiasm."

1914 JULY: Meetings in Regina to discuss ways of improving education in the province. Proposals rejected; Saskatchewan Teachers' Alliance formed. M.J. briefly acts as secretary.

AUGUST 4: First World War declared; Norah and M.J. move into their house in North Regina, to open new school.

AUTUMN: Alberta Teachers' Alliance formed, then B.C. Teachers' Alliance. M.J. takes leading role.

1915 APRIL 17: John Major Coldwell born, becomes ill soon after.

SUMMER: M.J. takes over St. Albans Anglican Church as visiting preacher.

1917 JUNE 26: Saskatchewan provincial election; Liberals win 51 seats, Conservatives 7; Jimmy Gardiner's first election. W.M. Martin premier.

M.J.'s first overt politics, as chairman of an election meeting, where he criticizes the minister of education.

DECEMBER 17: Unionist victory in the federal "Conscription" election. M.J. acts as poll captain, criticizes government action to disenfranchise many voters who oppose conscription, although he himself is in favour.

1918   The flu epidemic hits Regina.

1919   MAY 15: Winnipeg General Strike begins.

JUNE: M.J. offered job as a principal in Regina. Accepts.

JUNE 23: J.S. Woodsworth arrested in Winnipeg.

JUNE 26: Strike called off.

1920   DECEMBER: M.J. is asked to run for alderman. Declines.

1921   MAY 4: Margaret Coldwell born in Regina.

DECEMBER 6: General election won by Liberals, J.S. Woodsworth wins in Winnipeg North as an Independent Labour member. He is joined by William Irvine, to form the "Labour Group" in the House. Agnes Macphail, first Canadian woman MP, elected by United Farmers of Ontario.

DECEMBER 21: M.J. becomes a Regina alderman; he will be re-elected four times.

1922   Alderman Coldwell exposes meal rackets in Regina. Canadian Teachers' Federation formed.

1923   M.J. runs for alderman again, tops polls.

1924   M.J. and family visit Seaton. M.J. studies Labour party proposals.

1925   M.J. does not run for alderman, runs as a Progressive in federal elections. Defeated, and loses deposit.

Canadian Teachers' Federation meet in Toronto; M.J. is elected vice-president.

OCTOBER 29: Liberals defeated in general election, but Mackenzie King clings to power with the aid of Progressives. Not long after, Woodsworth comes to see M.J. in Regina.

1926   FEBRUARY 26: Jimmy Gardiner wins Saskatchewan Liberal leadership, becomes premier.

Teachers meet in Charlottetown. M.J. becomes president of Canadian Teachers' Federation.

SEPTEMBER 14: Liberals win the controversial "King-Byng" election.

1927   MARCH 17–18: M.J. one of three Saskatchewan reps on national committee for Canada's Diamond Jubilee. M.J. on Ottawa visit learns of immigration corruption.

Teachers meet in Toronto. M.J. hosts World Federation of Educational Associations.

NOVEMBER: M.J. breaks immigration corruption story.

1928   M.J. becomes national secretary of CTF.

Ottawa appearance re immigration scandal.

1929   JUNE 6: Gardiner Liberals lose Saskatchewan vote. KKK active. J.T.M. Anderson becomes premier, appoints M.J. chairman of Royal Commission into the Saskatchewan Public Service. Reports in early 1930.

SUMMER: M.J. begins Tuesday-evening lectures at Regina library.

AUTUMN: Clarence Fines, M.J., J.S. Woodsworth and a few others at the Western Conference of Labour Political Parties.

Independent Labour Party founded in Regina.

United Farmers of Canada (Saskatchewan Section) defeat resolution to take direct political action. Saskatchewan Farmers' Political Organization forms a splinter group.

OCTOBER 24: The Great Depression begins with stock market crash.

1930   Norah diagnosed with multiple sclerosis.

JULY 28: R.B. Bennett leads Conservatives to victory in general election.

1931   FEBRUARY: United Farmers decides to go into politics.

M.J. becomes president of the Independent Labour Party of Saskatchewan, which joins the United Farmers of Canada (Saskatchewan Section), to form the Farmer-Labour Group, of which he becomes leader.

AUGUST: League for Social Reconstruction proposed during an academic meeting in Williamstown, Massachusetts.

1932   April: Tommy Douglas writes to J.S. Woodsworth, who puts him in touch with M.J. M.J. and Jack go to Weyburn to meet Tommy.

LSR manifesto issued in Toronto, to become basis of the *Regina Manifesto*.

May 26: The idea for a new party is conceived at William Irvine's Ottawa office.

July 25: The Independent Labour Party re-elects M.J. as president.

July 27: The ILP joins forces with George Williams's United Farmers of Canada (Saskatchewan Section) to form a new party, the Farmer-Labour Party. M.J. becomes leader by acclamation.

August 2: CCF formed at a joint meeting of the Western Conference of Labour Parties and the United Farmers of Alberta, in Calgary. M.J. is chair of Policy and Program Committee.

December 31: M.J. resigns as alderman.

1933   July 19: The *Regina Manifesto* is adopted by the new CCF party, after three days of debate.

1934   June 19: Saskatchewan provincial election; M.J. defeated. He wants to call it quits, but Norah persuades him to try again.

March 3: United Farmers of Ontario quits the CCF, because of controversy about ties to the Communists, and J.S. Woodsworth disbands the Ontario party, which is reformed under stronger central control.

1935   June 3: The "On to Ottawa Trek" begins in British Columbia.

June 14: Trekkers arrive in Regina.

July 1: Regina Riot breaks out, Trekkers are disbanded, and leaders are arrested.

August 20: M.J. asks school board for permission to extend leave of absence to run in postponed federal election. Denied. He is fired for not returning to school.

August 22: Social Credit under William Aberhart sweeps to power in Alberta.

October 14: Liberals win general election, M.J. goes to Ottawa as CCF MP for Rosetown-Biggar. The new party wins seven seats, on 8.8% of the vote. George Williams becomes provincial leader.

1936   MARCH 23: New school-board motion to reverse decision, allow M.J. leave of absence. Tabled.

APRIL 27: School board reverses itself, reinstates M.J.

JUNE 24: M.J. resigns from principal's job.

JUNE 22: M.J. in the House denounces Sgt. Leopold, RCMP spy.

JUNE 26: M.J. speech on Regina Riot.

Norah is now unable to walk.

1937   JUNE 29: CCF fails to win a single seat in Ontario election.

1938   M.J. becomes national chairman of the CCF.

1939   SEPTEMBER 3: Britain declares war on Germany.

SEPTEMBER 6: Three-day meeting of the CCF National Council debates a resolution to approve Canada's involvement in the war. J.S. Woodsworth will voice his opposition, but the party will give limited approval.

SEPTEMBER 9: M.J. speaks for the party in the House of Commons in debate on the war. J.S.W. speaks against Canadian participation.

SEPTEMBER 10: Canada declares war; one dissenting vote — J.S.W.

SEPTEMBER 13: J.S.W.'s last speech in Parliament, calls for conscription of wealth for war.

SEPTEMBER 28: CCF war policy set.

1940   MARCH 26: Liberals win big federally, M.J. re-elected. Agnes Macphail loses. She will run as CCFer in Ontario in 1943 and win.

M.J. begins attempt to unseat George Williams as CCF leader in Saskatchewan.

MAY 18: National Council meeting. J.S.W. has stroke.

OCTOBER 28: Woodsworth named honorary president of CCF.

NOVEMBER 6: Caucus elects M.J. acting house leader.

1941   JANUARY: Leadership job divided from presidency in Saskatchewan. Williams remains president, but loses leadership. He enlists.

JULY: Heavy infighting over Saskatchewan leadership; Douglas becomes president, Fines vice-president.

Williams conducts letter war.

NOVEMBER 13: M.J. calls in at Seaton on visit with MPs to troops.

1942 FEBRUARY: In York South by-election, Joe Noseworthy defeats Arthur Meighen, becomes first CCF MP in Ontario.

MARCH 21: J.S.W. dies.

APRIL 22: M.J. named House leader, job he has held since late 1939.

JULY: Saskatchewan provincial convention chooses Douglas as CCF leader.

JULY 27–29: National convention in Toronto elects M.J. national president without contest. M.J. proposes "Total mobilization for war."

1943 AUGUST: In Ontario, CCF becomes official Opposition, under Ted Joliffe, with 34 seats to the Conservatives' 38.

SEPTEMBER: Canadian Congress of Labour endorses CCF as its political arm. Pat Conroy lukewarm.

The hate campaign against CCF led by Gladstone Murray takes off. It will last more than a decade.

OCTOBER: Attempts to get Roman Catholic ban on CCF lifted come to nothing.

1944 JUNE 15: Saskatchewan election. CCF under Douglas wins 47 seats; Liberals get 5.

SEPTEMBER: M.J. and other Canadian CCFers go to London for meeting of Labour and Social Democratic parties. M.J. stresses the need to free India and other colonies at war's end.

NOVEMBER: M.J. moves amendment to conscription resolution.

National convention accepts a mixed economy, will restrict public ownership to banks and monopolies.

First Political Action Committee of the CCL formed.

1945 APRIL: M.J. is offered a cabinet post in the King government. He declines.

JUNE 11: Liberals re-elected, but down heavily, from 181 seats to 127. CCF picks up 12 seats in Saskatchewan; total 18 there. But nationally, CCF has only 28 seats — 18 of them in Saskatchewan, on 11% of the vote.

In Ontario, CCF drops from 34 to 8 seats in provincial election — the Gestapo Affair.

1946   First health-care card granting free medical care to all old age pensioners issued.

1947   JANUARY 25: Woodsworth House opens in Ottawa.

M.J. calls for price controls.

FEBRUARY 13: Leduc oil strike changes Alberta politics forever.

APRIL: Row in Parliament as M.J. tries, in vain, to get old age pension increased to $50 from $25 a month.

1948   JUNE 7: CCF again official Opposition in Ontario, with 21 seats. Bill Temple defeats George Drew, who becomes federal leader of Conservatives.

JUNE 11: In Saskatchewan, CCF wins 31 seats, down from 47; Liberals under Walter Tucker get 19, but lower vote than in 1944.

Battle against the Communists in B.C. CCFers win.

1949   JUNE 27: Liberals win again federally, while CCF drops from 28 to 13 seats. CCF membership plummets; half is lost in 1945–1947, another one-third after 1949 election.

1950   M.J. urges updating *Regina Manifesto* at national convention. A committee set up, but bogs down.

MAY: Battle over NATO divides the party.

1951   MARCH 8: M.J. attacks "Socialist Fellowship" in B.C. as a "threat to liberty." National executive bans it from party later in March.

SEPTEMBER 29: Margaret Coldwell marries Douglas Carman.

NOVEMBER: CCF thrashed in Ontario election in midst of McCarthyism, down to 13 seats.

1952   Douglas wins again in Saskatchewan; Liberals down to 11 seats.

W.A.C. Bennett scrapes win over CCF in B.C.

Frank Underhill ousted from board of Woodsworth Foundation.

M.J. has surgery (prostatectomy).

1953   JULY 2: Norah dies during election campaign. M.J., after funeral, returns to campaign trail.

AUGUST 10: Liberals win again in general election. CCF gets 23 seats, only two east of Manitoba, on 8.7% of the vote.

NOVEMBER: Donald MacDonald becomes Ontario leader.

1954   Economic slump.

OCTOBER: M.J. visits Israel.

1955   Quebec issues dog the party.

APRIL: Canadian Labour Congress unites TLC and CCL.

JUNE: Donald MacDonald elected in York South.

1956   MAY 31: Uproar in Parliament on Black Friday, the Pipeline Debate.

JUNE 1: M.J. calls the Speaker "A tyrant, a Hitler."

AUGUST 3: *Winnipeg Declaration* replaces the *Regina Manifesto*.

M.J., Lorne Ingle, MacDonald and Lewis make final revision.

AUGUST: M.J. visits Seaton and Exeter, speaks at Hele's School.

1957   FEBRUARY 25: M.J. has first heart attack, brought on by hardening of the arteries.

JUNE 10: Progressive Conservatives under Diefenbaker win minority government federally, CCF up to 25 seats, including three in Ontario, on 10.7% of the vote.

AUGUST: Stanley Knowles offered Speakership of the House of Commons; he turns it down.

SEPTEMBER 23: Ingle letter re M.J. leaving country.

NOVEMBER: M.J. leaves on tour of India for two months.

1958   MARCH 31: PC landslide, M.J. defeated in Rosetown-Biggar. CCF back down to 8 seats on 9.5% of the vote.

APRIL 21: M.J.'s column begins in the *Toronto Star Weekly*.

APRIL 23: Caucus elects Hazen Argue House leader; M.J. remains president and national leader.

CLC Winnipeg convention calls for the "creation of a new political movement."

JULY 25: CCF National Convention in Montreal authorizes council and executive to explore "the proposed broader political party."

DECEMBER: M.J. on UN mission tour to India.

1959   FEBRUARY 23: M.J. returns from India.

Frank Underhill heads committee to raise money for M.J.

JUNE 13: New party proposals: M.J. letter to Clarence Fines "It may work out, but labour has been for us a weak reed."

1960   APRIL 25–29: CLC Montreal convention endorses executive Council, pushes new party forward. M.J. becomes honorary national leader.

JUNE: CCF wins the "Medicare Election" in Saskatchewan.

AUGUST 9–11: CCF convention authorizes executive to go ahead with new party proposal.

M.J. steps down as national leader when vote at the convention is not unanimous.

Convention names Hazen Argue national leader, setting off battle with administration, who want no part of him.

OCTOBER: Walter Pitman wins Peterborough by-election as the first new party MP.

M.J., Lewis pressure Douglas to run; Lewis tries to talk Argue out of standing.

1961   AUGUST 4: NDP Founding convention. Tommy Douglas is elected national leader on first ballot.

OCTOBER 13: Saskatchewan Medical Care Insurance Act introduced by Tommy Douglas.

NOVEMBER 1: Tommy steps down as premier.

1962 FEBRUARY 25: Hazen Argue quits NDP, which he calls "a dark and sinister threat to democratic government in Canada."

JUNE 19: Tories win again federally, with a minority; NDP gets only 19 seats and 13.5% of the vote.

Only 23% of labour votes NDP; 38% votes Liberal. Tommy Douglas loses.

1963 APRIL 8: Liberals under Pearson win minority government; NDP gets 17 seats federally on 13.1% of the vote.

NOVEMBER 29: M.J. writes to Angus and Grace MacInnis with concerns about the NDP.

1964 APRIL 22: Ross Thatcher, Liberal, wins in Saskatchewan.

OCTOBER 14: Pearson appoints M.J. to House of Commons Advisory Committee on Election Expenses, which reports to Judy LaMarsh, whom M.J. charms. Committee reports in 1966, but legislation does not follow until 1974.

JUNE 25: Pearson appoints M.J. to Privy Council.

1965 NOVEMBER 8: Another Liberal minority government federally.

NDP elects 21 MPs on 17.9% of the vote.

1966 JULY 1: Federal medicare begins.

Thatcher wins again in Saskatchewan.

JULY 3–6: NDP convention in Toronto endorses "special status" for Quebec.

DECEMBER 16: M.J. appointed to Royal Commission on Security.

1967 JULY 1: M.J. awarded a companion of the Order of Canada.

1968 JUNE 25: Trudeaumania sweeps the nation; Liberals get 155 seats, NDP 22 on 17.0% of the vote.

1969 APRIL 29: The Waffle is born in Toronto; new name for an old party split.

JUNE: Royal Commission on Security reports.

JUNE 7: Ed Schreyer becomes NDP leader in Manitoba.

JUNE 25: Schreyer wins snap Manitoba election.

1970   OCTOBER 16: War Measures Act invoked.

1971   APRIL 21–24: T.C. Douglas resigns as federal NDP leader.

National convention elects David Lewis leader on fourth ballot.

JUNE: Allen Blakeney wins Saskatchewan back.

By the end of 1971, NDP has tripled MPs, doubled popular support.

OCTOBER: Ontario election; Stephen Lewis, who has unseated MacDonald, misses becoming Opposition leader by one seat.

1972   JUNE: Waffle thrown out of Ontario party.

SEPTEMBER: Dave Barrett wins in B.C.

OCTOBER 30: Narrow Liberal victory federally; NDP gets 31 seats on 18% of the vote.

NOVEMBER 5: M.J. gets LLD from St. Francis Xavier.

1974   JULY 8: Liberals win again federally, NDP gets 16 seats, fewer than in 1953, on 15.1% of the vote. Wage and price controls are the big issue.

AUGUST 25: M.J. suffers fatal heart attack, due to a ruptured artery.

NOTES

INTRODUCTION

1 "Rosetown, Sask.: The Place to Be!" undated pamphlet, p. 3.

2 Ibid.

3 Rosetown *Eagle*, October 17, 1935.

4 John Robert Colombo, *Colombo's Canadian References*, Toronto: Oxford University Press, 1976, p. 120.

5 Interview by Walter Young with Frank Scott, July 13, 1962.

6 Co-operative Commonwealth Federal Programme, adopted at First National Convention, held at Regina, Saskatchewan, July 1933; hereafter, the *Regina Manifesto*.

7 David Lewis, *The Good Fight: Political Memoirs*, Toronto: Macmillan, 1981, p. 377.

8 *Ottawa Citizen*, August 23, 1974.

CHAPTER ONE: THE MAN IN THE AISLE

1 The phrase is from William Kilbourn's *Pipeline: Transcanada and The Great Debate: A History of Business and Politics*, Toronto: Clarke, Irwin & Company, 1970, p. 14. And no, I cannot explain why Trans-Canada is spelled "Transcanada" in the title but nowhere else in the book. It is now spelled "TransCanada."

2 House of Commons Debates, May 9, 1952.

3 Kilbourn, op. cit., p. 33.

4 House of Commons Debates, May 8, 1956.

5 Kilbourn, op. cit., pp. 116–117.

6 Dale C. Thomson, *Louis St. Laurent, Canadian*, Toronto: Macmillan, 1967, p. 425.

7 He repeated the phrase in his history of the period, *The Search for Identity: Canada Postwar to Present*, Toronto: Doubleday, 1967, p. 143.

8 Kilbourn, op. cit., p. 111.

9 Ibid., p. 112.

10 Thomson, op. cit., p. 435.

11 House of Commons Debates, June 1, 1956.

12 Ibid.

13 House of Commons Debates, June 6, 1956.

[14] Walter Stewart, *Divide and Con: Canadian Politics at Work,* Toronto: New Press, 1973, pp. 113–114. Trudeau mouthed the words, so they would not appear in Hansard, and later claimed that what he had said was "fuddle duddle." George Bain, then of the *Globe and Mail,* made journalistic history by putting the real words into print for the first time in a Canadian newspaper.

CHAPTER TWO: SEATON DAYS

[1] *The Penguin Atlas of World History: Volume Two,* Middlesex: Penguin, 1982, p. 103.

[2] See the discussion in *Harold Laski: A Life on the Left,* by Isaac Kramnick and Berry Sheerman (Middlesex: Penguin, 1993, p. 38 ff.). Many of the early Fabians, like Sidney Webb and George Bernard Shaw, were convinced eugenicists, with, in some cases, an overlay of racism. Sidney Webb lamented the fact that those sections of the populace who had "thrift and foresight" tended to small families, while "children are being freely born to the Irish Roman Catholics and the Polish, Russians and Jews…This can hardly result in anything but national deterioration; or, as an alternative, in this country gradually falling to the Irish and Jews."

[3] Edward Bellamy, *Looking Backward,* New York: Modern Library, 1951, p. 76.

[4] Herbert Spencer, *Principles of Biology,* 1867, Part III, Chapter 12.

[5] Quoted in Eric Kierans and Walter Stewart, *Wrong End of the Rainbow,* Toronto: Collins, 1988, p. 78.

[6] G.G. Munford, *Seaton, Beer and Neighbourhood: Through the Famous Landscape to the Gates of Devon and Dorset,* Yeovil: Whitby & Son, Third Edition, 1893, p. 6.

[7] George P.P. Pullman, *The Book of the Axe,* Fourth Edition, Bath: Pitman Press, 1875, p. 836.

[8] Ibid., p. 848.

[9] Quoted in Ibid., p. 10.

[10] *White's Directory,* 1850, p. 385.

[11] John F. Travis, *The Rise of the Devon Seaside Resorts, 1750–1900,* Exeter: University of Exeter Press, 1993, p. 103.

[12] *Memoirs 2,* "Childhood and School Days." Sometimes the page numbers are missing, or not legible, so I have dropped them. Coldwell Papers, National Archives of Canada.

[13] I am indebted to Nigel Cole, Solicitor, of Axminster, whose firm has an office at No. 1 Major Terrace, Seaton, who dug out these papers from the firm's vault.

[14] The elms are gone now, but everything else in St. Gregory's Anglican Church yard remains as M.J. described it, down to, or up to, the rooks.

[15] There is a portrait of M.J. in this suit, clutching a badminton racket and standing on a chair. His hair is in curls, and he looks game for any fate, despite the get-up.

16 That is, at the Bloody Assizes conducted in Exeter by Judge Jeffreys in 1685; these resulted in 300 hangings, 800 transportations and hundreds more finings, floggings and prison sentences.

17 Papers from Nigel Cole, Axminster.

18 Ibid.

19 M.J. Coldwell, "Experiences as a Boy," radio script; undated, no page numbers. It is marked in writing, "After the War." Coldwell Papers, National Archives of Canada.

20 Down on the waterfront. There is a new assembly hall, now, in the Town Hall, and the place M.J. refers to here has become, ah, an assembly room for the local Conservative Association.

21 1898.

22 "Some Childhood Recollections," radio script.

23 Closer to 25, actually.

24 This was written shortly before the Second World War, and helps explain M.J.'s mixed feelings about that conflict.

25 "Some Childhood Recollections."

26 One of the ironies that attend M.J.'s life is that nearly all the buildings, places and views he knew as a boy are still much as they were, while almost all of those in his second home, Saskatchewan, are gone.

27 This is from an unsigned booklet called *Hele's: An Account of the Making of a School in Exeter, 1850–1950*, in the Devon County Library in Exeter.

28 Ibid.

29 Ibid., p. 12.

30 Ibid.

31 The old station is gone now, as is the branch line of the South West Railway, but there is a recreation station there for tourists in the summer, and an open, sort of Toonerville Trolley line that runs along the same route up the Axe Valley to Colyford.

32 *Memoirs 2.*

33 "Experiences as a Boy," p. 10.

CHAPTER THREE: AN EDWARDIAN IN EXETER

1 Both quotes are from B.W. Clapp, *The University of Exeter, A History*, Exeter: University of Exeter, 1982, pp. 18–19.

2 Ibid., p. 27.

3 Walter Young, "M.J. Coldwell: Leadership in a Democratic Party," conference paper, March 4, 1976, p. 18.

4 "I Remember," transcript of an article Coldwell wrote for the Exeter College magazine in 1963.

[5] Ibid.

[6] "Experiences as a Boy," radio script.

[7] Clapp, op. cit., p. 30.

[8] Ibid.

[9] Interview of Mrs. Real by Walter Young, 1967; the quote appears in Young's 1976 paper cited above, on p. 17.

[10] "Experiences as a Boy."

[11] Letter, M.J. Coldwell to Major A.B. Gay, curator, the Royal Albert Museum, April 14, 1954.

[12] Letter, Major Gay to Jean Lesage, April 21, 1954.

[13] Ibid.

[14] *RAM*, vol. 5, no. 2, 1909.

[15] Joseph Chamberlain, the Conservative colonial secretary during the Boer War, became convinced that Britain should abandon its free trade policy for what came to be called "Imperial Preference," to bolster the Empire. The change was eventually adopted through the work of his sons, Austen and Neville.

[16] *Memoirs 2.*

[17] Clifton Daniel, editor, *Chronicle of the Twentieth Century*, London: Dorling Kindersley, 1995, p. 13.

[18] Anne Daltrop, *Charities*, London: B.T. Batsford, 1978, p. 62.

[19] Ibid., p. 58.

[20] John Grigg, *Lloyd George: 1902–1911, The People's Champion*, London: Methuen, p. 194.

[21] Robert Newton, *Victorian Exeter, 1837–1914*, Leicester: University Press, 1968, p. 179.

[22] Ibid., p. 278.

[23] Ibid.

[24] Ibid., p. 282.

[25] Ibid., p. 292.

[26] Ibid., p. 280.

[27] Quoted in Ibid., p. 308.

[28] Both men switched sympathies. M.J. ran into Northam years later, during a vacation visit to Devon in 1924, and discovered that he had become a Conservative. He later became Sir Reginald Northam, director of the Conservative Party Training School at Masham, in Yorkshire. Despite their — now reversed — political differences, the two men remained friends and corresponded for years.

[29] "I Remember."

[30] *RAM*, V, no. 2, 1909.

[31] Margaret Norah Carman, "My Father, M.J.," private paper, 1993.

³² Usually, but not always, hymns.

³³ "I Remember."

³⁴ *Memoirs 2.*

³⁵ Ibid.

³⁶ "I Remember."

³⁷ *Memoirs 2.*

CHAPTER FOUR: PRAIRIE PROSPECTS

¹ The Toronto Board of Trade amended this to read, "Good! By God, I'm going to Canada!"

² *Memoirs 1.*

³ Ibid.

⁴ *Memoirs 1.*

⁵ *Canadian Global Almanac,* 1998, p. 42.

⁶ Ibid., p. 49.

⁷ It still is. The now-bustling town is just west of a line between Edmonton and Calgary, south and a little east of Wetaskiwin.

⁸ M.J. had been a sturdy churchgoer in England and trained as a deacon in the Anglican Church.

⁹ McNally did, in fact, give M.J. an excellent report, but did not remember the new schoolteacher being quite as exuberant about his duties as this account suggests. In fact, he wrote some years later, "Because he had never had to cope with a large school where grades ranged from one to eight, nor with a rigid curriculum, he was frustrated and discouraged… He was quite the best-qualified teacher I had seen in many visits, and I was very anxious to hang onto him." McNally said he talked M.J. out of quitting. G. Fred McNally, *G. Fred: The Story of G. Fred McNally,* Don Mills, Ontario: J.M. Dent, 1964, p. 34.

¹⁰ Reverberations from the outpourings of hatred surrounding the Manitoba Schools Act of 1890 were still shaking all of Western Canada, and bigotry on both sides of the religious and language barrier found expression in the perennial debate about how much, and which, religious influences would govern the schools.

¹¹ M.J. makes this point with characteristic, but perhaps undue, caution. The fact is that the influx of newcomers set off a barrage of racist complaints that the native population was about to be swamped. Kenneth McNaught, in his *History of Canada* (London: Praeger, 1970, pp. 192–193), quotes a typical burst of vitriol: "So long as Britons and northwestern Europeans constitute the vast majority there is not so much danger of losing our national character. To healthy Britons of good behaviour, our welcome is everlasting; but to make this country a dumping ground for the scum and dregs of the old world means transplanting the evils and vices that they may flourish in a new soil."

Chapter Five: The Reluctant Politician

[1] This contract appears in Dean Robinson, *The Hills of Home: North Easthope Township, 1827–1997* (Stratford, Ontario: North Easthope Book Committee, 1998), p. 737. I am grateful to Bill Brown, sometime of Stratford, now a resident of Sturgeon Point, Ontario — but not on the school board — for bringing this to my attention.

[2] *Memoirs 1.*

[3] *Reminiscences, 2.*

[4] See Escott M. Reid, "The Saskatchewan Liberal Machine Before 1929," in *The Canadian Journal of Economics and Political Science,* II, no. 1, 1936.

[5] Ibid.

[6] Ibid.

[7] *Memoirs 1.*

[8] Ibid.

[9] Ibid.

[10] *Memoirs 2.*

[11] *Reminiscences, 2.*

[12] James Cappon, "Current Events," *Queen's Quarterly,* July 1917, p. 115.

[13] Quoted in J. Murray Beck, *The Pendulum of Power: Canada's Federal Elections,* Scarborough: Prentice-Hall, 1968, p. 307.

[14] R. MacGregor Dawson, *William Lyon Mackenzie King: A Political Biography, 1874–1923,* Toronto: University of Toronto Press, 1958, pp. 260–262.

[15] *Reminiscences, 2.*

[16] *Memoirs 1.*

[17] Mason Wade, *The French Canadians 1760–1967,* Toronto: Macmillan, 1955, p. 750.

[18] O.D. Skelton, *Laurier,* vol. II, Toronto: Oxford University Press, 1921, p. 529.

[19] *Reminiscences,* no. 3.

[20] Ibid.

[21] *Memoirs 1.*

[22] There were ten aldermen, five of whom were elected in alternate years for two-year terms. M.J. was elected in 1921 and 1923, dropped out in 1925 when he ran for the Progressives and was re-elected in 1928 and 1930. He headed the polls in 1923, 1926, 1928 and 1930.

[23] *Memoirs 1.*

[24] Ibid.

[25] Ibid.

[26] Quoted in Walter Stewart, "Strike Me Pink," in *But Not in Canada,* Toronto: Macmillan, 1976, p. 206.

[27] *Memoirs 2.*

[28] Grace MacInnis, *J.S. Woodsworth: A Man to Remember,* Toronto: Macmillan, 1953, p. 145.

[29] *Reminiscences,* no. 2.

[30] *Memoirs 1.*

[31] Ibid.

[32] *Reminiscences,* no. 3.

[33] *Reminiscences,* 2.

[34] Ibid.

[35] *Reminiscences,* 1.

[36] Letter, Lorne Ingle to the author, June 7, 1999.

[37] William Stevens Fielding, who had been King's finance minister but who was in retirement at this time.

[38] Forke had succeeded Crerar as leader of the Progressives and then succumbed to the same blandishments, and followed Crerar into the King cabinet in 1926. M.J. had been quite critical of him.

[39] This was already a hot topic in eastern newspapers, but M.J. never saw these and had no idea that he had stepped into the middle of a hornets' nest that had already been stirred.

[40] *Reminiscences,* 3.

[41] *Reminiscences.*

[42] Doris French Shackleton, *Tommy Douglas,* Toronto: McClelland and Stewart, 1975, p. 60.

CHAPTER SIX: PLAN OR PERISH

[1] *Memoirs 1.*

[2] Ibid.

[3] *Memoirs 2.*

[4] Ibid.

[5] Ibid.

[6] The farmer got two and a half cents.

[7] *Memoirs 2.*

[8] Sandy Leslie of Sedley, whom we met in Chapter 4.

[9] Later Churchill Falls.

[10] *Memoirs 1.*

[11] Shackleton, op. cit., p. 63.

[12] Ibid., p. 64.

[13] Quoted in Ibid., p. 63.

[14] *Reminiscences,* no. 5.

[15] Lewis H. Thomas, editor, *The Making of a Socialist: The Recollections of T.C. Douglas,* Edmonton: University of Alberta Press, 1982, p. 264.

[16] In brief, M.J. was referring to the Communists, who were constantly trying to take over the ILP, as well as any other left-wing parties.

[17] Quoted in Shackleton, op. cit., p. 64.

[18] J.F. Conway, *The West: A History of a Region in Confederation,* Toronto: Lorimer, 1983, p. 128.

[19] *Memoirs 1.*

[20] Ibid.

[21] Ibid.

[22] Interview of Frank Scott by Walter Young, July 13, 1962, Walter Young Papers, University of British Columbia.

[23] Underhill gave me this account of the *Manifesto* during a series of interviews for a radio documentary I did on him in 1968.

[24] Ibid.

[25] House of Commons Debates, May 2, 1932.

[26] MacInnis, op. cit., p. 263.

[27] Ibid., p. 266.

[28] *Reminiscences.*

[29] Quoted in Shackleton, op. cit., pp. 64–65.

[30] M.J. reproduced the *Regina Manifesto* as an appendix to the only book he ever wrote, *Left Turn, Canada* (New York and Toronto: Duell, Sloan & Pierce, 1945), and this summary is drawn from that.

[31] "External Relations," Section 10, of the *Regina Manifesto.*

[32] Ibid.

[33] J.F. Conway, op. cit., p. 115.

[34] Pierre Berton, *The Great Depression 1929–1939,* Toronto: McClelland and Stewart, 1990, p. 208.

[35] *Memoirs 2.*

[36] Berton, op. cit., p. 207.

[37] Margaret Stewart and Doris French, *Ask No Quarter, A Biography of Agnes Macphail,* Toronto: Longmans Green, 1959, p. 169. The Margaret Stewart here was my mother; Doris French became Doris French Shackleton. They noted that, a short time after Macphail's ultimatum, while a resolution dealing with labour was on the floor, Angus MacInnis, a B.C. delegate — and J.S. Woodsworth's son-in-law to be — said with a wry smile, "I could threaten to leave if this measure is not accepted, except for the sobering thought that you would probably get on very well without me."

[38] Letter, M.J. Coldwell to Frank Eliason, June 20, 1934, Coldwell Papers, National Archives of Canada.

CHAPTER SEVEN: P.S.: THE HORSE IS DEAD

[1] Quoted in Shackleton, op. cit., p. 59.

[2] Stewart and French, op. cit., pp. 177–178.

[3] *Memoirs 1.*

[4] Walter Stewart, *But Not in Canada,* op. cit., p. 64.

[5] *Reminiscences,* no. 5, 1963, p. 6.

[6] *Memoirs 2.*

[7] Jean Bannerman, *Leading Ladies of Canada, 1639–1967,* Galt, Ontario: Highland Press, 1967, p. 173. See also Jean Love Galloway, "Nora [*sic*] Coldwell: Gallant Lady of the CCF," in *Saturday Night,* June 14, 1949.

[8] Interview, Ottawa, August 27, 1998.

[9] James H. Gray, *The Winter Years,* Toronto: Macmillan, 1966, p. 155.

[10] Ibid., pp. 20–22.

[11] James H. Gray, "Canada Flirts With Fascism," *The Nation,* October 9, 1935.

[12] House of Commons Debates, June 20, 1936.

[13] *Reminiscences,* 5.

[14] Shackleton, op. cit., p. 49.

[15] Minutes, Board of Education, Regina School Division, August 20, 1935; August 27, 1935, February 25, 1936; March 23, 1936; April 14, 1936, June 24, 1936 (M.J.'s letter of resignation).

[16] Quoted in Shackleton, op. cit., p. 85.

[17] To keep the banks from simply foreclosing every time a farmer got behind in payments, the Credit of Alberta Regulation Bill required the licensing of all bank employees, and their activities were put under the control of the Social Credit Board. The legislation was later disallowed.

[18] Letter, T.C. Douglas to M.J. Coldwell, December 6, 1936, CCF Papers, Public Archives of Canada.

[19] J. Murray Beck, *Pendulum of Power,* op. cit., pp. 220–221.

CHAPTER EIGHT: DAYS OF GLORY, DAYS OF GRIEF

[1] J.M. Beck, op. cit., pp. 220–221.

[2] *Reminiscences,* 4.

[3] Interview, Ottawa, July 21, 1998.

[4] *Reminiscences.*

[5] Stewart and French, op. cit., p. 232.

[6] David Lewis, op. cit., p. 116.

[7] Ibid., p. 118.

[8] Letter, J.S. Woodsworth to J.A. Martin, December 22, 1932, Woodsworth Papers, National Archives of Canada.

[9] Lewis, op. cit., p. 90.

[10] Shackleton, op. cit., p. 92.

[11] Regina *Leader-Post*, July 14, 1947.

[12] Interview of Arthur Kroeger, Ottawa, June 17, 1998.

[13] This, again, is a battle being refought more than half a century later.

[14] He did this every year.

[15] W.A. Riddell, Canada's delegate to the League of Nations, vastly underestimated the extent to which Mackenzie King was willing to go to avoid any international entanglements. The oil embargo, if successful, would certainly have brought Mussolini's tanks to a halt. King didn't care. "Do honourable members think it is Canada's role at Geneva to attempt to regulate a European war?" he asked. Since that was precisely supposed to be the role of the League of Nations, he got no meaningful reply from his own members.

[16] Interview of Arthur Kroeger.

[17] James Struthers, *How Much Is Enough?* Toronto: University of Toronto Press, 1994, p. 83.

[18] Quoted in Kenneth McNaught, "The 1930s," in *The Canadians, 1867–1967*, J.M.S. Careless and R. Craig Brown, editors, Toronto: Macmillan, 1967, p. 269.

[19] Radio broadcast, April 18, 1939, Coldwell Papers, National Archives of Canada.

[20] Records of the National Convention, Toronto, August 3–5, 1936, CCF Papers, National Archives of Canada.

[21] Toronto *Globe and Mail*, February 15, 1937.

[22] House of Commons Debates, February 15, 1937.

[23] Ibid.

[24] Regina *Leader-Post*, August 13, 1937.

[25] Minutes, CCF National Council, February 26–27, 1938, National Archives of Canada.

[26] *Commonwealth*, April 27, 1938. The headline the paper ran over this bit of dynamite was "Government Betrays Seed Wheat Trust."

[27] House of Commons Debates, May 24, 1938.

[28] Letter, M.J. Coldwell to David Lewis, September 17, 1938, Coldwell Papers, National Archives of Canada.

[29] In the original transcript of the taping, this was given as "limited support." Coldwell later scratched out the word "limited."

[30] Actually, on September 6, three days after Britain declared war and four days before Canada did so.

31 In short, the National Council sided with M.J., and a deal was struck that Woodsworth, the party leader, would make his own statement first, but that Coldwell would then present the party's official position in the debate on September 7. The vote was 15 to 7.

32 Transcript, Public Archives History Club, May 18, 1966, Coldwell Papers, National Archives of Canada.

33 House of Commons Debates, September 7, 1939.

34 Quoted in MacInnis, op. cit., p. 304.

35 Ibid., p. 307.

CHAPTER NINE: M.J. TAKES THE HELM

1 The figures are all in the Report to the National Convention, 1938, in the CCF collection of the National Archives of Canada.

2 Lewis, op. cit., p. 118.

3 Letter, J.S. Woodsworth to M.J. Coldwell, September 9, 1938, Coldwell Papers, National Archives of Canada.

4 Joseph E. "Holy Joe" Atkinson, then the *Star*'s publisher, had created the newspaper out of a strike, and was always sympathetic to left-wing causes and social issues. Comedian David Broadfoot once described him as a "small-l Conservative."

5 Transcript, Public Archives History Club, May 18, 1966.

6 It was reduced from $4,000 as part of the measures to fight the depression.

7 Transcript, Public Archives History Club.

8 J.W. Pickersgill, *The Mackenzie King Record: 1939–1944,* Toronto: University of Toronto Press, 1960, p. 60.

9 *Canadian Forum,* April 1940.

10 Beck, op. cit., pp. 238–239.

11 Transcript, Public Archives History Club.

12 King's minister of justice and Quebec lieutenant.

13 Transcript, Public Archives History Club.

14 Ibid.

15 Ibid.

16 Ibid.

17 Ibid.

18 Mackenzie King's private secretary at this time.

19 John Blackmore, then the Social Credit leader.

20 Transcript, Public Archives History Club.

21 Minutes, CCF National Executive, March 21, 1942.

22 *Report of the National Convention,* 1942, CCF Papers, National Archives of Canada.

23 Lewis, op. cit., p. 180.

24 "Conservatism, Liberalism and Socialism in Canada," in *Party Politics in Canada,* Hugh G. Thorburn, editor, Toronto: Prentice-Hall, 1967, p. 70.

25 Samuel A. Martin, *An Essential Grace,* Toronto: McClelland and Stewart, 1985, p. 54.

26 Pickersgill, op. cit., p. 571.

27 Ibid., p. 601.

28 Horowitz, op. cit., p. 71.

29 Transcript, Public Archives History Club.

30 Interview of Stanley Knowles by Walter Young, June 1972, Walter Young Papers, University of British Columbia.

31 Interview of M.J. Coldwell by Gad Horowitz, March 28, 1962, in Horowitz, op. cit., p. 71.

32 Ibid.

33 Shackleton, op. cit., p. 119.

34 Cameron Smith, *Love & Solidarity,* Toronto; McClelland and Stewart, 1992, p. 99.

35 J. Harvey Perry, *A Fiscal History of Canada: The Post-War Years,* Toronto: The Canadian Tax Foundation, 1989, pp. 550–554.

36 The Veterans' Charter of 1944, passed with the approval of all parties, provided returning veterans with low-cost loans to purchase land, a home or furniture, or to start a business, rehabilitation grants, a clothing allowance, war service gratuities, life insurance, and tuition and grants to aid education.

37 Transcript, Public Archives History Club.

CHAPTER TEN: MILLSTONES

1 Interview, Ottawa, July 20, 1998.

2 *The Making of a Socialist: The Recollections of T.C. Douglas,* edited by Lewis H. Thomas, Edmonton: University of Alberta Press, 1982, pp. 264–265.

3 This was 612 Bank Street, where they lived from 1941 to 1948.

4 Margaret Norah Carman, "My Father, M.J.," private paper, March 23, 1993.

5 Interview, Ottawa, July 20, 1998.

6 Interview, Ottawa, August 2, 1998.

7 Smith, op. cit., p. 105.

8 Ibid., p. 98.

9 Ibid.

[10] A number of accounts have now been written about this, the best of them David Lewis's detailed examination in his own autobiography, *The Good Fight*. Gerald Caplan also wrote about it in *The Dilemma of Canadian Socialism: The CCF in Ontario*, and a much briefer account appears in my own book, *But Not in Canada*, under the title "Water Me No Gates."

[11] Reg Whitaker and Gary Marcuse, *Cold War Canada: The Making of a National Insecurity State, 1945–1957*, Toronto: University of Toronto Press, 1994, p. 274.

[12] Lewis, op. cit., p. 274.

[13] *Parliamentary Guide*, 1946.

[14] Beck, op. cit., p. 250.

[15] M.J. wrote a set of separate memoirs dealing with specific subjects; these were to be worked into his autobiography. The one quoted here was written on July 13, 1964.

[16] In 1936.

[17] *Memoirs 2*.

[18] Interview, Guelph, Ontario, September 2, 1998.

[19] For years the key mandarin in external affairs.

[20] *Memoirs 2*.

[21] Blair Fraser, *The Search for Identity: Canada Postwar to Present*, Toronto: Doubleday Canada, 1967, p. 40.

[22] Cameron Smith, op. cit., pp. 106–107.

[23] J.T. Saywell and Walter D. Young, "The CCF and the Communist Party in Canada, 1932–1955," unpublished paper.

[24] Between 1943 and 1959, when it was illegal to belong to a communist party, it was actually known as the Labour-Progressive Party; same thing.

[25] *Memoirs 2*.

[26] Saywell and Young, op. cit., p. 23.

CHAPTER ELEVEN: MAN ABOUT THE HOUSE

[1] Interview, Toronto, September 1, 1998.

[2] House of Commons Debates, May 7, 1947.

[3] M.J. Coldwell, "Why Parliament Fails Us," in the *Star Weekly*, September 16, 1958.

[4] Ibid.

[5] Ibid.

[6] Interview, Toronto, June 25, 1998.

[7] House of Commons Debates, September 30, 1974.

[8] *Stratford Beacon Herald*, January 24, 1945.

[9] Young, op. cit., pp. 25–26.

[10] The story is told by Eric Estoric, in the Preface to Coldwell's book *Left Turn, Canada,* op. cit.

[11] Blair Fraser, *The Search for Identity: Canada Postwar to Present,* Toronto: Doubleday, 1967, p. 115.

[12] Ibid., p. 116.

[13] Beck, op. cit., p. 279.

[14] Letter, Ingle to the author, June 7, 1999.

[15] Interview.

[16] He told John Bird of Southam News Services in 1948, "If I had to choose between so-called socialism without democracy on the one hand, and democracy without socialism on the other, then I would choose democracy without socialism."

[17] Young, op. cit., p. 30.

[18] Interview of Stanley Knowles by Walter Young, June 1977.

[19] Interview with Walter Young, 1966.

[20] Ibid.

[21] Actually, the post he didn't hold was that of secretary of state for external affairs.

[22] At that time, the MP for Lake Centre, Saskatchewan.

[23] Later, attorney general of British Columbia.

[24] So it did; the entry was never changed.

[25] Transcript, Public Archives History Club.

[26] *Left Turn, Canada,* p. 56.

[27] M.J. approved of Groome's comments and pointed to her thesis as guidance for Walter Young, his chosen biographer.

[28] Agnes Jean Groome, "M.J. Coldwell and CCF Foreign Policy, 1932–1950," M.A. thesis, University of Saskatchewan, Regina Campus, 1967.

[29] *Report of the Tenth National Convention, Co-operative Commonwealth Society,* Winnipeg, Manitoba, August 19–21, 1948.

[30] Ibid.

[31] Groome, op. cit., p. 214.

[32] House of Commons Debates, March 28, 1949.

[33] Thomas Garrigue Masaryk, Benes's predecessor and mentor.

[34] In the House of Commons, the papers could have been claimed by the new Czech government after the coup, and they would have had to be surrendered.

[35] Transcript, Public Archives History Club.

[36] Lewis, op. cit., p. 383.

[37] Ibid., p. 386.

[38] Letter, Grant MacNeil to M.J. Coldwell, March 4, 1951, Coldwell Papers, National Archives of Canada.

[39] Letter, M.J. Coldwell to Grant MacNeil, March 8, 1951, Coldwell Papers.

[40] CCF National Council Minutes, March 17, 1950, CCF Papers, National Archives of Canada.

[41] Letter, M.J. Coldwell to P.E. Wright, MP, November 7, 1950, Coldwell Papers, National Archives of Canada.

[42] Beck, op. cit., pp. 272–73.

[43] Lewis, op. cit., p. 360.

[44] Report, CCF National Convention, 1950, CCF Papers, National Archives of Canada.

[45] Ibid.

[46] Carlyle King, *Canadian Forum*, April 1952.

[47] *Canadian Forum*, September 1953, p. 121.

[48] *Halifax Chronicle-Herald*, July 17, 1953.

[49] Interview, Ottawa, August 2, 1998.

[50] Jack was working for Air Canada.

CHAPTER TWELVE: THE CCF STALLS

[1] Beck, op. cit., pp. 286–287.

[2] Frank Underhill, *Canadian Forum*, September 1953, p. 121.

[3] *Halifax Chronicle-Herald*, July 17, 1953.

[4] Ibid., July 30, 1953.

[5] Interview, February 28, 1999.

[6] Lewis, op. cit., p. 413.

[7] *The Canadian Almanac*, 1987, p. 38.

[8] Research director of the Canadian Labour Congress.

[9] Interview, Guelph, September 1, 1998.

[10] Lewis, op. cit., p. 416.

[11] Quoted in Lewis, op. cit., p. 428.

[12] Young, op. cit., p. 32.

[13] Quoted in Young.

[14] Minutes, National Council, January 13–15, 1956, CCF papers, National Archives of Canada.

[15] Leo Zatuka, *A Protest Movement Becalmed: A Study of Change in the CCF*, Toronto: University of Toronto Press, 1964, p. 93.

[16] C.A.R. Crosland, *The Future of Socialism*, London: Jonathan Cape, 1956.

[17] Minutes, National Council, January 13–15, 1956.

[18] Lewis, op. cit., p. 441.

[19] Interview with Lorne Ingle, Toronto, September 1, 1998.

[20] Quoted in Becker, op. cit., p. 297.

[21] Letter, Lorne Ingle to Stanley Knowles, M.P., September 23, 1957.

[22] Letter, Knowles to Ingle, September 27, 1957.

[23] Interview, Toronto, September 2, 1998.

[24] Beck, op. cit., pp. 326–327.

[25] Cooper got 9,962 votes to Coldwell's 8,051. In his previous elections, Coldwell had won by majorities of 2,446 (1935), 2,902 (1940), 4,866 (1945), 3,527 (1949), 5,888 (1953) and 4,295 (1957). *Parliamentary Guide*, 1958, p. 384.

[26] *The Independent*, Biggar, Saskatchewan, June 13, 1957.

[27] Lewis, op. cit., p. 485.

[28] Return of Electoral Expenses, National Archives of Canada, Coldwell Papers, Vol. 59.

[29] Ingle was trying to be admitted to the Ontario bar; it took a while.

[30] Arthur Blakely, of the Montreal *Gazette.*

[31] Stanley Knowles, defeated in Winnipeg North Centre, became executive vice-president of the CLC.

CHAPTER THIRTEEN: ANOTHER NEW PARTY

[1] Stanley Knowles, *The New Party,* Toronto: McClelland and Stewart, 1961, p. 35.

[2] The wording of the resolution adopted by the CLC embraced "the CCF, interested farm organizations and other like-minded individuals and groups," Report, Canadian Labour Congress Convention, April 21–25, 1958.

[3] *Canadian Global Almanac 1998,* p. 48.

[4] Cameron Smith, op. cit., p. 152.

[5] Lewis, op. cit., p. 447.

[6] National Archives, Coldwell Papers, MG 27 III C.12, vol. 62.

[7] Lewis, op. cit., p. 486.

[8] Interview, Guelph, September 2, 1998.

[9] Quoted in Lewis, op. cit., p. 460.

[10] *Left Turn, Canada,* pp. 90–91.

[11] Donald Creighton, *Canada's First Century,* Macmillan: Toronto, 1970, pp. 141–143.

[12] Letter, David Heaps to Allen Seager, April 29, 1996. Seager was preparing a paper on M.J. and had asked for Heaps's comments. The crack about no one in the national office speaking French is not quite true; Frank Scott, national chairman from 1943 to 1951, and David Lewis, were both fluent, if not bilingual, and François Laroche, national vice-chairman, 1946–1949, was francophone.

[13] Stanley Knowles, op. cit., Appendix B.

[14] *Toronto Star Weekly,* July 5, 1958.

[15] Interview, Guelph, September 2, 1998.

[16] Lewis, op. cit., p. 499.

[17] Ibid., p. 500.

[18] Doris French Shackleton, op. cit., p. 253.

[19] Interview, Guelph, September 2, 1998.

[20] Susan Mann Trofimenkoff, *Stanley Knowles: The Man from Winnipeg North Centre,* Saskatoon: Western Producer Prairie Books, 1982, p. 165.

[21] Interview, Guelph, September 2, 1998.

[22] This is from an interview with Doris French Shackleton, quoted in her biography of Douglas, op. cit., pp. 256–257.

[23] Quoted in Smith, op. cit., p. 154.

[24] John C. Courtney, *The Selection of National Leaders in Canada,* Toronto: Macmillan, 1973, p. 177.

[25] Ibid., p. 257.

[26] Ibid., p. 259.

[27] Interview, Guelph, September 2, 1998.

[28] Peter Newman, *The Distemper of Our Times: Canadian Politics in Transition, 1963–1968,* Toronto: McClelland and Stewart, 1968, pp. 74–75.

[29] Ibid., p. 75.

[30] *Canadian News Facts,* vol. 23, p. 4, 088 and vol. 25, p. 4, 393.

[31] Beck, op. cit., p. 348–349.

[32] Ibid., p. 343.

[33] Ibid., pp. 370–371.

[34] These were removed because Quebec used the terms in reference to itself.

[35] Letter, M.J. Coldwell to Angus and Grace MacInnis, November 29, 1963. This letter is not in the Coldwell Papers.

CHAPTER FOURTEEN: "A DEAR AND LOVELY MAN"

[1] Interview, Toronto, September 2, 1998.

[2] Interview with Carl Hamilton, Guelph, September 2, 1998.

[3] *Ottawa Citizen,* January 15, 1962.

[4] Ibid.

[5] In 1971; it was a bitter battle and a rowdy convention.

[6] William Mackay Carman, "My Grandpa," private paper, March 23, 1993.

[7] *Memoirs 1.*

[8] Quoted in *Ottawa Citizen,* June 22, 1963.

[9] W.T. Stanbury, *Money in Politics: Financing Federal Parties and Candidates in Canada,* vol. 1 of the Research Studies, Royal Commission on Electoral Reform and Party Financing, Toronto: Dundurn Press, 1991, p. 29.

[10] Ward Smith, "A Tribute to M.J.," *Ottawa Citizen,* September 5, 1974.

[11] Ibid.

[12] Ibid., pp. 32–33.

[13] Ibid., p. 34.

[14] Walter Stewart, *But Not in Canada,* Toronto: Macmillan, 1976, p. 179 ff.

[15] Quoted in Peter Newman, op. cit., p. 403.

[16] Stewart, op. cit., p. 174.

[17] *Report of the Royal Commission on Security,* Ottawa: Queen's Printer, 1969. There is only one copy of this report in the National Archives, and it is in dreadful shape, with some parts unreadable.

[18] Ibid., p. 100.

[19] Ibid., p. 111.

[20] He told his daughter, Margaret, about this, with mixed amusement and indignation. Interview with Margaret Norah Carman, Ottawa, July 20, 1998.

[21] *Canadian News Facts,* June 16–30, 1969, p. 283.

[22] From the citation, St. Francis Xavier University, Antigonish, Nova Scotia, November 5, 1972.

[23] Interview, Regina, February 22, 1999.

[24] Interview with Margaret Carman, July 20, 1998.

[25] Norman Ward, "A Tribute to M.J.," *Winnipeg Free Press,* September 5, 1974.

CHAPTER FIFTEEN: THE DRAWBACKS OF DECENCY

[1] Trofimenkoff, op. cit., p. 185.

[2] "M.J.," pamphlet of the Douglas-Coldwell Foundation, Ottawa, 1974.

[3] Interview with Ed Whelan, Regina, February 22, 1999.

[4] Southam News Services, August 27, 1974.

INDEX